HANDBOOK OF MANAGEMENT DEVELOPMENT

Handbook of Management Development

EDITORS: DEREK P. TORRINGTON
DAVID F. SUTTON

Gower Press

First published in Great Britain by Gower Press Limited
Epping Essex
1973

ISBN 0 7161 0154 8

Contents

CONTENTS

CONTENTS

CONTENTS

Illustrations

ILLUSTRATIONS

Notes on Contributors

DEREK TORRINGTON is Principal Lecturer in Industrial Relations at Manchester Polytechnic where he is responsible for developing courses in personnel management and management of human resources. Before working at the Polytechnic he was Manager of the Personnel and Training Division of Oldham International Ltd. He is a member of the Institute of Personnel Management and of various IPM committees. His extensive lecturing activities include a five-year run of seminars for the British Institute of Management on successful personnel management. He has published various articles in management journals, and two books: *Successful Personnel Management* (Staples 1969) and *Face to Face* (Gower Press 1972). He also edited *Handbook of Industrial Relations* (Gower Press 1972).

DAVID SUTTON commenced his career as teacher and consultant in the fields of management and organisation development as a part-time teacher at Salford College of Advanced Technology while he was still employed as Production Manager for James Halstead Ltd, of Whitefield. After a short spell as a Production Manager with the Michelin Tyre Co. Ltd, he moved into full-time employment as a management teacher when he joined the staff of the High Wycombe College of Technology and Art as a Senior Lecturer. This marked a change in a career pattern which had taken him from graduation at Manchester University in 1951 into the technical and production management side of the rubber and plastics industries with the Dunlop Co. Ltd, Turner Brothers Asbestos Co. Ltd, Halsteads and Michelin over a period of 13 years. After two years at High Wycombe, Mr Sutton returned to the Northwest as Principal Lecturer and Deputy Head of the Department of Management at Manchester Polytechnic, a post from which he has recently resigned in order to further develop his work as a freelance consultant and as a founder member of Action Learning Projects International.

REX ADAMS is Director of Studies at Ashorne Hill, the steel industry management college. He is responsible for the college's teaching and research work. After service in the Army, he worked at Pressed Steel Company and Nuffield Exports for three years before going to Birmingham University, where he read economics, politics and sociology and took a master's degree in industrial relations. He was on the research staff at Nuffield College, Oxford, for two years and then taught in the University of Sheffield for four years. He first went to Ashorne as Adviser on Studies in 1962. Mr Adams's publications include three books written jointly with Hugh Clegg, on various aspects of industrial relations. He was visiting lecturer at London Business School, Autumn 1971.

DEREK DE BELDER served an engineering apprenticeship with the Ministry of Supply and received a BSc (Engineering) degree from London University. After four years in the Far East as an Engineer with the City Council of Singapore, he joined the Royal Navy as an Instructor Lieutenant at HMS *Caledonia*, the engineering training establishment. In 1959 he joined the Education, Training and Personnel Department of AEI. Since 1965 he has been with Ashley Associates and from 1970 to 1972 he was Managing Director when, on the amalgamation of Ashley Associates with the Knight Wegenstein Group of Management Consultants, he was appointed Deputy Director of their UK Recruitment Division.

MEL BERGER graduated from the University of California at Los Angeles, obtaining a BSc in business administration and an MBA in behavioural science. He has lived in England for the past eight years where he has been involved in management training, industrial consultancy and research. He has worked in the Management Department of the University of Leeds, in the Management Department of the Polytechnic of North London and currently in the Department of Occupational Psychology at Birkbeck College. At present he is primarily involved in researching and advising on management and organisation development in Reed International. He is an associate member of the European Institute for Transnational Studies in Group and Organisational Development (EIT) and treasurer of the Group Relations Training Association.

DAVID CASEY is Director of Training and Development at Wall Paper Manufacturers Limited. He taught for three years before entering industry as a research chemist. Three years later he was appointed Technical Manager of Berger (UK). A second change of direction came after a further three years when he decided to combine his interest in the process of management with his early liking for teaching and moved into the training field as Personnel Development Manager, responsible for training and development as well as industrial relations. Moving to Reed International in 1967 when the organisation was expanding rapidly provided an opportunity to work as Senior Training Officer at the Corporate Centre, running residential programmes and acting as training adviser to a major division, the Wall Paper Manufacturers Limited. Mr Casey was a member of the group of three which produced the Owen Report in 1971 and is serving on the Executive Committee of the Association of Teachers of Management.

JOHN H. DAFFORNE is Deputy Regional Training Officer of the Manchester Regional Hospital Board where he is responsible for mounting courses including those for professional and technical staff. Mr Dafforne has wide experience of management in hospitals. He is a Fellow of the Institute of Chartered Secretaries and Administrators and of the Institute of Health Service Administrators; he is also an Associate of the Institute of Company Accountants. He has contributed articles to *The Hospital*.

HAWDON HAGUE is Managing Partner of CONTEXT, an organisation providing help with in-company management development and training. He read philosophy, politics and economics at Oxford and has had wide experience of training management and general management including a period as managing director of Caithness Glass, consultancy with Urwick, Orr & Partners and the Oxford Consultants. Mr Hague is a frequent lecturer and has contributed articles to *The Guardian*, *The Financial Times*, *The Engineer* and *Industrial & Commercial Training*.

GEORGE HAYWARD is Principal Lecturer in Management Studies at Danbury Park Management Centre where he is responsible for full-time and block-release courses leading to the postgraduate Diploma in Management Studies. He is also responsible for a course leading to the Diploma in Management Studies (Agriculture) and for the coordination of research activities. His industrial experience was gained in the UK, Canada, the USA, Finland and Denmark marketing capital equipment. He spent two years on research into the diffusion of innovation and has an MSc from Bradford University Management Centre; he is presently carrying out further research as a Doctoral Candidate in the Faculty of Applied Science, University of Nottingham. Mr Hayward is a member of the Management and Supervisory Working Party of the Agricultural, Horticultural and Forestry Industry Training Board.

JACK HOWARTH is Regional Training Officer of the Manchester Regional Hospital Board where he is responsible for management training for all grades of hospital staff. He has had 10 years of teaching experience in England and Canada and was a tutor organiser in HM Prison Service for eight years.

SAMUEL HUGHES is Headmaster of Burnage High School, Manchester. He read modern history at Oxford. His educational career, interrupted by war service in the Guards Armoured Division, has taken him into modern, technical and grammar schools at both assistant and headmaster level. His present school is a large 11–18 comprehensive with an annual intake of 300 pupils.

NOTES ON CONTRIBUTORS

L. C. JARMAN is Head of the Department of Management at Manchester Polytechnic. He spent six years as an electrical and production engineer before joining the Ministry of Labour as an Instructor. His subsequent career has been mainly in training and education in a variety of industries, including Bristol Aeroplane Company, RTB Limited, the Merseyside and North Wales Electricity Board and Metal Industries Limited. In 1962 he joined the Manchester College of Science and Technology. Mr Jarman is a member of the Institution of Electrical Engineers and of the Institution of Production Engineers. He is a member of the Education Committee of the Institution of Works Managers.

JEAN K. LAWRENCE is a Senior Tutor at the Manchester Business School where she is working on the newly developed action-centred programmes for experienced managers. Miss Lawrence read mathematics, physics and philosophy at Glasgow and worked for Cadbury Brothers Ltd where she was Production Manager, responsible for chocolate assortments and Easter eggs, and Operator Training Manager responsible for training all women operatives at Bournville. She then worked as a Senior Consultant with the Anne Shaw Organisation Ltd, where she managed assignments in the food industry, shipping, retailing, cinemas and potteries. She now teaches project management—the management of large-scale, one-time changes.

K. C. LAWRENCE is Director of Training of the Distributive Industry Training Board where he aims to help the industry make wider use of systematic, practical and relevant methods of developing people to achieve the objectives of their company and to increase their own job satisfaction. Mr Lawrence's career in training management (with Carreras and Dunlop) has involved most aspects of training and development, including training semi-skilled machine operators, sales representatives, supervisors and managers although he has specialised in management selection, training and development.

ROGER LYONS is National Officer of the Association of Scientific, Technical and Managerial Staffs. He is 30. He read economics at University College London and was Merseyside Divisional Officer of ASTMS before his present job.

ORLANDO OLDHAM is Deputy Chief Executive of Royal Worcester. He was previously Chairman and Managing Director of Oldham International. He is a Harvard MBA. Mr Oldham is a member of the Court of Manchester University and Chairman of the University's Appointments Board; he is also a member of the Fellows Committee of the British Institute of Management and of the Council of the Royal Society of Arts.

A. REID is Corporate Planner of Tennent Caledonian Breweries Ltd, the Scottish subsidiary of Bass Charrington Ltd. He was appointed Management Adviser to the company in 1969 when management by objectives was introduced. He had previously had 20 years' experience in the licensed trade in Scotland, mainly in sales and sales administration.

ROY L. SPIERS is Group Personnel Services Manager of the Taylor Woodrow Group where he is responsible for providing an advisory service on recruitment, selection, placement, training and development of all staff team and young operatives. He trained as a civil engineer and ultimately became a planning engineer for major civil engineering contracts. He joined Taylor Woodrow in 1963 with special responsibility for the introduction and use of network analysis techniques for planning and programming of construction work. He was appointed Group Training and Education Officer in 1966, and a Director of Taylor Woodrow Services Ltd in 1969.

GARETH THOMAS is Personnel Officer with Kent Instruments Ltd with a wide range of responsibilities including recruitment at professional and managerial level. His CNAA degree in electro-mechanical engineering was gained by sandwich course at North Staffordshire Polytechnic and GEC. He also has a Diploma in Industrial Administration from Bradford University Management Centre. Formerly he was responsible for personnel research with Simon Engineering Ltd.

G. B. TICEHURST is adviser to Ford Motor Company operational and staff components in Europe on organisational development and management education activities. He was born at Cheltenham where he was educated from 1932 to 1937, followed by a career in the Royal Marines until 1958. After a number of industrial appointments, he joined Ford in 1962. He is a member of the Executive Committee of the Association of Teachers of Management and a contributor to ATM Occasional Paper No. 5 on the role of the training officer in industry. He is currently concerned with a variety of interventions and programmes to assist managers and managements to improve performance, and in the development of internal personnel resources to help in this process.

VERNON WALKER JONES is Manager (Personnel) of the Legal & General Assurance Society, where he is responsible for management development, manpower planning and training (with particular reference to management training). In 1970 he was responsible for installing the Society's new management development scheme. He has worked in many departments of the Society, including New Business, Pensions and Sales, and was Life Superintendent, Central London, from 1964 to 1968.

J. G. WOOLHOUSE is director of the Kingston Regional Management Centre. From 1967 to 1972 he was company education and training officer of Rolls-Royce Ltd, where he was responsible for education, training and management development. Born in London in 1931, he graduated in law at Brasenose College, Oxford, and served in the Army and in the Royal Auxiliary Air Force before joining Rolls-Royce as a graduate trainee in 1954. In 1961 he became education officer of Rolls-Royce's Aero Engine Division and made a special study of management development and training in the UK. During the last ten years he has been engaged in a wide range of training and development programmes, and has worked closely with the staff of leading British and American business schools. From 1965 to 1967 he was director of personnel of Rolls-Royce & Associates Ltd, a subsidiary of Rolls-Royce. He is an associate member of the Institute of Personnel Management, is a member of the British Institute of Management, and has been a frequent contributor to the BIM's Management Development Workshops.

Preface

Any organisation—manufacturing, educational, governmental, service, charitable or whatever—has its managers, even though some organisations might shun the term 'manager'. Those who exercise authority and responsibility for the time being need to develop those who will reign tomorrow. They have to avoid the temptation to develop replicas of themselves, but rather to develop managers able to cope with a rapidly-changing situation. This development process requires planning, the provision of skills and knowledge and the opportunity to acquire maturity and judgement.

This book gathers together a symposium of experience in widely-differing fields on how managers are effectively developed. It is offered as a pattern for action by management development officers, personnel managers, training managers, and those managers at all levels who share the responsibility for improving the managerial performance of colleagues.

There are three main sections. First we have some considerations of those aspects of organisation which have far-reaching effects on the success or failure of management development. Many promising schemes have failed through lack of the right environment; plants not being able to take root in inappropriate soil. We therefore start by considering the setting that is needed.

The second section deals with the management development activity, and our contributors discuss the different elements that have to be combined for a successful programme for both groups and individuals.

In part three we have a series of case histories of what organisations have done to grow the managers they need. Interesting here is the range of organisations which are now attempting systematic programmes of development as they seek ever-greater managerial ability in the future.

We have been fortunate in receiving the support of such excellent contributors, and we know that the material within these pages will be of lasting and real value to those who read them.

Derek Torrington
David Sutton

Acknowledgements

We wish to thank the following for permission to use their material.

The publishers of *The Will to Manage* by Marvin Bower : the extract quoted in Chapter 6.

The Engineering Industry Training Board : the job description and training needs analysis example in Chapter 8 which appear in the Board's Booklet No. 6 *The Training of Managers*, obtainable from EITB Publications Department, 54, Clarendon Road, Watford, Herts WD1 1LB.

The editor and publishers of *Personnel Management* : the bulk of the material in Mr Casey's chapter appeared in *Personnel Management* October 1971, under the title 'Individual growth in a company context'.

Mr Tony Giles : the figures used to illustrate Chapter 19.

Part 1

THE SETTING OF MANAGEMENT DEVELOPMENT

'The climate must be right' is one of the axioms used for almost any innovation; otherwise the new plant will wither and die.

For management development to succeed there has to be a variety of favourable factors in the setting. In this opening section we consider some aspects of the activity of the organisation that may contribute towards the ultimate success or failure of the management development objectives.

1

The Nature of Management Development

*L. C. Jarman, Head of Department, Manchester
Polytechnic*

In a report recently commissioned by the National Economic Development Organisation carried out at The Institute of Manpower Studies at Sussex University, Dr Timothy Legatt estimated the 1971 managerial population of the UK at 450,000, increasing to 500,000 by 1975. Management can thus be seen as a major activity in modern society and one for which, until comparatively recently, little or no training was forthcoming. In the past the managed 'just growed' as a result of being placed in a management post by virtue of birth, favour, marriage or the 'natural powers of leadership'.

Our present complex, technologically sophisticated society demands more than selection by choice and development by opportunity. Because we need more managers, more people without the obvious skills are being obliged to undertake the managerial role. The situation is heightened because we are also demanding many more skilled professionals : lawyers, doctors, scientists, entertainers, and these ranks must be filled from that body of the population which could have been expected to fill the managerial void. Certain sociological factors have worked together to help the situation : class barriers have largely disappeared enabling all levels of the population to aspire to managerial posts, education for all has removed another 'have / have not' barrier, women are increasingly taking their place in our economic society. Nevertheless, the demand for managerial talent has resulted in a realisation that we have here a human activity which makes peculiar and particular demands upon those who undertake it and that the numbers needed—if these demands are to be met—are steadily increasing. The ratio of managers to workers is rising as technology advances and greater demands are made on each management post. As a result not only are more managers needed but the level of skill and knowledge required of the individual manager is also rising.

It is only within comparatively recent years that a critical examination has been made of the management job. In the United Kingdom, management was being studied at Manchester College of Science and Technology as early as 1922, the British Institute of Management was founded in 1947 and many technical and professional bodies included management as a subject in their examinations before the Second World War. The real impetus for management training and development has, however, only appeared since 1945 and most specifically since the Franks Report of 1963 and the foundation of the Business Schools at London and Manchester in 1965. Now the flood gates are open; courses abound, management schools are legion, reports appear with the seasons, experts pounce from every angle, a new wave of corporate planners appears with each batch of MBAs; but still many firms remain at worst unconvinced, at best puzzled. An understanding of management development depends on an understanding of the true nature of management which is, in many cases, only partially understood so that many people still cannot see the ordinary mortal as being capable of practising management.

If we are to examine management development we must carry out a needs-cost-fulfilment analysis by studying total manpower requirements, determining what is needed to fulfil these requirements, assessing personal needs, examining the learning process and the activities of learner and teacher and placing all of these concepts within the framework in which they must operate in the working situation. Within this working situation where management is in action, management development must also be in action and learners, trainers and managers must develop the expertise needed to produce the managerial team of the future by using the managerial arts and skills in a manner appropriate to the technology, the style and the market. These arts and skills—delegation, counselling, leadership, assessment of performance—all form part of the management learning process and also of the management task.

The practice of management is a way of life. It is one of the inherent characteristics of man; one of the arts practised from time immemorial. Like other arts, it is based on a body of knowledge; the more exact the knowledge, the more likely is the practice of the art to reach heights of achievement.

Management is a feature of every aspect of our society. Manufacturing industry, the service industries, local and central government, educational institutions, churches—all need to be managed.

If we accept that there is a common (management) component in all these activities, this component should be capable of conceptual isolation, and a body of knowledge devised which can be taught and on the basis of which skills can be developed. It should also be possible to devise programmes of training which will provide the community with a body of trained managerial talent in the same way that it can be provided with trained teachers, chemists, engineers, economists and clergymen.

Management is a practical activity, based upon a wide range of academic disciplines each of which needs to be studied to a considerable depth. As a result, the teaching of management has become a highly generalised activity in which a team is involved in relating a wide range of academic concepts to a strictly practical situation by means of highly developed analytical abilities, creative problem solving and skill in personal relationships.

The problems of a particular manager's programme of training are multiplied when we come to consider programmes of management development for an organisation. Such programmes must not only cater for the requirements of the individual manager—they must also encompass the activities of managers at all levels throughout the organisation and provide for management succession—anticipating growth, technical change and legislative changes and providing the managerial talent necessary to motivate and control the organisation in a changing growing environment.

A management development programme should have a fivefold objective :

1 To improve the job performance of the managers currently in post
2 To provide adequate 'cover' in the event of unexpected short-term

      changes such as death, transfers, resignations or unanticipated new developments

3 To raise the general level of management thinking and understanding in all branches and at all levels in the organisation

4 To provide a supply of managerial talent which will meet the anticipated needs of the future development of the organisation in terms of commercial change, growth and increased technological and managerial expertise

5 To extend the frontiers of knowledge in the understanding of the management function.

If the management development programme is to fulfil these five requirements it must call upon the entire range of resources of the organisation and of the national and international facilities available in this field. Commitment and understanding is demanded from top management, cooperation and skill in imparting knowledge and skill from senior and middle managers, and an eagerness to learn at all levels. In many cases the organisation will employ its own management development specialists. Close links will exist with local and national authorities—educationalists, academics, consultants, management practitioners. Lectures, seminars, books, films, case studies all abound and are available for use. The objective of the management development programme is to obtain the 'best fit' in terms of effectiveness and economics not only for the organisation as a whole but also for each individual. It can be as wrong to produce a standard company mould which restricts the occasional vibrant personality as it would be to concentrate on training a few 'prima donnas' in the hope that they will leaven the whole lump in some mystical manner.

    Education, training and personal development are all part of the pattern of management development leading to an organisation-wide atmosphere of learning in which everybody has a part to play. It is common on management courses for students to say that they have learnt more from other students than they have from the instructional staff. This is often said without implying any criticism of the instructional staff and is an indication that the staff have succeeded in a major objective— the creation of a learning situation in which the student can learn and develop by using all of the resources available to him. The skill of the staff has been in providing the resources, bringing them to the attention of the students, imparting sufficient knowledge for learning to commence and catalysing and guiding the learning process.

A successful management development programme will achieve all of these effects in the company situation by marshalling and presenting the necessary resources, creating learning situations and monitoring and evaluating the degree of effective learning as expressed in job performance.

In common with other management activities, management development can be seen as having two stages of activity:

1　Making decisions—a strategic activity from which a policy emerges. The material upon which these decisions are based comprises the corporate planning of the organisation, the manpower plan, an understanding of the learning process, an assessment of strengths, weaknesses and needs (both corporate and individual), knowledge of the resources available and a clear understanding of the desired objectives.

2　Implementing these decisions—a tactical activity involving making operational decisions, motivating and controlling staff, coordinating the activities of superordinates, subordinates and colleagues—in short, achieving the results and objectives designated at the strategic stage.

A major decision must be that of deciding who is to take responsibility for the successful operation of the management development programme. The responsibility must rest finally with the chief executive because of the organisation-wide nature of the exercise. Obviously this responsibility must be delegated but the delegatee must be an executive who has the ability to represent the activity at board level. Responsibility for the continued development of existing managers and the creation of their future colleagues and their replacement must involve all of the management staff—not merely those in the management development department.

Each management post calls for an accurate matching of the job description, based upon the work which needs to be done, with the skills of the incumbent of the post. In order to fill a specific management job, a man or woman needs to cultivate a range of abilities, some of which will be in common with every other management post while others are peculiar to that one job. The basic function of the management development programme will be to isolate the present and future requirements of each job, to compare these requirements with the managerial abilities

THE NATURE OF MANAGEMENT DEVELOPMENT

available and to develop means whereby these two can be paralleled. Each management job calls for:

1 Background knowledge
2 Knowledge for application
3 Tool subjects, such as statistics or mathematics
4 Management techniques, such as value analysis or critical path analysis
5 Management skills.

Business schools, universities and colleges have tended to:

1 Identify the areas of accepted academic disciplines seen to be relevant to the management function (economics, psychology, sociology, statistics, mathematics, and so on)
2 Tack on to these subjects the quantification subjects seen as being directly related to the management activity (accounting, operational research, applied statistics, computer sciences)
3 Offer a mélange of subjects which purport to provide the embryo manager with the tools of his trade.

This approach is analogous to providing a journeyman joiner with saw, plane and adze and then turning him out to operate in a chair-making factory alongside a group of experienced workmen.

Because of the realisation that management ability can be proved only in the work situation, the teaching of academic disciplines has been supplemented by the development of a range of teaching techniques designed to relate the academic learning to the work situation and to simulate the actual management task. By using exercises of this nature—case studies, role plays, in-tray exercises, business games—and providing the situation in which the students can act as managers in a simulated situation with an analysis provided by the teacher or (more effectively) by the group itself, the teacher of management takes his student body close to the live situation and gives them the opportunity to practise as managers without the risks (to the profitability of the organisation and to the morale of the trainee manager) which attend the live situation.

Even simulation is not, however, seen as being a sufficiently close approach to the management situation and the attention of progressive teachers of management has been directed recently towards training managers while they are engaged in the real-life situation. In this way the management teacher achieves:

1 Complete integration of the working and the learning processes
2 A heightened sense of learning because the learner is in a position to learn from his own actions, with the help of tutors
3 Involvement of the management teacher in the work situation, thus enabling him to relate the learning to the action more directly and enabling him to be seen as a realistic aid to improvement in the performance of the actual job
4 Active participation between the academic trainer, the trainee and the trainee's own superior aided by any management development services which exist within the organisation.

The realisation that management ability can be proved only on the job brings a full appreciation of the nature of management development. Management development is an activity designed to improve the performance of existing managers, provide a supply of managers for the future and extend the understanding of the management activity by drawing from three resource areas:

1 The knowledge, skills and teaching abilities manifested by the academic world and exercised through the academic tutor
2 The experience, local expertise and resources provided by the organisation within which the trainee operates
3 The trainee himself.

Without a true rapport between these three constituent elements, each aware of its own contribution and the contribution of the other partners, management development will be a two-horse troika with the third horse not merely immobile in the shafts but also positively hindering the efforts of the other two.

2

Planning Managerial Manpower Needs

G. Thomas, Personnel Officer, Kent Instruments Limited

Materials, money and men—the three resources an enterprise utilises to achieve its aims.

Traditionally, our supplies of industrial and commercial manpower were thought to be governed by the same complex market forces that apparently determined our demand for this resource. More recently, however, governments and industrialists have realised the inefficiency of such forces in producing supplies of suitably qualified people, especially at the right time. Gradually, manpower planning has started to evolve. It is still very much in an embryonic stage but active research is being carried out. Some companies, with the aid of computers, are even using quite sophisticated techniques and some very high-brow mathematics.

It is certainly not my intention to expound any such techniques in this chapter. Mathematical models can be extremely useful when trying to plan manning requirements in large assembly-line production units. In such cases the sheer numbers involved, the typically rapid turnover of semi-skilled tasks required and the host of local labour market and national employment factors encountered probably warrant their use.

Even in the largest corporation, however, management manpower planning should not normally require this approach. Nevertheless, a step-by-step method based on a continuous review of one's forecasts and other data is required. It certainly is my intention, therefore, to discuss how to plan systematically the needs of the enterprise's most important resource, its managerial manpower.

Components of the plan

Any resource plan contains two essential elements, namely, forecasting the demand for the resource and assessing the means of supply. A complex arrangement of factors influence the supply and demand elements and the manpower plan must therefore be constantly developed to highlight where action is required to reconcile the two.

The most important overall consideration of the plan necessarily follows from realising that managers are the most important resource of the enterprise—the need for managerial manpower and the objectives of the enterprise are completely interdependent. By analogy, a new product should not be developed without market research and without market research it is not possible to know what types of product the enterprise should produce.

Figure 2:1 illustrates the essential components of a management manpower plan and the main factors influencing those components. The sequential steps involved in developing the plan will now be discussed.

Company objectives and operations

The starting point of the whole exercise must be to determine and realise the *purpose* of the enterprise. All other objectives within the enterprise necessarily stem from the purpose and contribute to its achievement. The predominant technology, the definition of functions and the organisation of activity are therefore relevant both to the purpose of the enterprise and its need for managerial manpower.

The company objectives, and in turn its operations, are subject, however, to a range of internal and environmental influencing factors. Within the company, technological changes are often associated with or give rise to organisational and other operational changes. In turn, repercussions on

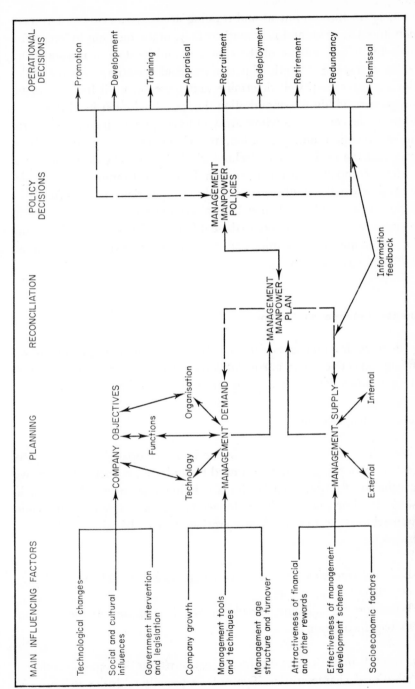

Figure 2:1 Flow diagram of the management manpower plan

the management recruitment and training needs are inevitable. Diversification into new fields and new markets may, in the medium to long term, change the whole outlook of the company and its style of management. In other cases, the strength of personality and versatility of a particular senior manager may well determine and preserve, until his retirement, idiosyncrasies within the organisation that possibly hinder its objectives.

Outside the company a whole array of forces prevail, including government intervention and legislation, the changing cultural demands of society and the rapid pace of technological change. The development of subsidiary companies in the European Economic Community countries will open new outlets and the burden of the Industrial Relations Act 1971 will pose new problems. Somewhere along the line, however, the company must reconcile its purpose to these influences. Its objectives, including those for management manpower, must thus be developed within an enlightened environment.

Managerial manpower demand

The demand for managers can now be assessed in the light of known company objectives. The particular forces of change have to be isolated and some prediction made of their effect on management manpower.

Forces affecting demand

Perhaps the greatest influencing factor is the company's *growth* objectives: for example, that there is a need to double a product output in two years, that a 'dead-cert' market for a slow home-selling product exists in New Zealand or that certain no longer profitable activities of the company need to be written off. Consideration of such objectives leads to two questions:

1 Does the company need more or less managers to achieve its desired objectives?
2 What sort of skills and knowledge will be required in the resultant management team?

The second most important factor concerns the company's internal organisational characteristics. Typically, especially with the assistance of management consultants, large organisations tend to rotate every five years or so from centralised to decentralised structures and vice versa. While this is going on the status and role of a department may rise and fall or appear and disappear. Intermingled in this planned (or confused!) organisational change is the demand for more or less managers. Bearing all this in mind, however, it is extremely important that management manpower requirements should be carefully assessed to ensure that the organisation retains the right management balance to remain effective. Some of the questions that should be asked in this context are:

1 Are responsibilities effectively and sensibly divided and/or grouped?
2 Is there any unnecessary overlapping of responsibilities?
3 Are the lines of communication and authority clear and effective?
4 Do managers know and understand their own responsibilities and those of others with whom they are concerned?

Another influencing factor is the management tools and techniques the company uses—or does not use. The age of the computer is certainly not over yet and may well be with us for good. Operational research and cybernetics are still unknown in many companies. Discounted cash flow and overhead value analysis are, however, becoming more common and widespread. The existence or otherwise of these sophisticated management practices should nevertheless help throw more light on both how many and what types of managers are needed.

The age structure and turnover in the company's management hierarchy are, in themselves, extremely important determinants of managerial manpower demand. Retiring executives often have to be replaced by internal promotion or by external recruitment. For various reasons, managers at all levels move on to work elsewhere and again they very often have to be replaced. It is certainly easier to draw up retirement schedules than to predict wastage rates. Management succession plans should therefore try to cater for the expected and unexpected turnover in managerial manpower to indicate the quantity and quality of managers required.

In summary, a company's demand for managers is influenced by a number of factors. The change in demand that these factors create has to be determined in order to ascertain the numbers and the types of managers required. Although the number and the type are in some ways interdependent, it is more difficult by far to assess the latter, especially where changes in knowledge and skills are concerned. It is misleading to assume that today's and tomorrow's managers are cast from the same mould.

Management development concerns itself especially with the types of manager the company requires. To ensure that the relevant facts are available it is imperative that the company should develop an administrative system that both describes the present and future managerial functions and indicates the personal attributes required in the managers that occupy or will have to occupy those functions.

Job descriptions and specifications

Job descriptions are a useful tool in a number of different activities, including recruitment and selection, job evaluation, training and management development. Managerial jobs need to be described within the context of the company's objectives, technology and the organisation of its operating functions. If the company does not already have a method of describing the jobs that its existing managers occupy, it is certainly well advised to do so. A manual of job descriptions could then be quite easily drawn up and maintained to take account of future managerial requirements.

For the purpose of planning the company's managerial manpower needs, and then its management development programme, job descriptions are instrumental in a number of ways. It is insufficient in a managerial job description to describe only the main duties and responsibilities, the status and relationships in the organisation and the authority for the use of resources. These factors indicate only the static requirements of a job and could bear little relation to the company's objectives. A manager's job description, therefore, should summarise his function in terms of his job objectives and the standards he is expected to reach. In this way, job descriptions can be instrumental in :

1   Specifying, in line with company objectives, the positions to be filled and functions to be performed in the organisation
2   Providing objective criteria by which performance standards can be assessed and hence individual managers appraised
3   Subsequently identifying areas of strength and weakness in individual managers and thus determining their potential and training needs
4   Identifying areas of weakness in the organisation structure so that,

MANAGERIAL JOB DESCRIPTION

Designation

Accountable to

Accountable for

I   Purpose of the position

2   Job objectives and standards

  (a)

  (b)

  (c)

  (d)

  (e) Planned development of subordinates

3   Other duties and responsibilities

  (a)

  (b)

  (c)

Figure 2:2 **Managerial job description form**

through effective replanning and management succession, these problems can be overcome.

Figure 2:2 shows a layout for a job description that could be used to cover all managerial positions in a company.

Job specifications are a necessary tool in determining what skills, knowledge, experience and aptitudes are required in the incumbents of managerial posts. They are usually developed in line with the job description. During the job analysis stage, the checklist of items to be looked for should include:

1 The desirable age range, if it is felt to be an important factor
2 The educational standards deemed necessary, including professional qualifications
3 The particular kinds of experience required, such as type of industry/ company or involvement in line/staff functions
4 The particular skills that are essential, such as fluency in a European language
5 The necessary personal attributes, such as cultural interests or an ability to communicate at all levels in the management hierarchy.

Quite obviously, job specifications must be absolutely realistic. The company must not lose its head in the clouds and try to stake its claim on, for example, a non-existent marketing genius. Moreover, the specification should steer clear of vague intangible characteristics. One thing it could possibly include, however, is an indication of the attributes that are definitely *not* required in the incumbent of the job. There is often a tendency to forget this vital point during the selection or promotion of managers, especially at the more senior levels.

Managerial manpower supply

A company's source of present and future managerial manpower may be tapped from two lines of supply:

1 Its existing internal resources
2 The external labour market.

Both the numbers and types of managers that are available must now be assessed. Like the demand function, however, the supply of managers is subject to a number of internal and external forces of change. These will be examined briefly before discussing the two supply sources in more detail.

Forces affecting supply

The company objectives can influence its supply of managerial manpower, both internal and external, in a number of ways. If the company decides to set up a component-manufacturing factory in an area with government development grant attractions, an array of problems could present themselves. Could existing managers be adequately attracted to move to the new location? Would the local supply of managerial manpower contain managers of the right calibre and experience? These problems may be even further enhanced if the company decides, for example, to operate overseas for the first time. On the other hand, prior investigation may show that the supply of adequate managerial manpower creates few problems.

Other in-company factors that can affect the supply function include the attractiveness of rewards, employee benefits, security of employment and the effectiveness of the company's management development programme. The last item is an extremely important one as it can, in itself, be a major determinant in the turnover of high-calibre managers. If a company continuously loses high-potential managers, it is a sure sign that their potential is either not being adequately identified or that the company's whole management development scheme (assuming it has one!) needs a complete overhaul.

Environmental influences are rather more subtle. Issues as near to home as housing difficulties and travel problems created by the closure of a railway line can seriously affect supply sources almost overnight. Supplies of prospective junior managers in the retail and distribution industries have been adversely influenced by the increased opportunities for young people to go to university. In such cases, the industry has had to rethink its recruitment and training policies with respect to school-leavers. In many other industries, phases of high national and international demand for certain types of specialists often create scarcities, and hence, high buying prices, for this type of managerial resource. On reflection, the reverse usually applies when the demand, as in the computer software industry, starts to drop off.

Most companies, especially the large ones, are well advised systematically to consider these far-reaching environmental influences on manpower supply. Local factors must, of course, be analysed and solved in the most economical way. Departments of the local government, bodies like the local chamber of commerce and universities and colleges may provide advice and research to this end. On a national scale, industry-wide research is often available from academic institutions or consultants. Looking optimistically more to the future, however, one might be able to foresee more information on managerial manpower supply emanating from the new National Training Agency as well as the still-existing industry training boards.

Internal supply

As a starting point in assessing the company's existing supply of managers a management inventory should be established. This inventory should record all the pertinent information about the company's managers so that subsequent analysis may indicate trends in changes of supply.

Personal history or career sheets should be drawn up for all managers in the company. The majority of the information that should be contained in these should be available from the personnel department. It is essential, however, that the record be maintained and updated. This is a simple task, demanding a straightforward and systematic approach. The basic facts that need to be recorded are:

1 Age and retirement date
2 Education and qualifications
3 Experience prior to joining the company
4 Experience with the company, with allocation for the length of time spent in each designation
5 Special training relevant to the profession or designations held
6 Special skills, attributes, interests or other accomplishments relevant to the profession or designations held.

This sort of information, logically recorded over a period of time, will enable the company to prepare age-structure and retirement schedules, turnover and wastage rates, and indications of the range of skills, knowledge and experience existing in its management structure. The analysis may be prepared according to grade of manager, department, specialisation, and so on, as required. It should certainly provide an insight into

MANAGERIAL JOB APPRAISAL

Designation

Accountable to

Review date

Period covered

1   Performance comments in respect of each objective

(a)

(b)

(c)

(d)

(e)

2   Potential and development plans

(a)

(b)

(c)

Figure 2:3   Managerial job appraisal form

the talents available in the company and may even indicate where information is lacking.

The management inventory could also be extended to contain information from the company's management review schemes. In this way, analyses of management appraisal ratings can be developed which will enable the effectiveness of the company's managerial manpower supply to be assessed.

Traditional management appraisal schemes tend to relate very much to a review of personality traits. An assessment on the basis of these factors is extremely susceptible to variations in rating standards and prejudice or bias. The results of such assessments are therefore highly subjective and open to a great deal of doubt. The more objective appraisal schemes, which are certainly more favoured in the enlightened sectors of industry and commerce, concern themselves with 'performance' and 'potential' based on the results achieved by the manager. Perhaps the most popular technique in use in this context is management by objectives.

Management by objectives is basically a particular approach to the running of an enterprise. As one of its concepts it embraces a method of improving the effectiveness of managers by appraising their performance and developing their potential. Although assessment schemes based on management by objectives distinguish between performance and potential reviews, it is also recognised that the two factors complement each other in some ways. The fact that a manager performs well in one particular job is usually a good indication that he has potential for similar work at a higher level. In predicting a manager's potential for a different kind of work, however, the performance assessment for his current job is rarely a good indicator. Some research has been carried out in order to test the validity of a range of predictions (including performance, salary progression and personality tests) for identifying potential, but there is still a lot more to be done.

The job description form illustrated in Figure 2:2 is based on the more objective approach of defining a manager's job, that is, within the context of the objectives of the organisation. The form may be quite easily developed into an appraisal form as shown in Figure 2:3.

External supply

It is important for a company, in the light of its demand for managerial manpower, to assess also the external sources of supply. Moreover, the company should try to identify the threats to and opportunities in the valuable reservoir of managers existing outside its own organisation's boundaries. Because their knowledge crosses company and industrial boundaries, management consultants who provide a recruitment service can be extremely useful in this sense. When it is found necessary to recruit from outside a senior manager of a particular type, it is often worth while to employ a recruitment consultant to 'head-hunt' the man you want.

Companies should, nevertheless, attempt to conduct some labour market research themselves. They can do this either, for example, by surveying the appropriate sections of industry themselves or by calling on information provided by the various local and national bodies described earlier. In this way the company can determine how it compares with its competitors in the labour market and, indeed, if the quantity and quality of managers it seeks do in fact exist.

Reconciliation: the management manpower plan

Having defined the demand and assessed the supply for its managerial manpower, the company must now attempt to reconcile the two functions and determine what policy and operating decisions it is to take. The conclusions to be made at this stage are still somewhat tentative and will normally need some revision. Each aspect of the reconciliation must, however, be examined in some detail.

Time span

A company's corporate plans are normally geared to the most appropriate time scales predominant in its industry. In the petroleum refining in-dustry, for example, a time span of ten years is regarded as medium to long term. A long-term plan in the consumer durables field, however, is normally regarded as being between three and five years. In all, the time span of the company's forward business objectives will primarily deter-mine how far ahead the management manpower plan looks.

Some companies can forecast their supply and demand with fair accuracy over a period of two or three years. The possibility of changes in circumstances will, however, make longer-term forecasts much more liable to error. In short-term forecasts, it is usually possible to name individuals who are to fill particular vacancies due to arise through retirement, expansion or other causes. For the longer term the same degree of precision will not be practicable. The aim should be therefore to try to ensure that enough managers of sufficient calibre are being developed to provide a foundation for the future, in so far as it can be envisaged. This may indeed sound very vague but it at least allows the company to prepare and plan its managerial manpower needs to some degree—which is better than not at all.

As far as the development of individual managers from raw recruits is concerned, the time span is somewhat longer. It seems common experience in industry to take about fifteen years to develop a promising recruit into a senior manager or director. Quite obviously, therefore, management planning is a long-term investment anyway.

Management succession plans

Management succession plans are an important integral part of the reconciliation process. However carefully developed, though, succession plans can never be perfect. Supplies often become short through promising managers leaving the company because of various attractions elsewhere. A sudden and necessary company reorganisation could throw the whole scheme out and create an excess of budding senior managers. It is, nevertheless, imperative to have succession plans in order to systematically sort out the 'mess' afterwards and minimise the losses.

Visual presentations of the company's succession plans are extremely useful. One of the more commonly used methods, as shown in Figure 2:4, is the managerial replacement organisation chart. The chart indicates the names of the current incumbents of the positions together with the names of their possible replacements. Each man's age and his current performance and promotion potential are also indicated. The chart can illustrate, in simple terms, the strengths and weaknesses of the company's managerial resources. It will probably show that for some posts a number of short- and medium-term replacements might exist. For others no obvious candidates will appear to exist at all. The chart should also enable the company to plan individual managers' development programmes.

Talent hoarding

Effective planning to meet future needs calls for a company-wide perspective. Conflicts may arise between, for example, departmental and com-

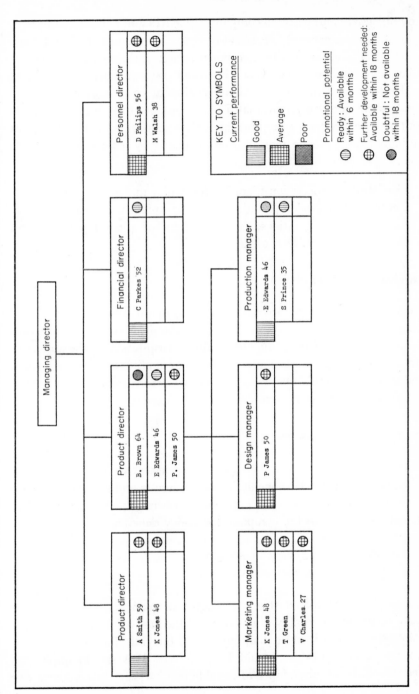

Figure 2:4 Managerial replacement organisation chart

pany objectives and between company objectives and personal ambitions. In all such cases every effort should be made to minimise the loss departments suffer when men with high potential are transferred elsewhere.

To help avoid possible 'talent hoarding' by some departments, and the frustration, turnover and high recruitment costs it may incur, top management could stipulate that a key objective of every major department was to produce a number of high-potential managers. In larger companies the problem may also be alleviated by a two-tier succession plan :

1　Decentralised succession planning for junior management position
2　Centralised succession planning, with responsibility to the main board, for more senior positions, the 'high fliers' of greatest potential and the overal coordination of the plan.

Individual career development

The individual manager's motivation and interest must be regarded as being of the utmost importance. It is undoubtedly better to try to reconcile the supply and demand functions with the aspirations of the ambitious and equally effective manager. Indeed, to ignore such factors could render the company's managerial manpower plans useless, especially in today's age of almost nonexistent company loyalty.

Reconciliation in perspective

To put the range of conclusions fully into perspective, it must of course be realised that perfect reconciliation of the supply and demand functions in the plan is impossible. Two alternative operating strategies therefore present themselves to the company for policy decision :

1　To have an overmanaged company, or
2　To have an undermanaged company.

It must be remembered that the 'degree of management' referred to above relates to the quality of managers utilised as well as to the quantity.

All other things being equal, one would imagine that the first of the two alternative strategies would be preferred. This should imply that there would be an abundance of capable managers in the company who could take over senior jobs at very short notice. The danger, however, would be in holding on to those managers until they could replace others —or, more optimistically, until they could expand the company and in doing so create jobs for themselves!

Realistically, however, the company should normally try to reconcile as closely as possible the supply and demand functions by revising them in the light of other known changes. This systematic revision, updated by a feedback of information from the managerial manpower plan, should be regularly maintained to keep abreast of changing company and environmental influences. In this way, the planning technique, if efficiently administered, becomes a closed-loop control system. Essentially, such a system aims to correct errors by feeding them back to the input functions, that is, the supply and demand forecasts of managerial manpower.

The regularity of updating information depends very much on the degree of accuracy required by the company. As a general rule, however, reviews should be carried out at least every three months in most industries. In this way, changes in policy and operating decisions regarding managerial manpower needs can be made more reliably.

Policy decisions

Certain fundamental policy issues must necessarily be determined to enable personnel, training and line managers to take operational decisions on management development. These essential policy matters include :

1   Does the company offer high financial and other rewards for high performance and potential, but low security?—or does it offer high security and average rewards?
2   Will the company give promotion on merit regardless of, say, sex?
3   Is it to be general company policy to try to promote from inside or does it try to fill senior posts from outside?
4   What degree of autonomy should be given to divisions and departments for developing their own managerial manpower?
5   How closely should the company try to reconcile the supply and demand managerial manpower functions?
6   To what level and extent should the company develop job rotation schemes for managers?

7   What will be the company's policy regarding trade union membership at senior manager levels?

The list could, no doubt, be extended to include numerous other important issues relevant to particular industries. The same point will, however, apply to them all : the policies must be determined in the light of the company's objectives and made explicitly known to all members of management who have to operate them. Moreover, as policies are changed either as a result of revisions in the managerial manpower plan or for other reasons, the alterations must be both communicated to management and fed back into the plan.

Operational decisions

As the final stage in the planning exercise is reached, the reader may feel that this, quite typically, is where all the hard work is about to *begin*. Elsewhere in this handbook the array of specific tasks, like recruiting managers, paying their salaries and developing them to do their jobs, are described in great detail. I intend to linger briefly in this domain, however, just to emphasise a couple of points.

I must certainly agree with the reader who realises that to establish firmly the company's management development programme a lot more work still has to be done. Nevertheless, the importance of the planning stage cannot be overemphasised for two specific reasons :

1   The managerial manpower plan often throws light on weaknesses in the company structure that may never have otherwise been isolated and can indicate new areas of exploration, especially in the management development field.
2   Through its systematic and objective development, the managerial manpower plan covers a lot of fundamental groundwork. This provides a framework on which the company's management development programme can be based.

Manpower planning, however, is a continuous process. The basic data required in the plan must therefore be kept up to date. Modifications should be noted and fed back into the system in order to maintain the required accuracy of the output data. In summary, the necessary components of a management manpower plan are:

1 To analyse the managerial manpower needs with respect to the purpose and aims of the company
2 To predict the potential of the company's existing managers in order to achieve its future needs
3 To assess the development requirements of the individual managers in order to utilise their potential
4 To assess the turnover and wastage factors that must be applied to the company's managerial supply and to analyse those forces affecting wastage
5 To determine the variance between the supply and demand functions in order to suggest recruitment and other corrective measures to reconcile the two functions
6 To maintain and review the necessary information system inherent in the plan to ensure that the company's managerial manpower needs are adequately sustained.

As in the past, market forces will continue to prevail and exert their influences on the supplies and needs of the enterprise's human resource. In the future, however, we must ensure that we have adequate control of those forces so that we might ultimately determine more precisely our needs of managerial manpower, our most valuable resource.

Further reading

Buzzard, R. B., 'People in Industry—Statistical Indices and Records', *IPM Journal*, September 1962.
Drucker, Peter F., *The Practice of Management* (New York: Harper & Row, 1954).
Humble, J. W., *Improving Management Performance* (London: Management Publications, 1969).
Humble, J. W., *Management by Objectives in Action* (Maidenhead: McGraw-Hill, 1970).
Pym, Denis, 'The Misuse of Professional Manpower', in *Industrial Society* (Penguin, 1968).

Roberts, B. S. and Smith, J. H., *Manpower Policy and Employment Trends* (LSE, 1966).

Roberts, T. J., *Developing Effective Managers* (IPM, 1967).

Whyte, William H., Jr, *The Organization Man* (New York : Simon and Schuster, 1956).

Woodward, Joan, *Industrial Organization: Theory and Practice* (London : Oxford University Press, 1965).

3

Recruitment and Selection of Potential Managers

Derek de Belder, Ashley Associates

Although many companies have sophisticated management training schemes they will always have to look at their own managerial ranks and outside for potential managers and compete in the market for the best management talent available. Not only will this need be in the large companies, but also in the medium and small organisations who cannot afford to have sophisticated management succession programmes, but must rely upon a transfusion of new management blood when a crisis in management promotion or appointment develops.

In looking at the situation in financial terms the recruitment of a manager at the age of 30 and who is being paid £4000 per year could mean an investment of around a quarter of a million pounds during the next 30 years. Consequently, it is of the utmost importance that every attention should be paid to all stages of the recruitment and selection process.

Analysis of the vacancy

It is not uncommon for a personnel department or recruitment consultant to be asked : 'Find us a works manager', or 'We want a sales manager— you know, a sales manager.'

Every company is different, not only in its products, but in its style of management, in its organisation structure, in the individuality of its management team and its specific requirements into personal characteristics of individuals who will be able to work in that particular environment. It becomes of paramount importance to identify clearly the appointment which has to be filled. The analysis of the situation can be done in a logical sequence by looking in depth at the total organisation, then at the function and finally at the specific location of the appointment in the whole. The objective of this identification is to reveal the interaction which will have to take place between the person appointed and other members of the management team. It is extremely rare that a member of the management team will have to work in complete isolation.

In considering the company and total organisation there are many items which need to be reviewed and the review should include trade trends and future plans, financial information, present organisation structure, methods of management, management controls, human and industrial relations, research and development, new product developments, production activities and policies relating to the relevant areas of activity.

The function must be analysed, especially in light of such items as future plans, trade trends and future of the company. If, for example, the recruitment requirement is for a replacement for the sales manager is it desirable to consider the appointment exactly as before? The market trend may indicate a larger proportion of business is now coming from overseas, and consequently one of the major requirements could be expertise in overseas negotiations.

Job description

The prime objective of undertaking this analysis exercise is to prepare the job description so that the major items of responsibility, duties and authority can be readily identified. The job description should be kept in relatively simple terms and not written in pseudo-legalistic terms. It should also be written in such a way as to allow initiative to be used. Basically the preparation of a job description is a discipline and when any management situation is analysed for the first time it can come as a surprise to find the wide range of multitudinous activities which a manager has to perform in the course of undertaking his duties.

The job description can be written in various forms and style, but irrespective of the layout of the job description form, the essential aspects of responsibilities, duties and authority should be included. As an illustration, parts of two job descriptions follow.

Job description of a general works manager

This appointment was for a general works manager in a metal-processing company with a labour force of over 400 personnel.

Responsibilities
1 The general works manager will be responsible to the managing director.
2 The general works manager will be responsible for:
   (*a*) The works manager, technical manager and all personnel in the works function
   (*b*) Complete control of the works function with the prime objective of achieving agreed targets, especially those related to production output and manufacturing costs
   (*c*) The preparation of annual budgets
   (*d*) All trade union negotiations and to ensure that all procedures are followed and that all agreements with the unions are in accordance with group policy
   (*e*) Submitting capital budget proposals to the managing director.

Major duties
1 To ensure that all systems and controls are operating in an efficient manner.
2 To appraise all production methods and to prepare a programme of projects for investigation with the objective of increasing efficiency.
3 To maintain constant surveillance on quality control.

4   To review the programme for new plant and capital plant being installed according to the overall production programme. . . .

Authority

1   He will have authority to recruit, promote, transfer and dismiss, subject to conforming to company policies and subject to keeping within budget requirements.

2   He will have authority to make agreements with trade unions subject to conforming to company policies. . . .

Job description for a financial controller

The financial controller was a new appointment in a public company employing 2500 and engaged in commercial activities. Reorganisation was taking place.

Responsibilities

1   The financial controller will be responsible to the managing director.

2   He will be responsible for :

   (*a*)   All personnel in the financial department, including four heads of department and head of statistics

   (*b*)   Ensuring that all accountancy activities are organised efficiently to enable all financial accounts to be prepared in accordance with the agreed schedule

   (*c*)   Submitting monthly accounts to the managing director and for ensuring that the accounts are a true and accurate record of the company's activities

   (*d*)   The safe transaction to the bank of all money received. (Note : the company received large sums of money each day and security arrangements were of paramount importance.)

Major duties

1   To assist the management team in the preparation of annual budgets and to submit final budgets to the board. Upon approval to ensure that monthly information is submitted to management and to investigate any variances from budget.

2   To consider the implementation of appropriate costing systems in order that the cost of each operation can be ascertained.

3 To advise the board on the detailed aspects of capital budget proposals.
4 To ensure that management are provided with appropriate and relevant statistical information. . . .

Authority
1 He will have authority to implement systems and controls as approved by the managing director.
2 He will have authority to approve expenditure up to an agreed amount. . . .

Setting objectives

Today management is being subjected to close scrutiny and their ability and achievements are being directly measured. Budgets and financial accountability are now accepted as part of management and more and more managers are accepting objectives as normal practice in their day-to-day activities. The setting of objectives can also be incorporated into the job description with the proviso that objectives are measured and kept under constant review so that the achievement or non-achievement of the objectives can form part of the management appraisal.

Appointment specification

Identification of the main areas of responsibility will then enable the appointment specification to be prepared—in other words, highlight factors which the successful applicant should have in the way of experience and knowledge to fulfil the requirement of the appointment.

The essential elements of the job specification will deal with such things as :

1 Managerial experience
2 Knowledge of the industry
3 Record of success
4 Knowledge of management controls
5 Ability to manage people
6 Technical ability.

It will also be necessary to identify the personal characteristics expected, not only for the person to do his work, but also for the person to become a member of the existing management team and fit in a harmonious manner with that team.

It is necessary to identify the likes and dislikes of the executives in that team and especially to obtain an appreciation of such matters as political, religious and other controversial subjects.

The job specification is the blueprint for making a successful appointment and is the basis from which selections can be made. There are, however, dangers in being too pedantic in the interpretation of the specification.

Identification of essential elements is a guide to success, but a too rigid specification makes the task of selection virtually impossible. If possible, each element should be weighted to establish degrees of essentiality and hence allow some latitude in the selection process.

The hundred-per-cent manager does not exist and consequently it is important that in the interview stage the areas of weakness of the applicant are identified. The technical areas of knowledge are relatively easy to define, and it is those relating to human behaviour which create the most difficulty in comprehension and analysis.

Using job descriptions given earlier, the following two specifications deal with the essential qualities required in each situation.

Job specification for general works manager

1 Must be a competent works manager with experience at controlling a similar size operation, preferably in an engineering processing batch production environment
2 Must have conducted trade union negotiations
3 Must have detailed knowledge of management control with experience at setting production budgets
4 Must have administration ability
5 Above all, must have leadership abilities
6 A professional qualification would be of value
7 A knowledge of retailing would be useful.

Job specification for financial controller

1 Must be a qualified accountant (CA, CWA or CIS)

2   Must have held a senior management appointment with control over a large accountancy operation
3   Must have administrative ability to deal with complex financial activities
4   Must be capable of introducing systems and controls
5   Must be capable of working to schedules and producing information as and when required
6   Leadership qualities are of paramount importance.

Finding the man

The job has been defined, the specification has been agreed. The next stage is often forgotten and it is to ensure that nobody in the present organisation has been overlooked. Later in this chapter a section has been devoted to the subject of management appraisals which help to identify potential management within the organisation. If it is absolutely certain that a search must be made outside, then the method of recruitment must be decided. What methods are available?

1   Public advertisement incorporating the company's name
2   Box number advertisement
3   Recruitment consultants
4   Head hunters
5   'Old-boy' network
6   Executive and Technical Register.

Recruitment advertising

Recruitment advertising has grown into a major industry and many newspapers and journals see the revenue from it as a major contribution to their economy. The object of a recruitment advertisement is to attract managers with potential ability to undertake the appointment and whose experience, ability and personal qualities meet the job specification. A good advertisement should, if possible, give the following information :

1   The title of the appointment
2   Identification of the company
3   Detail of the products

4   Location of the appointment
5   Major responsibilities
6   Essential requirements to meet the specification
7   The rewards
8   How to apply.

There is no rule which says that the success rate of an advertisement is directly proportional to the size of the advertisement and there are numerous examples where money has been wasted by over-elaborate advertisements. Copywriting and layout is becoming a skilled part of the recruitment process and the most successful advertisements give all of the above information in clear and concise terms. Above all, the cost of recruitment can escalate if the advertisement is too large and is placed in too many media at the wrong time. The ideal advertisement has one reply from the applicant who meets all aspects of the specification and who is appointed.

Many companies now have a standard style with the company symbol incorporated into the design. These advertisements generally attract attention and hence achieve the first objective.

Anonymity

There are specific occasions when anonymity is required and the use of box number advertisements has often been made. However, many of the recruitment consultants and advertising agencies offer confidential reply services which overcome many of the objections to the box number. There is always a fear that the applicant may be applying to his own company and consequently there could be some indication of disapproval at a later stage.

Application

In the requirements for the advertisement the last item refers to the method of application.

Most companies have their own application forms and for management recruitment there needs to be special care taken in the design of the form.

Basic information relating to family history, academic success, membership of professional bodies and training is required. Space must be allocated for information relating to the applicant's industrial and commercial career, leaving adequate room for sufficient information to be given about responsibilities and duties in each appointment. There is a need for some standardisation of applications, especially if a large number of applications are received. The experienced interviewer will be able to obtain the key points from the information given and assess whether the applicant's knowledge and experience is anywhere near the specification requirements.

The application form can be used as a basis for the interview, and the layout can be arranged to assist in the assessment of the individual, not only at the end of the interview process, but at the preliminary assessment of applicants. It is useful to bear in mind the usual classification of human attributes, the two most common being under the following headings :

Seven-point plan	*Five-point plan*
Physical make-up	Impact on other people
Attainments	Qualifications
General intelligence	Brains and abilities
Special aptitudes	Motivation
Interests	Adjustment
Disposition	
Circumstances	

Consultants

During the last two decades there has been a gradual increase in the number of consultancy organisations specialising in recruitment. Their methods of operation are very similar and many have established a first-class reputation for thoroughness and success.

Why use a recruitment consultancy, and what do they do? For companies that do not have any personnel management expertise within the organisation, a recruitment consultant can advise on the appointment in an objective manner, undertake a detailed assessment, examine the company organisation, prepare a detailed appointment specification, produce effective advertising and select appropriate media, assess and administrate the processing of replies, interview suitable applicants in depth and prepare a detailed short-list report.

In many large organisations the recruitment consultant can supplement the activities of the personnel director and his team and can also deal with situations which require a high degree of confidence and when there may be an overload situation.

The fees charged by consultants are generally in the region of 15 per cent of initial annual remuneration for the appointment, plus advertising costs.

A comprehensive list of management consultants that specialise in personnel selection is included in *Register of Management Consultants* (Epping : Gower Press, 1972). The British Institute of Management also has a comprehensive list of consultants who have specialist ability in recruitment activities. A decision on which consultancy organisation to use is a matter of judgment, not only of the reputation of the organisation for thoroughness, efficiency and acceptable fee levels, but also of the experience, expertise and personality of the consultant and his ability to appreciate the situation.

Head hunters

Much has been written about head hunters and their method of operation. Generally, they undertake assignments for appointments above a salary level of £5000 per year. They normally charge 25 per cent of the initial annual remuneration and many have a minimum fee of £2000. For this fee the first part of their operation is very similar to recruitment consultants in that they undertake a detailed examination of the company's activities to determine full information about the appointment and hence determine the specification. The method of finding the man can then vary, but generally by considering similar industries, they make a direct approach to a successful executive, maybe in a competitive operation. There are arguments for and against this technique and for many companies this method is not acceptable, although for others it proves to be an effective method.

Registers

Most consultancy organisations, including the head hunters, maintain detailed registers which contain information about applicants who have either applied to advertisements, or who have applied directly to them with the objective of being placed on the register.

Many vacancies can be filled from these executive banks and much depends upon the ability of the system to match up specification requirements to individual details. However, it is necessary to have detailed specifications, plus personal characteristic requirements to ensure that the major elements can be identified.

Preparing for the selection

Earlier in this chapter mention was made of the job analysis and the job description and hence the appointment specification. There are plenty of schemes for describing human differentials, and the seven-point plan has also been described.

Each of the subheadings of this seven-point plan can be further divided. For example :

Physical:
Health and physique
Speech
Appearance and bearing

Disposition:
How acceptable to other people
How dependable, how self-reliant

Circumstances:
Need for promotion, financial situation, domestic circumstances.

The appointment specification will also have given a list of essential and desirable qualities.

It is with all this background information that the interview can be planned. Far too many interviews take place without any preparation beforehand and unless the interviewer is skilled and practised in this particular profession then off-the-cuff interviews cannot cover all areas of the applicant's experience, ability and attitudes. Some industrialists claim that they can assess a person completely in five minutes—often with disastrous results.

It is necessary to assess what information is on the application form and what has been omitted, to decide what further information is required to assess the person's *actual* knowledge and what questions must be asked for a fair judgment to be made.

A checklist of questions prepared before the interview allows a logical sequence to be followed and ensures that there have been no omissions —and creates an excellent impression on the candidate.

Carrying out the selection interview

There is no magic formula for successful interviewing and each person develops his own style. However, there are several main points worth considering, especially in the selection of managers:

1   The interview should be relaxed, but not too relaxed
2   First impressions are not always true
3   Get the candidate to talk
4   Avoid leading questions, questions with a yes/no answer
5   Show interest and encourage at all times
6   Keep note writing to a minimum
7   Make a mental check that all areas have been covered.

In most management situations the interview must be searching and detailed in its quest for information. It is often of value to double-check various points and especially to take great care in identifying areas of individual responsibility. Too often a candidate will say 'We were responsible for . . .', without specifying his actual responsibility.

The length of the interview must be planned and it is doubtful if justice can be given in less than one hour. There are many occasions when an interview, especially in the higher echelons of industry, can last for three hours or more. However, a longer interview does not increase the success rate of the selection process.

An interview should always be closed as soon as the interviewer is satisfied that he has covered all aspects of his interview plan.

Qualifications

In many specifications there is a requirement for an academic or technical qualification, but it is very rare for companies to ask for evidence of achievement. In a recent survey it was found that only 30 per cent of companies made any check on the validity of an applicant's claim to a qualification, although the number found to falsify their claim is extremely small.

Assessing the candidate

Having completed the interview it is necessary for the interviewer to make his assessment and this should involve a systematic matching of evidence from all sources against the specification. It becomes absolutely vital to check between fact and inference and to judge between an opinion and a judgment.

Grading systems can be introduced covering all aspects of the specification. Some systems use a five-point system and, by indicating the level of achievement, the assessment can be made much easier.

It is essential not only to assess positive areas, but to identify the negative areas—areas where knowledge is weak, or where personal qualities are lacking. For example, a basic personality feature is an introvert or extrovert character and in certain management structures the extrovert character is considered to be essential. If the applicant does not display this requirement, then he must be marked accordingly.

One form of assessment for a works director appointment covered the following headings:

1   Family background
2   Academic and scholastic record:
    (a)   Academic (intellectual achievement)
    (b)   Social activities
    (c)   Leadership roles
3   Career pattern
4   Managerial qualities
5   Performance in present post
6   Languages
7   Domestic personal circumstances
8   Experience and understanding of working in a family business
9   Potential
10 Personality summary
11 Training and development.

Each of these assessment headings can be subdivided to enable a more detailed examination to be made.

RECRUITMENT AND SELECTION OF POTENTIAL MANAGERS

PERSONAL FACTORS	PLUS	AVERAGE	MINUS	COMMENTS
Presence/Authority	*			
Initiative/Self-confidence		*		
Self-expression/Clarity of speech		*		
Ambition/Motivation	*			
Intelligence/Clarity of thought	*			
Reliability/Loyalty	*			

TECHNICAL QUALITIES	ADEQUATE	DOUBTFUL	NOT ADEQUATE	COMMENTS
Academic attainments	*			
Professional qualifications	*			
Other				

MANAGEMENT EXPERIENCE	GAINED	LACKING	POTENTIAL	COMMENTS
	*			

JOB SPECIFICATION RATING	VERY GOOD	GOOD	FAIR	POOR
Knowledge and experience				
Essential	*			
Desirable		*		
Character/Acceptability	*			

DECISION AND COMMENTS	SHORT-LIST	DOUBTFUL	NOT SHORT-LISTED
	*		

Figure 3:1   Summary of candidate assessment for a works director appointment

For example, under the heading 'managerial qualities' can be the following subheadings:

1   Ability to gain acceptance for new ideas
2   Ability to learn from failure
3   Understanding and use of management information
4   Knowledge and understanding of manufacturing process, plant and equipment
5   Experience and ability to undertake negotiations with trade unions.

The overall assessment can then be classified into the major elements shown in Figure 3:1 and used to form a general profile of management ability and comparison with the specification.

The summary in Figure 3:1 shows that the overall profile is acceptable and that the applicant has been judged to have the appropriate experience to warrant further consideration. The process of assessment has been undertaken in a systematic manner using a planned framework which ensures that as many facets of human behaviour as possible have been considered.

Tests

Additional help can be given to the assessor by applying tests. These tests should, wherever possible, be specially designed and the interpretation of results should be undertaken only by qualified personnel.

Tests are best for finding specific aptitudes and abilities and generally they can be prepared to give an indication of statistical value rather than a true assessment of an individual.

There are projective tests such as the Rorschach Inkblot Test where the report is dependent on the interpreter, but in themselves they are not enough.

It is always advisable to discuss the application of tests with an experienced industrial psychologist in order that the correct test can be applied and the results given a professional assessment.

Selection from within

In the first paragraph of this chapter it was stated that many companies have sophisticated management training schemes which have been designed with the objective of providing management for the future. It is essential to identify potential management within the organisation and a systematic appraisal should be made at regular intervals. The appraisal of management need not be a complex task, but should be related to some of the other techniques mentioned—the job description and management by objectives being the two main techniques applicable. There are many forms of assessments, but basically they all set out to identify particular areas of performance so that a judgment can be given. It must be emphasised that the assessment depends upon the ability and experience of the person making the judgment and that it is not just a question of saying 'He is a good chap'.

One form of assessment which can be used covers the following main headings :

1 Quantity of work
2 Quality of work

3   Initiative
4   Adaptability
5   Attitude
6   Personality
7   Regularity.

Each of these headings can be considered in depth; for example, with the heading 'quality of work', it is necessary to consider accuracy, competence and reliability of work. For 'adaptability' it will be necessary to consider ability and willingness to learn new methods and availability to work under difficult conditions.

The rating of each activity need not be complicated and generally a five-point scale is adequate because it has been found that unskilled assessors have difficulty in making a fair judgment if a scale with more points is used.

In the overall assessment of any organisation there will be a natural distribution of talent and identification of those with management ability will be revealed.

The management development programme then plays its part and ensures continuity of trained management.

Costs of recruitment

Very little has been published about the cost of recruitment. It should be part of the management plan to assess the cost of every recruitment exercise. In considering the cost of a recruitment operation the following checklist will be a useful guide to ensure that all items have been considered.

1   Executive time for :
    (a)   Analysis of the appointment
    (b)   Preparation of job description
    (c)   Preparation of appointment specification
    (d)   Preparation of advertisement
    (e)   Assessment of replies
    (f)   Preparation of interview
    (g)   Initial interviews
    (h)   Assessment of candidates

(*i*)   Final interview of selected applicant
(*j*)   Replies to unsuccessful applicants
2   Secretarial time to deal with all correspondence and arrangements
3   Advertising costs
4   Candidates' travelling expenses to attend interviews
5   Cost of hotel room for interviews away from office
6   Cost of other executives' time involved in the selection process.

A summary of all these costs will then give some indication of the total cost of recruitment.

4

Motivating the Manager
Part I: The motivational framework

Mel Berger, Research Officer, Birkbeck College

The aim of this chapter is to examine the motivation of managers. What motivates some people to work hard and conscientiously and others to do as little as possible? Can we, in fact, do anything to increase motivation? While it is important to understand motivation in its own right, the understanding should lead to some practical solutions to management problems.

Although motivation is a commonly used term a brief discussion of its meaning is a good starting point. Motivation is the will to achieve a goal in order to meet a personal need. Thus, the point of motivation is to satisfy human needs—for example, to belong to a friendly group or to accomplish challenging tasks. Awareness of the need will activate a search for goals to satisfy the need. The need for accomplishment may lead the individual to look for interesting work, or, if there is none available, to look for interesting tasks in the community or within the union. If his need is sufficiently frustrated and he feels that the organisation is to blame, he may do creative, interesting things which will ensure that production is restricted or that a particular instruction is not carried out properly. Where the individual's primary need is for friendship, then his goal may be to behave in accord with the standards of the group he wishes to join and he may resist promotion if it leads to being rejected by the group. Although people are motivated by many different needs, at a given point in time and within the context of the organisation only one or two are likely to predominate.

How does motivation reveal itself in the organisation? A highly motivated manager (that is one who finds his job fulfils his needs) is likely to put forward more effort, to take more initiative and responsibility and to be more creative in his approach to the job. On the other hand, a manager who finds his job does not fulfil his needs is likely to put forward less effort, to look for another job and to be absent a good deal—usually as many days as he has sick leave with pay. Accidents, waste and other products of carelessness and neglect are further consequences of low job motivation.

Where the meeting of an important need is blocked, the usual result is frustration and counterproductive behaviour. For example, employees can use their initiative and creativity to make sure instructions are not implemented as intended and to keep production below maximum. Another alternative open to the individual is gradually to lose the desire he once had to fulfil his needs by achieving organisationally productive goals and try to do it in other areas of his life or give up altogether.

Lawrence Zeitland, who has done research into employee theft, points out that the motivation behind stealing is often to enrich a dull job rather than to improve one's financial situation.

> Theft serves as a safety valve for employee frustration. It permits management to avoid the responsibility and the cost of job enrichment or salary increases at a relatively low amount of money per man.[1]

He reports the experience of a few organisations who clamped down on theft with the result that job satisfaction decreased and labour turnover increased. It should be obvious that theft (or taking unofficial 'perks') occurs at all levels—management as well as the shopfloor. He concludes that before attempting to reduce theft, management should consider the cost of theft compared to the cost of controlling it and of alternative methods of motivating people.

Managers often talk about their work associates and subordinates as being either 'highly motivated' or 'unmotivated'. Putting people into two categories vastly oversimplifies human nature. Everyone has needs— therefore, everyone is motivated, although not necessarily to work hard for the organisation. Further, the strength of motivation to find ways of meeting these needs varies so that some people seem to have little energy to put into any activity while others are full of energy. Thus, better working conditions and a more interesting job will not be the answer to low job motivation for *some* people. But let us not exaggerate the number of these people; by doing so one runs a high risk of losing the many people in the third category: namely, those who *do* have the energy to fulfil their needs but find themselves in circumstances that frustrate their attempts.

The task of management is to find ways to achieve harmony, or to minimise inconsistency between individual and organisational goals. To say that people are either motivated or unmotivated may reflect the common view that people are by nature motivated to work hard or by nature lazy. If this view is accepted then one does not really need to consider motivation; it is necessary only to pick the right man for the right job. Thus, one can disclaim responsibility for trying to change the situation so that more people will be more motivated to work. The vast majority of people can be motivated to increase their effort and initiative in ways which are consistent with the goals of the organisation.

Motivation and performance

While motivation is one determinant of job performance, other factors are equally important, particularly the manager's skills and ability and the cooperation between people. Performance is a function of ability and motivation and organisation cooperation. If any factor is zero or minus, then performance will not be good. For example, if management development increases the ability of managers, but they are not motivated to work hard, then it is unlikely that the ability will be fully used. It is likely that they will look for another job, which their newly acquired skills should help them to attain!

Many theories and ideas about how to motivate people do not deal with all of these factors when considering performance. As the result of one or two good experiences of improving performance by increasing motivation or by developing managerial ability, a general theory is constructed. Unfortunately, however, the ideas which worked so well in one situation and with certain types of people, often do not work in another situation and with other people. This is because people are motivated by different things; they place different priorities on obtaining different goals. For some, making more money is the most important thing, for others a challenging job is essential, while for others, job security is the prime concern. In many cases, some training and development is necessary in order to qualify for a challenging job or to make their current job more challenging.

The important point to emphasise is that people will only work harder and produce more if they think that this will help them meet their needs. Working harder is seen by some as leading to promotion and by others as leading to less work to go around and hence to redundancies. Or it may be viewed as leading to loss of friends as the result of moving to another department or being promoted. In this case, friendship needs may be in conflict with obtaining more money or with being promoted. Here the individual must decide which need is most important for him. Job needs and family needs may also conflict—for example, when promotion and career progress means very long hours and moving home every few years.

It should be apparent by now that motivating people, whether at managerial or shopfloor level, is not a straightforward matter—where people are concerned, few things are simple. The solution, put in its simplest form, is to discover what needs people wish to satisfy at work and what organisationally acceptable goals will satisfy those needs. Of course, any change that is implemented in order to increase motivation has a cost which should be weighed against the likely return, including the hard-to-quantify but critical things such as goodwill and trust. It is also important to think through the consequences of improving the motivation of some employees and not others. For example, if one improves the management development activities and promotion prospects for some managers, this may have an adverse effect on other managers or shopfloor workers if they feel neglected.

The reader is probably thinking, 'Quite, but how can I motivate my subordinates?' Without wishing to frustrate the reader, and diminish his motivation to read the rest of this chapter, I urge him to hold the question and first consider the nature of motivation more closely. From this, the answers will be more apparent and methods of motivating can be linked more easily to situations where they are most likely to be effective.

Human needs and motivation

Many managers and academics have considered the question of motivation and human needs and developed their own list of the different types of needs people have. While few of the lists agree completely it is generally accepted that people have different needs which reflect their specific personality, background and current situation. At various times in one's life, one is likely to have a different priority of needs that one wishes to meet. The need for security is very great to the child but becomes less intense as one gets older. At a certain age, security will again become very important in terms of providing security for one's family. Further, the priority of needs may change rapidly, as when redundancy is a real possibility. Whereas one's prime need *was* a sense of achievement, *now* keeping the job secure is likely to become all important. In this situation, a manager is less likely to try out new ideas which involve some risk of failure and is more likely to stick with the old way of doing things or with the ideas of his boss.

Within the context of organisations and work the following four needs are of particular importance.

Security or physiological needs. This refers to the need to survive, which means, most basically, to obtain food, shelter, clothing, etc. and to avoid physical harm. Where this need is central to an individual, he desires a job which provides long-term security. He is motivated to work as hard as necessary in order to keep his security and to avoid actions which put his security at risk. As such, this type of person does what he is told and seldom takes initiatives.

Social needs. This refers to the desire to belong to a group, to have friends and to receive affection. Where this need is central, the individual will want a job that involves him in dealing with others with whom he is congenial. Once he has made friends, he does not like to lose them— for example, by being transferred to another unit—nor does he want to lose his standing with them—for example, by being made boss over his mates. This type of individual is motivated to maintain the cohesion and good feeling of his friendship group.

Esteem from recognition. This refers to the desire to be thought highly of by others and to have his accomplishments recognised. Where this need is central, the manager desires praise for his efforts and usually promotion, power and status. This type of individual becomes motivated when he thinks his efforts are likely to be rewarded or noticed.

Esteem from achievement. This refers to the wish to develop one's competence and ability, to do a job which is challenging and to accomplish worthwhile tasks. Where this need is central, the individual can be motivated by an interesting, challenging job to do and by having a certain degree of freedom to do the job in his own way, within some limits of course.

One of the best-known writers on motivation, Abraham Maslow, suggests that man is initially motivated to meet his most basic needs—physiological and security needs. When these needs are fairly well satisfied, other 'higher' needs will become most important—first, social needs and then esteem needs. The needs that are central at a given time will tend to be foremost in the individual's mind and he will organise many of his activities to meet these needs. Two important principles should be underlined. First, a need that is relatively well met will soon cease to be a motivator. Second, people develop new needs when old ones are satisfied.

Frederick Herzberg has proposed a theory of motivation based on some research studies. He suggests that certain aspects of the work situation are determiners of job satisfaction—these are achievement, recognition, the work itself, responsibility and advancement. Herzberg calls these 'motivators'. They correspond to the esteem needs previously described. On the other hand, certain aspects of work do not appear to lead to job satisfaction, but do lead to dissatisfaction when they are not adequately met: these include company policy and administration, supervision, salary, interpersonal relations and working conditions. Herzberg calls these 'hygiene factors'. They correspond to physiological and social needs, which, according to Maslow, are more basic than needs for esteem.

Another well-known researcher and writer, David McClelland, has investigated the achievement motive. He found that middle- and high-status managers are generally more achievement oriented than low-status, low-paid employees. One of McClelland's most interesting research findings was that achievement motivation seemed to relate to a country's economic growth. In countries where school textbooks contain frequent references to achieving, the economic growth rate usually increased in the subsequent twenty years to a greater extent than did countries whose school textbooks contained few references to achievement. For example, England appeared to be very high in achievement orientation in 1925 but was below the average of other western countries in 1950. His general conclusion is that economic growth is not so much the result of outside forces, war and political occurences as the result of the 'level of achievement need felt by its people'.[2]

McClelland found that managers who had a high achievement motivation desired challenging work, but not *too* challenging. That is, they liked to work towards objectives that were realistic and likely to be attainable. This has important implications for objective-setting systems —that the specific objectives should be clearly stated and that the manager should see them as attainable yet challenging or stretching.

Trends in society

So far, the differences between people have been emphasised. Things like one's age, size of family, health and money in the bank often do affect the needs one sees as most important. Yet, because we live in the same society, there are likely to be certain needs which are satisfied for most people and certain needs which are not. A broad look at the society of today and some of the changes which have taken place over the past several years can lead to some statements about the shared needs of people.

1   Social welfare, pension schemes and sickness benefits provide people with much greater security than was the case in the past. Therefore, the fear of being out of work is not so great.
2   People are more educated, more informed of rights, more mobile, and more independent. This probably stems from having a higher standard of living, having not experienced the scarcity of a depression, having increased educational opportunities and having more information through the mass media. People are, therefore, less likely to be satisfied with passively following orders and rules and with doing routine, menial jobs.

3 There are more job alternatives than in the past. Therefore, if one is dissatisfied with one's job, one can more easily find another. This provides people with security which gives them confidence to demand work that is more to their liking.

4 The values of people seem to be changing away from maximisation of income as the priority toward a greater concern with family relationships and the enjoyment of life. As Roger Williams and David Guest pointed out in a recent article, 'the status, purpose, challenge and achievement in the job may no longer be sufficient compensation for a financial return which is diminishing in relation to rising costs measured in terms of mental stress and social upheaval'.[3] Similarly, in America, 'corporations are meeting great resistance to free-and-loose transfer policies. Some [companies] . . . are deliberately putting the brakes on transfers'.[4] Thus there appears to be a shift in attitudes away from seeing hard work and promotion as the primary work incentive.

These changes imply that people are more oriented towards achievement and job satisfaction and are less likely to accept a job that is not to their liking. Threats, fear of losing the job and promise of more money are no longer very successful ways to motivate people, indeed they generally have the reverse effect. This is not to say that motivating people by meeting their security needs is never effective. For example, a research study that I conducted showed that money and security are sources of motivation for some low-paid, unskilled male labour and that friendship is a source of motivation for some low-paid, unskilled women. For most managers and highly-skilled workers, however, the meeting of esteem needs and achievement is the prime source of motivation.

At the same time that people are changing, so organisations are changing. Industrial technology is more complex and prone to becoming out of date quickly, thus requiring more highly trained specialists. This means that managers must be able to make lots of quick one-off decisions rather than rely on set procedures; they must coordinate the activities of different types of departments and specialists, consider long-term aspects of the business and cope with a rapidly changing market and technology. Therefore, to be a successful manager in most modern organisations, initiative, taking responsibility, leadership and the ability to work in and to coordinate teams is essential. Thus, organisations increasingly require managers who are achievement oriented and who want to get ahead.

Implications for management development—research findings

The theories of motivation have implications for formal and on-the-job management development as well as for job satisfaction and doing a good job. It is likely that individuals who are only concerned with meeting security or social needs will not be particularly interested in improving their skills and in learning how to do their job better. Of course, they will be motivated to learn if they feel that it will make their job more secure or improve the cohesiveness of their group. But they are not interested in development for its own sake. Similarly the individual who desires recognition will partake in management development if he feels that it will result in his getting ahead. It is primarily the achievement-oriented individual who desires to learn and to improve his skills. Indeed if he is not in a situation where he can develop himself, he is likely to be dissatisfied.

So let us briefly consider what conditions are conducive to management development. Put another way, in what situations are managers most likely to be motivated to learn and to develop their abilities?

I have recently tested the importance of various conditions as conducive to learning among managers attending different types of management training courses. It was found that, regardless of whether the course was dealing with human relations, quantitative techniques or the interrelationship of different management functions, the members who were most likely to apply what they had learned to their job were those in situations :

1 Where the manager is aware of information he lacks or skills that could be improved, and where he has clear learning goals.
2 Where he feels he will have the opportunity to use the new skills or to try out different ways of tackling problems or of organising the work.
3 Where he knows that sources of help or consultation are available when implementing new ideas, particularly when dealing with snags which may arise when translating theory into practice (this condition was an exception in that it was not relevant to application from human relations courses).

These conditions also apply to the learning or development potential on the job and should not be seen as relevant to courses only. For example I have also been involved in a large survey of how managers feel about the way their potential is being developed. The most important results are detailed below.

As expected, there were considerable differences between companies in the degree to which management development was carried out seriously. Where management development was emphasised, people felt the organisation was concerned about their future and was taking an interest in them. Where little emphasis was placed on management development, people often felt neglected and were concerned about their future. Emphasis on management development refers to 'actions'; carrying out activities and demonstrating active interest rather than just paying lip service to it.

Managers are becoming increasingly loyal to their careers rather than to their company. They will remain with an organisation only if they believe that their career will be enhanced by remaining. This means that they want advancement and development opportunities, interesting, challenging work and freedom to do the job without undue interference. Although this attitude is common at all levels of management, it is most common among managers who are young, who have considerable ability and who are motivated to achieve. The importance of this change in attitude should not be underestimated; keeping these people motivated and working for industry represents a major challenge.

People who are new to industry and to a job are often insecure about what performance standards are required and what it takes to get ahead. Young managers and trainees, before they have evolved their own standards of good and poor performance, are particularly dependent on the views of others. Without coaching and guidance at this time, they can easily become discouraged and evolve standards that are inconsistent with other members of the organisation. Further, if they feel that their prospects are limited, or if they are too hazy and uncertain, then they begin to look out for opportunities in other companies. And the more able the individual, the more likely he will be to find the opportunities. Thus, the organisation is likely to be systematically losing the best managers where it does not meet important needs.

In virtually all organisations, even where management development is taking place, the majority of managers do not feel they are receiving sufficient information about their job performance and future prospects. Even where companies have installed elaborate MBO and performance appraisal systems, the problem is not necessarily solved. Again, surveys into the effectiveness of these systems reveals vast differences between and within companies.

It is increasingly apparent that systems like MBO and appraisal performance work only where managers are committed to them in the spirit in which they are intended, and where they have the skills to implement them. For example, the theory of MBO implies that the senior manager should give up some control over how his subordinate does his job and requires that managers should deal with differences of opinion in a problem-solving way rather than by dictate. An appraisal system implies that managers are prepared to be open with one another about strengths and weaknesses and requires interviewing and counselling skills. Neither system will work unless there is a fair amount of trust and goodwill between the managers involved and unless discussion and review take place when necessary, which is certainly more frequently than the once a year that is required by the formal system.

Methods of motivating managers

The traditional approach to motivation is to consider the man and his job. Thus solutions are seen in terms of increasing the opportunities to carry out challenging work and to provide recognition for good performance—for example, by praise, more money and promotion. Another way of looking at the problem is to consider the organisation setting and climate—matters such as cooperation and communication between people, style of leadership, clarity of objectives, administrative procedures and the organisation structure itself. This approach is called organisation development and is generally tackled more participatively than the traditional, 'expert'-based, approach.

In implementing any new approach or technique, resistance to change is a common phenomenon. Resistance is most likely to occur where people lack information about the change, lack influence in the change process and lack trust in those introducing the change. Where solutions are arrived at participatively, commitment to change is greatest and resistance is minimised.

Another point to be considered is the nature of the business. Organisations based on a modern complex technology and in an uncertain market require managers who are achievement oriented and who desire job challenge. However, the organisation whose technology is relatively simple and not likely to change much and whose market situation is stable, require managers who are more security or group oriented. So the organisation should consider the situation it is in and decide what sort of managers it requires. There is no point in motivating managers unless challenging jobs exist, or are likely to exist in the future. Similarly, it would be counterproductive to develop and raise the hopes of 20 managers where only 3 or 4 challenging jobs exist.

In considering how to improve motivation, remember that people will work harder only if they think that in so doing they are more likely to meet their needs. Most people want to know 'what's in it for them', that is, how a particular new approach will satisfy them. Even where the benefits seem obvious to top management, the individual must *believe* that he will benefit and this is the result of goodwill and trust in the company. Results do not happen at once, often people watch and wait in order to make up their minds about how to react. Or they may have a go and see what happens so that in the short term the results may be very good. But if the person feels that ultimately he did not benefit, and that the organisation took advantage of him, then the level of motivation will fall, often below the original level.

In most organisations, potentially high motivation is depressed by things in the organisation that appear to hinder or block the meeting of their needs. For example, rigid procedures and the enforced use of a hierarchy of command may block initiative. Unclear goals, insufficient delegation and lack of cooperation between people and departments may hinder task achievement. In circumstances such as these, organisation development and job restructuring may lead to improved motivation.

The essential first step which must precede the introduction of any new methods or techniques is to find out what needs are most important to people and to what extent they are being met. This can be done most scientifically and on a wide scale by attitude surveys. However, it can also be done, often very effectively, by simply talking to people. This approach will work where people trust the individual doing the asking and do not fear adverse consequences of saying negative things about the job. Clues can also be obtained by observing what things seem to work and what things do not. For example, was there any difference in Joe's performance after you praised him? How did this differ from the time he was criticised?

Having considered what needs are important to people, remembering that there are likely to be individual differences, approaches to meeting these needs can be thought through. I have already looked at a few approaches and suggested that feedback about job performance and career prospects is important for those with high esteem needs. Although money has fallen into disrepute as a motivator it is often important as an indicator of good performance and of status, hence meeting recognition needs. Setting objectives for people to work towards, where freedom to meet them is given, is a motivator for those with needs for achievement, autonomy and taking responsibility. Sometimes, even where these needs are not obvious, objective setting may bring them out. For example, people who have had limited responsibility and showed little initiative in the past may develop initiative when given the opportunity. Of course, this will not be true in all cases. Participative decision-making and delegation is likely to be effective where people want to take more responsibility. Like most techniques, increased participation is not always easy to achieve. It involves some managers giving up more control and power than they wish and others having to take more responsibility than they wish.

Through an understanding of the needs of people, methods of motivating people can be evaluated. Is a technique, new policy or approach to man management going to succeed in improving motivation? Or will it be seen as a threat to people's needs? Motivating people is not easy, it is a challenging task which achievement-motivated managers ought to tackle.

Notes

1 *Psychology Today*, June 1971.
2 *Psychology Today*, January 1971. Mike Reynolds has written an account of achievement-motivation training in England in *Industrial Training International*, **8** (6), 1971.
3 *New Society*, 1 July 1971.
4 Packard, Vance, 'The rootless American : signs of a turnabout', *Los Angeles Times*, 17 September 1971.

Part II: The individual and the company

Orlando Oldham, Deputy Chief Executive, Royal Worcester

A number of recent surveys claim that money and other material incentives are not at the top of the list of motivational factors, but they are important to certain individuals and occupations and they do, in most cases, help to motivate those with high needs for material possessions or recognition—say, the salesman, but probably not the poet or the nuclear physicist, except in their own fields.

People do things because they want to, they think they ought to, or they have to. Motivation is desirable, but manipulation is not. Effective participation increases the sense of involvement and responsibility.

By 'motivation', I mean the harnessing of a person's drives and needs to an activity with which he can identify, while not improperly interfering with other influences that do something towards making him a relatively free agent. 'Manipulation' means getting somebody to do what you want him to do by any means at your disposal without regard to human dignity. There is no clear dividing line between the two, but if we think of a spectrum, with motivation at one end and manipulation at the other, we should try to be as near the motivational end as possible.

The responsibility for encouraging motivation in a company rests with the chief executive and his immediate subordinates. If the chief executive and his team provide positive leadership, show energy, drive, enthusiasm and competence, explain what they are doing and maintain good formal and human contacts throughout the organisation, then it will have an excellent motivational base.

Enlightened management practices and motivational techniques can go some way to achieving an environment in which the individual will do well. Of equal importance is the choosing of people who, because of their make-up, experience and personal needs and drives, will do well anyway. The need to motivate them will be minimal. Nevertheless, a good performer can be encouraged to become an excellent performer and people can be helped to climb to a higher plateau—given encouragement, help and a beneficial environment.

The effective manager will make it his business to recognise highly motivated people and will, if necessary, seek professional help in their discovery and in improving his own performance in the disciplined use of selection techniques.

Material incentives

Material rewards can help, especially early in a person's career, to get him to acquire the habit of working hard and effectively and to identify with the company's goals. Material rewards can also be a very real spur to those who want them for recognition or security. This is probably particularly the case with those attracted to selling, financial and entrepreneurial activity.

Material incentives can enable the senior manager to acquire capital in a manner relatively painless to the company, and thereby enable him to see things with an owner's eye. If his company prospers, he is identified with the success and material reward reinforces this. If the company does badly, then, as Robert Heller stated recently, he should be identified with the lack of achievement and feel the owner's pain.

Even if material rewards do not increase motivation, they will attract the more talented people. The reward actually may not increase their effectiveness, but it at least makes sure that they are there.

Forms of material reward

Money can mean many things to many different people. It can be seen purely as purchasing power, and those with high material needs are obviously going to be stimulated by this need and the chance of satisfying it.

It can be a measure of achievement, enabling the possessor to announce his achievement by display or by his own inner satisfaction with the value placed on him by others in monetary terms. It can represent security. It can provide the means towards an infinite number of ends.

Money *can* motivate, it *can* call forth that little bit extra that makes the difference between a good average performance and an outstanding performance. But money is not the only motivator, and in some cases it is almost irrelevant.

Harmonisation of company goals with personal aspirations

Each individual in a company has certain aims and ambitions, however great or modest. The company itself has goals and objectives. Motivation will be at its maximum if these coincide; therefore top management should see that the aims and objectives of the company are clearly set out and clearly conveyed to the individuals and, within reason, they should try to determine how the aims and ambitions of their associates fit in with these.

What are the factors that motivate individuals or groups who achieve much, either in the course of duty, in professional activities or through inner drives and compulsions or non-material inspiration? Can these be identified and used in the industrial setting? Let us start with the obvious : different non-material factors motivate different people. Some people seem to have an inner compulsion—one could call them 'self-panickers'—so that they do not need motivating, they need identifying and selecting for the jobs where their dynamic attributes are appropriate, and they can help to motivate others.

The opportunity to exercise one's various talents, to be fully stretched, can enable those internally motivated to give of their best.

Participation

The matching, as far as possible, of company objectives and personal objectives is unlikely to be achieved unless everybody has a chance of participating, to some extent, in the setting of these goals. Those dealing with overseas companies will be aware of the difference of enthusiasm and strength of motivation of overseas teams when they are working on something they have initiated themselves, compared with when they are working on something which they consider has been imposed on them, or strongly influenced from outside.

Promising schemes, theoretically correct, can founder if badly presented, whereas much more doubtful schemes can succeed when backed with enthusiasm and ingenuity.

Joint consultation between different levels of management and with shopfloor employees can do much to improve motivation and morale when carried out in a genuine, honest and well-prepared manner. At Oldham International, full information was given to all, including the Shop Stewards Committee, on company achievements, including financial achievements, and company goals, only through face-to-face contact, backed up by written and printed information.

The working environment

Conduct results from an interaction of what a person is and his environment. Not everybody flourishes in the same environment, so the composition of a working team can be as important as the choice of individuals. An organisational pattern should be chosen that will allow a wide variety of people to operate effectively and to grow. There are many different styles of management and organisation and there are good and bad examples to be followed in each style.

Whatever style and form of organisation is chosen, this should be clearly explained to those who compose it. Formal relationships and reporting should be discussed, but also informal relationships, and where there could be a conflict of roles or personalities, this should be discussed openly with a new member of the team. It should be recognised that there is an informal organisation as well as a formal organisation, the former being extremely dynamic, the latter more static. It will be hard to describe the informal organisation but it should be acknowledged to exist and a spirit of awareness created towards it.

In general, people do reflect the general tone of the organisation. A factory that is well laid out, with good housekeeping, attractive functional offices, good industrial design throughout, extending to packaging, letterheads and trade marks, will have a much better *esprit de corps*. The atmosphere of a successful company—or country for that matter—has an important effect on morale, and hence on motivation. It is desirable for a working group to taste occasionally the sweets of success arising out of their efforts. Success feeds on success until it collapses into complacency. Just as with individuals, this is largely a case of confidence building—if you believe you can do it, you can, and this belief is helped by past evidence.

Avoiding demotivation is perhaps as important as attempting to increase motivation. If you have chosen people with a high degree of internal motivation, then the main task will be to remove impediments and frustration without becoming involved in harmful short-circuiting. The morale of the team must be safeguarded, as well as that of the individual.

Infusion of talent and a variety of experience

Part of the environment that is conducive to good motivation is a sense of dynamism and creativity. To maintain this, it is generally necessary to have a continued infusion of new talent and to provide a variety of experience for those within the organisation.

To achieve this, an organisation has got to be able to recruit the kind of people it wants and this means, today, that those doing the recruiting must have a feel for what is going on in society outside and how the goals and objectives of society, however confused, are shifting.

Some of the most able people, the 'self-panickers', will tend to enter those organisations that enable them to get done what they want to get done. To paraphrase the first Lord Leverhulme, they are entering business, or some other occupation, because that is where things do get done. If business does not offer this opportunity to the most able, they will go elsewhere and industry will lose talent and a powerful motivating factor.

This means that if business affairs are carried out in a way that tends to the general good and to help in solving the world's problems, then business will attract the best people. One way to keep them is to offer a variety of experience to broaden the manager's knowledge and background, and enable him to try out various roles, some of which might give self-motivation a greater chance of becoming apparent.

Broadening experience includes outside courses, and here it is important not to disappoint a returned executive. A major course should be taken, if possible, before a promotion. The broadening of experience, including the taking of courses, should form part of a thought-out and written-down clear pattern, prepared with the active participation of the person it affects.

Consent of the governed

It has recently been said that power has passed to the shopfloor. In crude terms this is so; managements operate with the consent of the governed and at any time the governed can make it impossible to govern, it being perhaps easier to do this today than hitherto. Nevertheless, this power will be useless for good unless it is shared and the need for government recognised. This can be made explicit and understood by all within a company. I did this quite openly at Oldham International as in Glacier Metal but, on a quite informal basis, I sought periodically to obtain the consent of the governed, admitting quite openly that I needed it. Having got it, management can—and usually should be—firm and disciplined.

Where the consent of the governed is obtained and constantly renewed, morale and motivation increase.

Raising the sights and competition

There are specific techniques for concentrating attention and focusing on desirable achievements. The setting of clear targets, after full consultation, and the recording of success against these targets, can do much to improve performance and it can also raise the sights of the manager. People can be shown by example that they can achieve more than they ever expected. For instance, before the managerial revolution took place in Britain, it was just generally assumed by the young American manager that he could do things which his British counterpart at that time would not have attempted; the American was not more able, but his working environment, the expectations of those around him, and his own inner motivation were so much more stimulating.

In our society, for good or ill, competition is a great motivator whether this be competition between individuals, between companies or between nations. It is important that the effect and pressures of competition be experienced by all managers, particularly that those 'inside' feel the pressures from outside direct.

Thus, for example, a technical section should, on occasions, be brought face to face with those who are using the products they design and develop to experience first-hand praise, blame or analysis. This of course must be done in a controlled manner.

Information on competitive performances, whether through inter-firm comparisons or published figures, should also be made freely available and compared with one's own performance.

Annual comment on working relationships

A manager within a company should have the right, at least once a year, to comment on his job and his relationship with his working superior, in the presence of a third party, and he should be told in detail of how his working superior feels he is doing his job and be given advice, where appropriate, detailing what steps could be taken to do it better.

A properly structured discussion of this kind enables both parties to see how the job has changed and enables a fresh assessment to be made by the working superior of the talents and capabilities of his working subordinate. The former has the opportunity of again discussing company goals and how these relate to the particular job under review and of seeing how these match up with the ambitions and needs of the person being interviewed.

An effective scheme of this kind is described by W. L. T. Isbister in his book, *Performance and Progress in Working Life*. Similar techniques have been applied under the name of management by objectives.

In what has been described the structure of the company, the choosing of people, the study of their jobs, a balance should be sought. A company needs a variety of ideas and some creative friction. A bunch of happy, harmonious conformists will get you nowhere; a bunch of quarrelling individualists, pursuing their own private goals at the expense of the company, will get you into deep trouble.

Personal relationships

Satisfactory and satisfying personal relationships can motivate and the opposite can demotivate to an even greater extent. A manager should spend a considerable time fostering the right relationships with his working subordinate and those on the same level within the organisation.

Healthy personal competition, a desire to be first at the feed pail is good within reason, but it is harmful if it destroys trust and teamwork. Much corporate time is wasted on internal politics that could be better spent in achieving agreed results.

A company will not prosper or only rarely do so in an atmosphere of mistrust and fear. Few people work their best in these circumstances. Therefore, the manager must be alert for tell-tale signs of corrosive and personal rivalry and he must step in when these signs appear, to stop the corrosion spreading.

It may be necessary to move an effective individual if he renders his colleagues ineffective by his actions or in the last analysis even by his personality. His face has got to fit. However, faces can often be helped to fit by skilful counselling or even reorganisation.

Encouragement, praise, friendliness, warmth—all these things help to create a climate of trust and well-being in which people can flourish.

A company with a good reputation for personal relationships, friendliness and concern will attract and keep the best people and reinforce their territorial instincts.

5

Administration of Managerial Salaries

Derek Torrington, Principal Lecturer in Industrial Relations,
Manchester Polytechnic

For any programme of management development to work it has to
have an appropriate system of salary development running alongside it.
Managers being developed need to see their rewards and potential
rewards growing with their performance. This will ensure their continued
motivation and commitment to the development programme, and may
prevent them being picked off by a competitor.

There are, however, dangers in setting up a scheme of salary development for managers making progress in isolation from other managers who
are flying less high, or who may be standing still. Although this book is
concerned largely with accelerating the growth rate of the outstanding,
we must also be concerned with the management performance as a whole.
There is little value in grooming a handful of young managers to reach
expensive eminence in the organisation by the time they are 30 if they
are surrounded by other managers who are apathetic or obstructive.
Disenchanted barons can jeopardise the effective progress of a crown
prince.

ADMINISTRATION OF MANAGERIAL SALARIES

This chapter will consider a system of salary administration for all managers, which has within it the ingredients to ensure the commitment of managers that the organisation is attempting to develop without prejudicing the remainder of the management team.

Objectives of salary administration for managers

Four objectives of salary administration for managers are suggested : equitability, marking promotion, motivation and reward for achievement

Equitability

The scheme needs to be one which produces equitable salaries for the managers employed. The salaries need to be sufficiently high to retain the services of managers by being competitive with those offered by other employers, so that managers will not be lost to the organisation just because the level of payment is too low.

Salaries need to be sufficiently high to attract managers into employment from other organisations when the need arises for their recruitment.

The comment in the two preceding paragraphs might imply that the employer should pay salaries that are as high as possible, but there are two other factors to consider, apart from the differentials within the salary structure. First, the organisation will need to pay salaries which are low enough to make for an economically efficient operation. Second, salaries will need to be low enough to permit people to leave if they are genuinely anxious to do so. In any organisation there will be managers and others who would like to leave but who cannot, either because they are too old to be taken on by another employer, because they have specialised skills for which there is a dwindling market, because they are not willing to jeopardise their pension rights, or because they have an unexpired contract which they are obliged to honour. Here there is a focus of discontent in the company. When things generally are going well it is merely the individual who suffers, while everyone else gets on with the job. If the organisation is suffering a spell of doldrums, then the discontented individuals act as a focus of infection in the whole working community.

People who wish to leave, and who would were it not for the fact that their existing salaries are artificially high and no other employer can match them, will remain in employment because they 'cannot afford to leave'. This type of malcontent may well be more of a problem within the organisation, and it is necessary to consider to what extent it is ethically justifiable to limit the freedom of movement and job choice of the individual by paying premium salaries.

These considerations require a system of salary administration that achieves a delicate balance to avoid paying too much or too little.

Promotional pathways

Different salary steps can mark the route of promotion for the aspirant. Job advertisements and recruitment literature are full of lush promises about 'excellent prospects for the right man', and there is always a rosy future somewhere up ahead. Not always does the aspirant know where it is and in which direction he should travel.

The employing organisation will presumably attach the highest price tags to those jobs it most values. Most managers wanting to make progress are looking for the best-paying jobs, both because they want the money, and because they seek to enjoy the approval of those higher up the hierarchical ladder than themselves.

In wondering which route to take to the top, the young manager will have an amount of folklore to guide him, as well as his own aptitudes and predispositions. The folklore will consist of things like 'The sales people get paid more than anyone else' and 'There isn't any future' in the area of the person he happens to be talking to at that moment. The view that salesmen are the highest paid presumably stems from the fact that they put on the bravest show and are at pains to sound and appear affluent. The lack of prospects in the area of the person he is talking to presumably stems from the lack of progress of the person advancing the opinion, and lack of opportunity is a splendid excuse for lack of progress.

If promotional pathways can be defined in salary terms, the young recruit knows where to set his sights and he knows what he can expect. Also the man who has got stuck in a particular job, and who expects to be paid a little more each year for doing the same job, can be stimulated to attempt a move if he can see what the move is worth.

Motivation

Although the idea of hygiene and motivational factors has reduced the importance of money, it is still true that it does have a motivational effect in managerial performance, both from the point of view of the attractions to some of enhanced purchasing power and from the point of view of the recognition of one's worth that salary level indicates.

Money can be thought of as a hygiene factor in the situation of the disenchanted barons referred to at the beginning of this chapter. If the salary is right there is likely to be at least a marginally beneficial effect on performance. If the salary is wrong there may be a seriously adverse effect on performance.

Reward for achievement

The final objective of salary administration can be described as being to reward achievement, both of the individual and of the group to which the individual belongs. The objective is to avoid an indiscriminate share-out of salary increases in which the efficient benefit to the same extent as the inefficient. It has already been suggested that there are dangers in dissatisfying the average manager by ignoring him and concentrating all one's attention on the above-average. Equally we have to avoid dissatisfying the above-average manager through his above-average performance receiving no greater reward than the average performance.

Setting up a scheme

Since the Second World War piecework incentive schemes for manual workers have generally become so complex and out of control that there have been extensive attempts, through job evaluation, measured day work and similar schemes, to clean up the method of wage payment on the shopfloor. To the observer it seems sometimes that salary payment schemes will soon be in the same plight. Many company schemes are being developed with a degree of sophistication that may carry within them the seeds of their own decay. Complexity can lead to inflexibility, which in turn can lead to salaries being inappropriate and to the need to latch something onto the system in order to keep it working. A scheme of this nature can also become something of a cage, out of which it is both difficult and expensive to break. At first glance one might think that schoolteaching is an uncomplicated job from the point of view of salary administration, yet the latest agreement on teachers' salaries contains eight pages of explanation, forty-eight pages of closely printed appendices and eight pages of index—and there is widespread dissatisfaction with the scheme!

With this in mind, the type of scheme advocated here will be a simple one. It should adequately meet the objectives set out earlier, but it will not require the appointment of a large staff to run it, and it will doubtless incur the displeasure of the professional salary administrator by reducing the mystique with which he has carefully surrounded his job.

This section deals with how one might set up a scheme from the very beginning. A three-stage process is needed to establish the framework.

Salary groups

How large a group will the system cover? Salaries are generally regarded as the wages paid to the non-manual employees, so some organisations may set up a single scheme to cover all staff and management. Others may seek to differentiate between staff and management, or even between staff, middle management and senior management. A further consideration is that of who is included as a manager. The designer may be earning a higher salary than the office manager, although he has little managerial responsibility. Presumably he would be included within the same salary scheme.

The first decision is on who is to be included overall, and then a decision is made on the categories of people who should be grouped together on common salary ladders. This means that their jobs are to come in the same payment scale and subject to the same criteria. Having decided the grouping, the salary limits are then added to the group. If a system is being set up for managerial and specialist/professional employees, it might have the following:

Senior management group (All divisional managers reporting to a board member, plus company secretary and accountant)	£3000–£6500
Middle management group (All managers reporting to senior managers, plus senior technologists, plant managers and regional sales managers)	£2000–£3500

Supervisory group   £1500–£2500
(All managers and supervisors re-
porting to middle managers, plus
sales representatives and graduate
trainees)

The group has a general title for the sake of identification, but the different people who are to be in that group are described in the brackets following the title. The title of the group does not necessarily describe the duties of all the people in it.

It will be noticed that the maximum salary figure for middle managers is above the bottom figure for senior managers, and the top figure for the supervisory group is above the bottom figure for middle management. This is an important element in salary administration, as it recognises that ranking is not the sole determinant of salary level. There is an element of salary growth with experience as well as salary growth through status and responsibility. Furthermore it usefully blurs the edges between the groups, taking the sting out of possible grievances about a man seeing someone else in a higher salary group than himself, even though his job is obviously one which deserves more recognition than the other man's. This principle is carried further in the next stage of the framework.

Salary ladders

For each group, a series of ladders is set up. Each ladder has a number of steps and each step indicates a level of salary payment. The steps vary in size, or value, so that the higher the salary, the larger the step taken in making progress. Roughly, the steps are in proportion to the salary, thus ensuring that a salary increase is meaningful in terms of the earnings of the recipient. Also the top rung of each ladder is equal to the fifth rung of the ladder below, providing considerable overlap. To some extent this is again to take the edge off ranking differences, but it also enables people to earn the same salary despite the fact that their career position is different.

Consider the salary groupings given as an example in Figure 5:1 and a 55-year-old in charge of a smallish department. He is thorough and competent, but has probably reached his occupational ceiling and will doubtless retire while in the position he currently occupies. The appropriate salary step for him might be middle management A3 at £2400.

ADMINISTRATION OF MANAGERIAL SALARIES

Supervisory group		A	B	C
	1	1925	2150	2500
	2	1850	2075	2350
	3	1775	2000	2250
	4	1700	1925	2150
	5	1650	1850	2075
	6	1600	1775	2000
	7	1550	1700	1925
	8	1500	1650	1850
Middle management	1	2625	3000	3500
group	2	2500	2875	3300
	3	2400	2750	3150
	4	2300	2625	3000
	5	2225	2500	2875
	6	2150	2400	2750
	7	2075	2300	2625
	8	2000	2225	2500
Senior management	1	4750	5500	6500
group	2	4500	5250	6100
	3	4300	5000	5800
	4	4100	4750	5500
	5	3950	4500	5250
	6	3800	4300	5000
	7	3650	4100	4750
	8	3500	3950	4500

Figure 5:1   Salary groups, ladders and steps

This gives him the possibility of two further steps to his maximum of £2625. In contrast there might be a younger, better-qualified assistant manager in a larger department. He may have greater career ambition and greater potential, due to his age and qualifications. In this case it would be more appropriate to put him at middle management B6. Both men would receive the same salary, but the younger man with the greater potential would have a more attractive maximum figure attached to the job he was doing.

Slotting

Once the framework of salary groups and salary ladders has been set up, the next problem is of job slotting and step determination. What job goes where and what rung of the ladder is the incumbent placed on?

The answer to this question depends on whether there is a system of job evaluation. If there is, it does the job of assigning people to points in the scale and will determine the appropriate differential between jobs. If such a system is not in operation, there are at least the following factors to consider.

Recruitment problems. The slotting of a particular job may be influenced by the difficulty in recruiting people for that type of position. If there is a shortage in the region of the type of manager being sought, it may be necessary to establish a premium rate to attract them. Similarly, a premium rate may have to be established to attract managers of the appropriate calibre if the industry is unattractive to those seeking career prospects. Many managers would hesitate before joining a company in an industry that was clearly in decline. First, he would lack the opportunities that come most readily with expansion. Second, the decline might reach the point of leaving him without employment at all.

Market values. Apart from recruitment difficulties through shortage of appropriate people or the unattractiveness of the industry, there is the competitive position of management salaries. It is not just competitors in the marketing sense that are considered here; it is a question of the prevailing rates paid to managers by all companies.

Executive salary surveys show that salaries for comparable posts tend to move in accordance with two criteria : the number of people employed and the annual turnover. Each company needs to establish the level at which its own salaries are to be pitched in relation to those applying elsewhere.

In order to establish what the current going rates are, there are two suggested sources of information that can be generally recommended. The British Institute of Management (BIM) conducts an Executive Remuneration Service, which is the most comprehensive available in the country. A biennial survey of salary structures is conducted among some 400 member companies of the BIM who volunteer to take part. The information is then analysed and classified for information to the companies who have participated. Only those companies taking part are supplied with the information. The BIM also provides a service by putting in touch with each other companies wishing to exchange information on salary structures.

The second source of information suggested is the Salary Research Unit of Associated Industrial Consultants (AIC). A similar survey is conducted and then the information is available for purchase from AIC. Both these provide useful barometers of prevailing salary levels.

From time to time smaller-scale salary surveys are carried out, usually within a particular locality. Branches of the Institute of Personnel Management occasionally do this to provide some comparative information for participants. There are also attempts by groups of employers to get together to exchange information. It seems important that the identity of employing organisations is rigorously camouflaged and that the exact basis of the remuneration being reported is clear.

If company identity is to be revealed it may be that one or two participants will report their salary structures in an unduly generous light, as no one wants to appear publicly as a poor payer. If one company has a system of incentive payments for managers on top of salary while another does not, it would be of little value to compare directly salary only.

One of the most common methods of determining prevailing rates is fraught with danger, and that is to glance through the situations vacant in the Sunday papers. This is only likely to be of value if it is done with strict discipline, over a number of weeks and using a number of different publications. It will still be suspect, as a number of companies never reveal salaries in advertisements, and a number of managerial positions are filled without resorting to newspaper advertising.

Union pressures. A developing factor is that of pressure from trade unions which can either be directly on managerial salaries, if these are subject to negotiation with a union, or—more frequently—indirectly through union pressure on the rates paid to those reporting to members of the management.

If there is direct union negotiation on managerial salaries, this clearly restricts the degree to which there can be employer initiative and unilateral decision on the value attached to different jobs.

Where there is not direct union negotiation on staff salaries there may nevertheless be an influence on them from other negotiations. A steep negotiated increase for one section of employees that was higher than increases negotiated for others might tend to push up the salaries of the managers of the first group more than other managers.

Infrastructure comparisons. A frequent problem with salaries is that one person thinks his salary is out of line because someone else doing a less worthy job is paid the same or more. This is why employers pay such close attention to going rates in other firms in order to reduce the amount of dissatisfaction on an inter-company basis. There remains the question of comparisons within the organisation. Should the production manager be paid the same as the sales manager, or more or less? Is the production engineer on a higher salary than the safety officer?

Job evaluation is designed to prevent this type of indecision and potential sources of bickering and frustration by imposing a standard set of criteria by which each job is assessed. Another way—still more common than job evaluation among managers—is to have a policy of secrecy. Salaries are not disclosed other than to the individual recipient and the salary administrators. This can increase frustration by replacing knowledge with speculation. A half-way point between total secrecy and public knowledge may be to publish the ladder on which a person is placed without revealing the step of the ladder he is standing on, so that someone publicly acknowledged as being on a B ladder could still be earning more or less than someone on ladders A or C.

It remains important to get the infrastructure comparisons right, not only to avoid frustration, but also to facilitate promotion. If future foremen are to be found from among the ranks of able young technicians, then the salary prospects for foremen need to be better than those for technicians.

Present salaries paid. The greatest constraint in setting up a system where none existed before will often be the existing salary level. The slotting of jobs needs to be done on a logical and defensible basis, but it equally needs to take account of the present situation. Clearly no existing salary can go down, it is a question of how much they go up, and the scheme could get into disrepute fast if certain individuals or groups received rapid, steep and expensive increases simply to meet the requirements of a rigid system of job evaluation. Some flexibility is needed, but not so much that the criteria of job slotting become meaningless.

Job slotting involves slotting twice. First the job is slotted, then the incumbent. In the first exercise, group and ladder are decided; in the second exercise, step on the ladder is decided. Both exercises are straightforward enough, requiring careful but constant attention to each job, taking into account the various factors discussed above, and then reviewing the decisions made in case slottings done at the end of the exercise have jeopardised the slottings done earlier.

Eventually a framework is achieved with every job and every incumbent slotted. This should provide the basis of equity and justice that is so fundamental to any aspect of personnel administration, and it will provide the steps up which people can aspire to climb if they want to improve their position. It will also provide a ceiling so that the person who is feeling reasonably comfortable at a step 1 or 2 position has to make up his mind whether he is going to accept that as his ceiling or whether he is going to make the effort to get onto a different ladder.

In various ways people know exactly where they are and how they can make progress, if they wish to. The next section considers how salaries are to be updated.

Updating a scheme

The main objective here is to maintain the appropriate company differential; ensuring that the competitive situation *vis-à-vis* other employers remains sound. Other objectives are to reward achievement, and to eliminate anomalies.

There is some interesting evidence on company practice from one of the most useful recent surveys, *Salary Structures*, by the National Board for Prices and Incomes. This gives an account of what information was examined by companies before setting the size of their overall salary budget; 23 per cent of the 5307 respondent companies said that the question did not apply as they had no overall salary budget. The other factors were:

Information examined	*Percentage of firms*
Movement of salaries in other companies	49
Movement of wages against salaries in the company	49
Movement of salary bill since last year	36
Profit targets	32
Comparatios	4
Other information	12

This information is given in Table 18(i) of the report. A footnote quotes the most usual aspect given under 'other information' was the ratio of salary bill to turnover.

Consideration of these criteria will bring the management to a point of decision about what the salary bill for the forthcoming year should be. Then there is the problem of how this amount—assuming that it represents a potential increase for managers—can be translated into appropriate salary increments for individuals. We can consider three criteria.

Cost of living. In current economic conditions a salary set in January will be worth less in terms of purchasing power by the following December. For this reason salaries need regular topping up to account for the rate of increase in the cost of living.

Service. It is common in public service to have a salary structure allowing for significant increases in salary as a result of nothing more than the passage of time. The incumbent moves steadily up his salary ladder, one rung at a time, until he reaches his maximum for the post he is occupying after five or ten years. Mainly this method has value where there is a relatively flat hierarchy in the organisation and a large proportion of 'operatives', such as police constables or schoolteachers. Opportunities for promotion may not be great, due to the flat hierarchy, and competence may well develop steadily over a period of years. Service is rewarded with increasing payment.

In industry and most branches of commerce there is likely to be a steeper hierarchy with promotion more generally available and more socially 'OK'. It may be management policy to discourage people from settling down and staying in one job or at one level. Even so, many industrial schemes allow for some salary increment on the basis of service, even if it is only on the basis of holding back the full salary for a post until competence is proved after a few weeks or months of satisfactory work. In overall salary administration the question of service increments needs careful judgment, though it is unlikely to be an issue in management development schemes, except where trainees may be pursuing a lengthy programme of development, the length of which prevents them from making any significant contribution to company performance for some years after their career begins.

Achievement. The third criteria for salary adjustment is the increase as a result of personal achievement. This word is used in preference to the word 'merit', which is more common in this context, as it is important that the salary adjustment should be related to what the person has accomplished rather than what he is.

This type of increase is the most important from the motivational point of view, but it is also the greatest potential source of trouble when Fred gets an extra £100 and Bill gets only £50. The criteria for recognition of achievement have to be clear and acceptable. If this does not happen, then the incentive to one person is a *dis*incentive to a number of others. Again we remember the danger of disenchanted barons surrounding crown princes—with the bluest of blue eyes!

If increases are accorded for intrinsic merit they are more difficult to justify than if they are accorded on the basis of agreed objectives being fulfilled.

Normally salary adjustments of all three types should be made at the same time of year, so that the disease of salary speculation is eliminated for as much of the year as possible, and so that people can get on with the job for which their salary is paid.

The most common times for salary reviews are the beginning of April or the beginning of January, to coincide with the beginning of the new financial year and fresh budgets. Some organisations have moved the date to September. Their argument is that September and October are the most popular times of the year for executive job changes, and some people might not move if they knew their new salary. Another argument in favour of this time of year is the dampening of salary speculation.

The danger of salary speculation is not only that it is time-wasting, but also it can develop unrealistic expectations so that a genuinely generous increase can appear niggardly when compared with the unjustified hopes that had been carefully contrived. As summer months are usually a time of preoccupation with holidays and kindred activities, salary speculation may not loom very large on employee horizons and salary increases become a pleasant surprise on return from two weeks on the Costa Brava.

Setting the overall budget figure

A responsible and knowledgeable executive of the organisation makes a careful estimate of the amount extra that the organisation needs to add to its salary bill for the forthcoming year to allow for salary increases. He may also need to allow for salaries to be paid to an increased number of employees.

Normally this executive would be the personnel manager, or one of his subordinates in a large organisation. He needs to consider all the salary-influencing factors, such as going rates, recruitment problems, cost of living and so forth. He will then produce a two-part figure for his management colleagues to approve. One part will be the percentage increase that he sees as being appropriate for cost-of-living increases; the other will be an amount to reward achievement. If the organisation is one in which service is recognised in a formal way by granting annual increases, there will then be a third part to the submitted figure, although this will need calculating with some care as increases to those with service may well be cancelled out by a proportion of relatively new recruits starting well down the scale from their predecessors. There may even be a small economy here. With a salary bill of £1,000,000 annually the submitted figure might look like this:

Present salary bill	£1 000 000
Proposed cost-of-living adjustment ($7\frac{1}{2}\%$)	£ 75 000
Adjustments for achievement	£ 50 000
Net service adjustments	£ 5000
	£1 130 000

It is unlikely that his managerial colleagues will accept the figure without debate, and it may well be trimmed down before final agreement. Although this is almost inevitable, it becomes difficult when the determination of next year's salary bill becomes freely negotiable, with the personnel manager asking for more than he needs because he knows it will be trimmed; and his colleagues then trimming it down because they know he has asked for more than he needs.

Having got agreement to his overall figure, the personnel manager starts work.

Divisional salary lists

Within the organisation there will be various senior managers with authority to influence the salaries of their subordinates. This is not the authority to decide unilaterally, but the authority to influence.

Name	Present salary	Ladder and rung	New salary	Line manager recommendation
Atkins	2,300	A4	2,473	
Brown	2,000	A8	2,150	
Clark	2,300	B7	2,473	
Davies	2,400	B6	2,580	
Evans	2,400	B6	2,580	
Farr	3,000	B1	3,225	
Gray	2,000	A8	2,150	
Hill	2,400	B6	2,580	
Inman	2,750	C6	2,956	
Jones	2,150	A6	2,311	

Total budget increase for next year: £ 2,962

Cost-of-living element: £ 1,777

Balance available for awards: £ 1,185

Figure 5:2 Divisional salary list

ADMINISTRATION OF MANAGERIAL SALARIES

For each of these managers the personnel manager will prepare a working sheet of salaries within his area of influence, like the one illustrated in Figure 5:2, showing for each person his present salary, his new salary after adjustment for cost of living, space for the award of additional sums and a note of the lump sum available to the manager for allocation among his staff. This is then sent to the line manager together with a list of the salary groups, ladders and steps.

Line manager recommendations

The line manager now pencils in on the sheet his recommendations, as shown in Figure 5:3, for the distribution of his lump sum, working within certain important limitations:

1   He cannot award less than one step on the ladder
2   He cannot take someone above the top of the ladder
3   At this stage his figures are only recommendations.

The limitation on not being able to award less than one step is to prevent the salary ladders becoming meaningless and to ensure that money spent on increases is spent to some advantage. Sums available for achievement awards can be wasted if dissipated in insignificant amounts. The decision to shift someone to a different salary ladder has to be taken in conjunction with someone outside the line manager's area, so as to avoid salaries in one functional area of the organisation getting out of step with those elsewhere.

Centralised check

The personnel manager then receives the lists back, being agreeably surprised at how quickly this paperwork moves, and checks through the recommendations for any problems.

The types of problem he may find are forgotten undertakings of the past, particularly obligations under career plans or failure to stick to the limitations of the salary groups and ladders. His most careful check will need to be on interdepartmental anomalies, and the possibilities of 'blue-eyed-boy' allegations.

If he finds any such problems he should sort them out quickly over the telephone or by face-to-face conversation, so that he soon has a

Name	Present salary	Ladder and rung	New salary	Line manager recommendation	
Atkins	2,300	A4	2,473	100	(A3)
Brown	2,000	A8	2,150	150	(A6)
Clark	2,300	B7	2,473		
Davies	2,400	B6	2,580	225	(B4)
Evans	2,400	B6	2,580	225	(B4)
Farr	3,000	B1	3,225		
Gray	2,000	A8	2,150	150	(A6)
Hill	2,400	B6	2,580		
Inman	2,750	C6	2,956	125	(C5)
Jones	2,150	A6	2,311	150	(A4)

Total budget increase for next year: £ 2,962

Cost-of-living element: £ 1,777

Balance available for awards: £ 1,185

Figure 5:3   Divisional salary list with line manager's recommendations complete set of managers' recommendations which he is prepared to accept as being consistent with company policy and sound from a personnel point of view.

By this means the personnel manager has provided a system that is supported by some expertise, and he has provided centralised control to ensure consistency and fairness. The line manager has made the decisions about awards to his own staff, but with the safeguard of the personnel manager's subsequent agreement.

Salary notifications

The personnel manager now sends final salary lists for each area to at least three people. First to the line manager who has confirmation that the salary awards are now final; then to the accountant who can finalise his salary budget for the forthcoming year; finally to the cashier or the computer so that the revised payments are actually made.

He will also send to each line manager a set of individual notifications for each of his personnel, giving the details of the award. The line manager then informs each member of his staff about the increase personally. This may well be an opportunity to have a general progress discussion with the man, and endorses the fact that the salary adjustment is one that has been decided by the line superior rather than a distant central authority, but that the central authority has endorsed the wisdom of the decision. He can then give the individual the note to place close to his heart.

Incentive payments

A substantial minority of managers receive some part of their annual remuneration from their employer in the form of a bonus payment that is agreed beforehand and linked directly, and in a calculable way, with performance. The objective is to link achievement with payment, the payment being subject to fluctuation up or down.

The performance to which the payment is linked may be the performance of the working group, or a formula based on the performance of the individual. By far the most common arrangement is a payment geared to the profit achievement of the undertaking, which focuses the mind of the executive on profit as the prime criterion by which he will be judged and ensures that the payment made will fluctuate according to the ability of the employer to pay. The possible drawback to this scheme is that everyone is the father of success, but failure is an orphan.

Alternative criteria are usually sales turnover or production figures within the area under the direct control of the individual manager. Sometimes a criterion is the meeting of the departmental or divisional budget. The advantage of this type of arrangement is that the attention of the individual is concentrated on his own personal performance. The difficulty is that targets need very thorough thought before setting to ensure that individual managers do not set off in opposite directions. The production manager might reach very high volume of output, but be insufficiently sensitive to detailed marketing requirements.

There are several difficulties about any form of performance-linked incentive payment for managers. Usually the period over which the performance is to be measured is twelve months, and it may be several weeks after the end of the period before calculations are completed, leading to a situation in which payment is made in midsummer for performance in a period which ended in the previous December. Is the payment close enough to the working period and is it frequent enough to be regarded as an incentive?

What happens in the poor year? Is it practicable to expect the manager to manage without what he has become accustomed to regard as an integral part of his remuneration; or is there a gesture made in paying something in lieu? This is not an uncommon practice, but immediately destroys the whole purpose of an incentive payment. This is a particular problem when the general level of payment is a high proportion of total remuneration. Levels of 20 per cent or more are common. Is there a danger of losing some of your best men when things get tough—just when you need them most?

The most effective practice seems to be either to pay incentives linked very carefully to individual or small-group performance, with payments being made either monthly or quarterly, or to pay an incentive based on company profitability, which represents no more than 10 or 15 per cent of total annual income. In this way it becomes a yardstick of performance rather than an integral part of the manager's family budget.

Career plans

The final short word in this chapter is on the question of salary progression under career plans of the type becoming more popular in management development programmes for the graduate entrant and similar young managers.

The contribution of the manager designate is limited by the fact that he is under training in the hope of enhanced performance in the future. His salary will still have to remain competitive with those of similar age and qualifications elsewhere, so it is usual to plot out specific salary steps he will reach during his development programme, subject to satisfactory progress. An approach similar to management by objectives can provide a series of milestones along the development road each of which has a salary label attached to it.

Further reading

Merrett and White, *Incentive Payment Systems for Managers*, London, Gower Press, 1968.

McBeath, *Management Remuneration Policy*, London, Business Books, 1969.

McBeath and Rands, *Salary Administration*, Business Publications, 1969.

National Board for Prices and Incomes, *Salary Structures* (Report Number 132, Cmnd 4187), London, HMSO, 1969.

Some Salary Surveys:
Institute of Physics, *Remuneration Survey*.
Associated Industrial Consultants Salary Research Unit, *Survey of Executive Salaries and Fringe Benefits in the United Kingdom*.
Council of Engineering Institutions, *Survey of Professional Engineers*.

6

Organisation and Team Development

John Woolhouse, Director, Kingston Regional Management Centre, and formerly Company Education and Training Officer, Rolls-Royce (1971) Limited

Whether a management development programme is designed to improve the performance of existing managers, or to provide for future succession, success will depend on two basic factors: the calibre of the people who have been selected for managerial jobs and the scope and opportunity available to them.

This chapter is concerned with the environment in which managers work—with the style, structure and climate of the organisation. This brief introduction to the complex subject of organisation and organisation development is divided into five main sections:

About organisations: Some observations on the nature of organisations and the ailments from which they suffer.

Organisation development: Methods of building more effective organisations.

Training managers: The limitations of conventional management training courses.

Unit development: An example of a programme designed to improve the efficiency of a manufacturing unit.

Development of an executive team: An experiment in executive training.

Lessons from experience

Because the subject is a difficult one, I want to begin with some very simple ideas about organisations.

A really well-managed business or military operation is characterised by a sense of achievement and satisfaction that comes from being a member of a team which knows where it is going and how to get there. There is an atmosphere in an efficient business, school or service unit that is far easier to recognise than to describe.

Anyone who has had the demoralising experience of working—or trying to work—in circumstances where the 'system' has virtually broken down will know that nobody seems to know what is happening, it is almost impossible to get anything done, more time is spent in conflict and argument than in useful and constructive work and the buck is being passed so fast that you have a job to find it, let alone discover who is responsible for it!

Some organisations do not fall into either category. They are neither particularly dynamic nor completely disorganised. They are just dull. They are often run by people who have been running them in the same way for a long time, who do not see any particular reason to change and who treat their subordinates with consideration, but without any great interest in anything they have to say. The rigid attitudes of their senior executives stifle any attempt at initiative or change, and older men are frequently heard to say, with regret, that they see so few young men today who have any real 'drive' or 'spark'.

It is interesting that when people talk about 'the best time of my life' or 'the best job I ever had', many of their stories, apart from wartime ones, are about the achievements of relatively small groups of people who did something for the first time. The story usually includes the phrase 'we opened . . .', 'we were the first . . .', 'we designed the original . . .'—'and there were only six of us in the whole department'. The natural manager has something about him of the innovator, the pioneer, and finds satisfaction in working with others to bring about change and improvement.

These comments are an indication that there are certain factors within an organisation that have a very significant effect on how well people do their jobs, and on how much satisfaction they derive from them.

Some organisations tend to create the type of climate we all enjoy, and others have the opposite effect. In the following sections of this chapter I want to examine some of these factors, and to suggest what can be done to create the type of climate in which managers can give of their best, because in the end this will determine how well the organisation's present managers do their jobs, and how successful it is in developing their successors.

About organisations

Organisation is a means of accomplishing strategy.

> The successful implementation of strategy requires that the general manager shapes to the peculiar needs of his strategy the formal structure of his organisation, its informal relationships and the processes of motivation and control which provide incentives and measure results. He must bring about the commitment to organisational aims and policies of properly qualified individuals and groups to whom portions of the total task have been assigned. He must insure not only that goals are clear and purposes are understood, but also that individuals are developing in terms of capacity and achievement and are reaping proper rewards in terms of compensation and personal satisfactions. Above all, he must do what he can to insure that departmental interests, inter-departmental rivalries and the machinery of measurement and evaluation do not deflect energy from organisational purpose into harmful or irrelevant activity. (Edmund P. Learned *et al.*, *Business Policy: Text and Cases.*)

Figure 6:1 illustrates a number of the 'processes' which are fundamental to most organisations, and indicates some of the 'qualities' or 'values' that are inherent in a successful organisation.

Most organisation and team development programmes are concerned with one or more of these 'processes' shown in Figure 6:1. Most, if

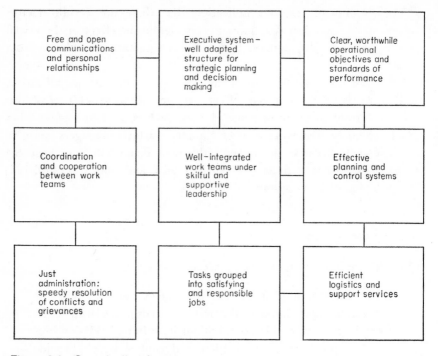

Figure 6:1   Organisational processes

not all, of these processes are interlinked and interdependent. In practice this often means that an attempt to solve a problem in one area will have very little effect on performance unless essential changes are made in other parts of the system. Many 'management-by-objective' projects have failed in practice through lack of proper control information, or through a failure to realise that the introduction of joint target-setting and performance reviews may involve a significant change in the style of the departmental managers concerned.

Organisational problems and diseases

Organisations, like people, are prone to a host of problems and diseases. The first problem in reviewing the effectiveness of an organisation is to find out what it is trying to achieve, and to diagnose the problems that are limiting its performance. Diagnosis, as will be seen later, is of crucial importance.

This section describes some common organisational problems.

The executive system

'The will to manage must include the will to organise' (Marvin Bower, *The Will to Manage*). The structure is not a set of organisation charts, it is a system for taking decisions, and for allocating executive duties, responsibilities and authority, determined by the purpose, technology, markets, geographical dispersal and the 'dynamics' or rate of change of the organisation. A highly centralised 'monolithic' organisation may, like a dictatorship, appear to be the most efficient way of running a business—at least in the short-term—and there are moments of crisis in which it is necessary to bring all one's forces under a single centre of control. But in the longer term a highly centralised structure is probably the worst possible environment in which to develop future managers. They will never learn to run a business if all the important decisions are taken in London, New York or some other 'corporate capital'. The most important contribution of the chief executive, apart from the selection of senior managers, is not merely to support an organised programme of management development, but to create the structure in which managers can experiment and learn. He must create the maximum number of independent companies, profit centres and cost centres consistent with effective control of the business. He should create divisional boards or executive teams accountable for the successful operation of their sector of the business, even though this may involve additional risks and some sacrifice of personal power.

Conflicting, overlapping and ill-defined executive responsibilities are another common source of trouble, and these structural problems can rarely be solved solely by the preparation of written 'terms of reference'. The real trouble is more likely to be caused by genuine difficulties and illogicalities in the structure, and by personal conflicts and misunderstandings which can only be cured by mutual efforts to negotiate a working solution.

Many senior executives hold dual roles as heads of a major department, and as executive directors of the company. The development of a board capable of taking a 'corporate' as opposed to a 'departmental' view often calls not only for considerable skill on the part of the chief executive, but for a planned programme of 'education' in the tasks and priorities of an executive board.

Objectives and standard of performance

The current enthusiasm for management by objectives is an indication that lack of clearly defined objectives and standards of performance is one of the most common organisational problems. The larger and more complex the organisation, the more specialised the jobs, the greater the likelihood of confusion about objectives and work priorities.

Most organisation or team development programmes involve some redefinition of objectives, but at a more fundamental level they attempt to create a new climate. A climate in which the formal master/servant or superior/subordinate relationship is replaced by a 'partnership' approach; in which targets are mutually agreed by managers and staff, and in which efforts are concentrated on working together to solve the problems that arise in meeting agreed performance goals. Management-by-objectives programmes, like appraisal schemes, can only flourish under an appropriate style of leadership. We have all heard the story of the manager at a departmental meeting, who shouted 'I am going to have participation in this outfit, if I have to force it in!'

Planning and control systems

To do an effective job, people need clear, consistent instruction and continuous feedback on the performance against programme.

Planning and control systems must be integrated into an overall information structure, but systems must be specifically designed to meet the needs of each department and level of business. Many supervisors in industry carry the burden of control systems designed to provide information for top management when they themselves are desperately short of simple, workable controls by which to manage their own operation. Organisation development programmes are concerned with 'people' problems rather than with 'systems' problems, but in practice there are few programmes which do not reveal the need for changes in methods of planning and control.

Jobs

The work of any organisation has to be divided into tasks or groups of tasks that an individual or a team can perform and for which they are responsible. The actual allocation of tasks and responsibilities depends on two main factors. One is the technology in which the organisation is engaged, and the other is its assumptions about people. A plantation can be run efficiently with slave labour or through a partnership scheme. In either case the technology will to some extent determine what has to be done, but the way work is allocated and the degree of responsibility of the people involved is largely a matter of values.

Many businesses today are run on the rather contradictory belief that it is reasonable, and necessary, for people to spend most of their lives on boring, repetitive work with little or no responsibility for the results; but that it is important to 'treat them properly' while they are doing it, and even to consult with them about various extraneous subjects, provided that such discussions do not affect the two fundamental issues of work or pay. This is sometimes called 'joint consultation'!

The growing interest in programmes of joint problem-solving, of 'job enrichment' and in the creation of more satisfying jobs within a modern technological society, is part of an attempt to close the 'responsibility gap'—the gap between the desire and ability of most citizens in a reasonably well-educated democracy to perform a responsible and worthwhile job, and the monotonous routine in which so many of them are actually engaged.

Teamwork

Teamwork is the foundation of any successful joint venture. Effective teamwork is largely the result of sensitive and skilful leadership.

Styles of leadership must be adapted to the situation, and, in moments of crisis, strong and authoritative leadership may be essential to survival. Nevertheless, leadership is a complex activity. It requires not only the establishment of a sense of direction and purpose, but a high degree of skill in understanding the factors that affect human motivation and, as John Adair's concept of action-centred leadership shows, in reconciling task, group and individual needs.

The 'managerial grid' approach developed by Blake and Mouton in a different way stresses the need to achieve the optimum balance between 'concern for production' and 'concern for people'.

Because teamwork is the core of all organisation development programmes, managers who take part in these programmes must have an opportunity of re-examining their own leadership styles; they must be willing to accept comment and criticism and, if necessary, to modify their style to meet the needs of today's situation.

A manager who cannot generate the necessary interest and commitment to the task in hand, or create a sense of pride in achievement in what has been accomplished, will never realise the full potential of his team. Individual motivation is determined by individual aspirations and inner 'drives', but the effectiveness of a team is a matter of mutual effort, cooperation and understanding. It is the task of the leader to create a climate in which these conditions can be fulfilled.

Coordination and cooperation

Misunderstandings and lack of coordination between departments can often cause more waste of time, money and effort than any limitations of individual skill or effort. There is nothing more heartbreaking than the experience of finding that days or weeks of effort have been nullified through failure to communicate a change of plan.

Conflicts between 'line' and 'functional' departments, or between one line department and another, are a frequent source of inefficiency and irritation. The more complex the organisation the greater the risk of confusion. This is well known and yet so many managers are 'too busy' to organise the regular personal contacts or even the occasional 'off-the-job' meetings and social contacts that are so essential to the maintenance of cooperative effort.

Logistics and support services

The success of any operation depends on efficient logistics and support services. Problems frequently arise through inefficient horizontal communications; for example, between a manufacturing plant and purchasing, tooling, maintenance, transport and other departments that provide essential materials and services. It is all too easy at the end of a long day to discover that the specification or programme has been changed, but that 'they' forgot to tell us. A relatively small improvement in cooperation can result in significant improvements in performance.

Administration and government

Managers do not always fully appreciate that any sizeable commercial or industrial organisation incorporates a 'system of government' by which the pay, promotion and conditions of its members are regulated.

A vital part of this process is the provision of a just and speedy system for the resolution of conflicts and grievances. The experiment carried out at the Glacier Metal Company was a remarkable attempt to evolve a 'representative' system through which the views of employees could be expressed, considered and incorporated into the company's practices and procedures. It is remarkable that so many companies have failed to develop any effective procedures for the proper administration of justice in industrial affairs. Managers are hurt and surprised to find that employees often have no alternative but to take direct and sometimes violent action to make their voices heard on matters which *directly and materially affect their working lives*. The growing interest in new forms of group problem-solving, joint consultation and partnership is a significant move towards the development of a more mature and rational form of 'industrial government'.

Communications

Underlying all the processes described in Figure 6:1 is the fundamental process of communication. Without communication there is no organisation.

One of the main difficulties about this subject is that even in a relatively simple organisation there is a whole series of communications systems associated with every aspect of its activities. Each of the processes I have described requires its own distinct set of communications procedures. 'Communications' cannot be tackled as if it were a single problem to be resolved by some universal panacea. Improvements can be achieved only by detailed studies of the information needed to run the business, and to tell people what is going on. These studies must include an examination of the purpose, form, frequency, method and content of the information systems in every area of the organisation. There is no easier way of reducing efficiency or of lowering morale than by isolating people from the information that they need if they are to carry out their work efficiently and play a mature and intelligent role in the organisation to which they belong.

As will be seen in the next section, one of the main objectives of an organisation development programme is to bring about a freer and more 'open' style of communication and, at a deeper level, to develop better understanding between people.

Organisation development

The previous section considered some of the more common problems that tend to limit the efficiency of an organisation. Sometimes these problems can be solved by straightforward executive action, and in a sense it is true that any effective manager is continuously engaged in the task of adapting and improving his organisation, by the changes he makes in responsibilities, appointments or by the introduction of new systems and procedures. What is new about the idea of organisation development?

In its simplest form an organisation development programme is a planned attempt, led by the senior people in the organisation, to change the 'style' and climate in which people work. It is a programme of *action*, not solely a programme of education, planned over a considerable period of time, and using *teams* rather than individuals as the 'agents of change'.

Most of the organisational weaknesses that have been discussed have their roots in much deeper problems of personal attitudes, outlook and prejudice. The way in which people behave, their attitudes to what is going on, their style of management, and their ability and will to cooperate are influenced by their understanding of the external situation, and of themselves.

I am personally a little sceptical about changing attitudes by any form of training. I am convinced, however, that considerable changes can be achieved by helping people towards a better understanding of each other's problems and points of view, and by feedback on the way their own behaviour and actions are seen by others. The task of carrying out major changes, particularly in a large organisation, is only practicable if the people concerned understand and are committed to the process of change. Commitment is achieved by involving people in the task of working out and implementing the changes that are needed. The best way of improving teamwork and collaboration between departments is to give the people concerned an opportunity to work together on a common solution to their problems.

The focal points of an organisation development programme are, therefore, the actual 'work teams' which make up an organisation and, where necessary, interdepartmental teams specially set up to deal with problems affecting two or more departments or functions.

Content of organisation development programmes

A typical programme will begin with a day or two of discussions, preferably away from the plant, between the senior executives and an outside adviser who has experience in this field. From then on, a plan will be devised to clarify the objectives to be achieved, and to carry out any necessary analyses of the situation. The importance of this 'diagnostic' stage cannot be overemphasised. You cannot cure a patient if you cannot diagnose the disease.

A typical organisation development (OD) programme may include the following phases:

1 Introduction to the general aims of the programme and to the ideas and concepts underlying it—often based on a preliminary discussion of problems that are of immediate concern to the participants
2 Team development: an attempt to resolve some of the problems of understanding, communication and conflict within the team, and to apply some of the lessons learned to day-to-day problems
3 Inter-team training: to try to achieve better understanding between departments and functions, and to improve vertical and horizontal communications
4 Setting improvement targets, examining potential problems and difficulties, and considering alternative plans of action
5 Selecting and implementing agreed changes, and modifying original plans in the light of experience; providing effective on-the-job support
6 Monitoring results, maintaining and adopting the newly established methods and procedures.

These teams, usually meeting on a part-time basis, are given the opportunity to analyse problems, to call on specialist help or advice, to study with the help of a trained adviser some of the human and 'behavioural' problems involved and, by a re-examination of their own working experience, to evolve and apply new solutions.

It is vital than an OD programme is designed to implement the strategy of the business and to suit the particular circumstances of the company. Every situation is different, and the actual design of the programme will vary considerably with that situation. Some programmes, particularly in the US, make extensive use of 'sensitivity training', 'grid seminars' or other special educational processes as a first stage in the programme, but in the UK most people prefer a more informal approach relying mainly on learning from experience, and on building discussion and 'coaching' sessions into the programme. After initial help from external consultants, a number of major British companies are now training members of their own staff to act as advisers to line managers, and to help in the design and administration of programmes. A typical organisation development programme will involve scores or hundreds of managers and will be run over periods from one to four or five years. It is relatively easy to start a programme, but a very different matter to sustain it.

It is very difficult to describe an organisation development programme in words. It is like marriage, if you want to find out what it is like, you have to try it! Nor is an OD programme a 'bed of roses'. The process is still experimental, and if not skilfully managed it can easily create more problems than it solves, but its potential as a means of bringing about lasting change is far greater than any other approach yet developed.

Uses of organisation development programmes

Organisation development programmes are appropriate in a number of different circumstances:

1 To improve the efficiency of an existing organisation
2 To help a newly created organisation to move more rapidly into effective operation—a unique opportunity and yet one which is rarely taken
3 To adapt an organisation to cope with changes in strategy, markets, products or operations
4 To deal with a new situation created by new ownership or management, by mergers, takeovers or other changes in corporate structure.

Programmes may be designed to deal not only with organisation change but with specific problem areas. The course programme of a leading business school for 1971, for example, includes sessions on industrial relations strategy, motivation, work-group development, problem-solving and managing conflict.

Whatever the objectives may be, all programmes have this characteristic in common; they are attempts not only to recognise the symptoms and effects of organisational problems, but to understand the underlying causes, and to use this knowledge to create strong and vigorous new organisations, or to improve the health and efficiency of those which are already in operation.

Training managers

During recent years it has become increasingly apparent that conventional management training 'courses' usually have little or no effect on individual or departmental performance. There are of course individual exceptions, and even the occasional dramatic 'conversion', but the doubts of many experienced managers about the value of management courses appear to have been justified.

From time to time managers—and particularly senior managers who are in a position to influence events—may find an external course a valuable and stimulating experience and may bring back important new ideas which can be applied in the company. Newly appointed managers will undoubtedly benefit from a properly planned programme of briefing, coaching and instruction. Intensive training will be necessary when a new procedure or new techniques are introduced. But, in general, there is remarkably little evidence that the efforts devoted to management training in the last twenty years have been justified by identifiable improvements in company or departmental performance.

This section will discuss some of the reasons for this apparent failure.

As a means of improving performance of *existing* managers, the conventional training course tends to suffer from three basic weaknesses, which are illustrated in Figure 6:2.

Problem A is that the manager of any business or department is faced with a series of operational problems which do not normally fall into the tidy categories or 'subjects' found in so many course programmes.

When a manager returns from a course, pressure of work, lack of support from supervisor or colleagues—who did not go on the course

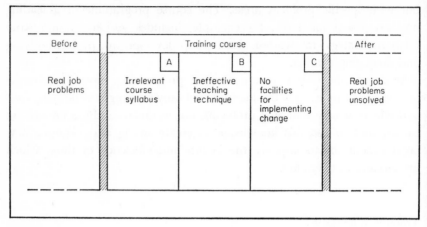

Figure 6:2   The conventional external course

—and the sheer difficulty of bringing about change if he is only the 'man in the middle', will probably mean that another management course is just a pleasant memory and a 'club tie'. It is no exaggeration to say that in some training programmes, any correlation between the most important problems in a business or department and the content of the management course is entirely coincidental. The mismatch between operational problems and educational courses is in itself enough to reduce the efficiency of the process to an uneconomic level.

Problem B is that long and sustained practice, preferably under expert tuition, is necessary to develop competence in even the most elementary management skills, and practice in a real situation is an essential part of the learning process. Nobody ever learned to fly an aeroplane merely by sitting in a classroom, or even in a flight-simulator. There is all the difference in the world between getting a quick appreciation of an idea, and putting it into effect. The conventional course cannot, and does not, provide the opportunity for on-the-job practice, which is an essential part of learning to manage.

Problem C is probably the most serious of all, and it follows from what has been said about Problem B. If an organisation is going to become more efficient, or to adapt to meet a new situation, there must be some significant change in systems, procedures, methods and in the behaviour of the people concerned.

In a conventional course, the time and effort that can be devoted to the problem of implementing changes is usually *totally inadequate*. The process of converting ideas into action is, as every manager knows, the most difficult part of the whole operation. If it is not planned, it will not happen.

Problem C also has an important corollary, that if managers from a single level in the organisation are sent *individually* on company or external courses, the impact will be seriously reduced. The vast majority of managers—and employees—work in *teams*, and it is almost useless to send individuals away on training programmes if improvements can only be achieved by a team effort.

Unit development

This section gives a brief account of the development programmes which are gradually replacing traditional management training courses in many leading companies. A particular example will be discussed which is based on a 'unit development programme' in an engineering factory employing about 1400 people. Although not strictly a full-scale organisation development programme, it is perhaps a more useful example for many readers because it is an approach which can be used by the manager of any operating unit, at a relatively modest cost, and which is likely to achieve considerable improvements in the performance of his management and supervisory teams.

This particular programme was introduced by the general manager with the purpose of improving overall performance on delivery, quality and cost.

The programme incorporated three parallel activities:

1   Redefining the aims and operating objectives of the department
2   Adapting the organisation structure to achieve these objectives
3   Developing personal awareness and a more effective management style.

These three strands of activity were run in parallel; each stage was planned by managers themselves with the help and support of the training department. In the early stages of the programme outside consultants were retained to advise on the design of the programme, but the company's own training staff have now taken over full responsibility for all unit development programmes.

The senior management team of twelve to fourteen people responsible for monitoring the programme met for two hours once a fortnight throughout the programme. The tasks of this group were to identify priorities and performance targets, to take action to resolve problems identified during the programme, to review the structure of the department and to establish the necessary control systems. Chairmanship was rotated among members of the group.

On alternate weeks the same group met for two hours with the heads of the departments responsible for supplies and support services to the department, with a similar agenda of setting improvement targets, establishing control systems, reviewing the organisation, identifying training needs, devising follow-up programmes and quantifying improvements on delivery, scrap, costs and other measurable factors.

The 'audit' or diagnostic phase of the programme was based on :

1 Personal interviews about job problems with every member of the management team
2 Group interviews with managers from different specialist departments or functions to highlight operational, manning and organisational problems
3 Foremen's group discussions, chaired by superintendents and devoted to clarifying the role of the foreman and re-examining his authority, responsibilities and working relationships with line and service departments
4 Activity sampling of results against work programmes.

In the next phase of the programme a series of ten three-hour discussion and feedback sessions were held with foremen in four separate groups.
The agenda for each session included :

1 A review of the existing system, procedure or method
2 Discussion of problems and improvements
3 Recapitulation and allocation of actions and report-back dates.

The subjects included :

1 Purpose and method of the programme
2 Scheduling and issue of work

3 Control and movement of work
4 Planning, estimating and tooling
5 Performance and maintenance of machines and equipment
6 Quality and inspection procedures
7 Costs and budgets
8 Control and programming of departmental work loads
9 Training
10 Recapitulation and reporting.

The main phase of the programme, involving managers, superintendents, and more than sixty foremen, lasted just over a year.

Specific targets were set for manufacturing time cycles, engine turn-round time, inspection times, scrap reduction and also on a number of special factors such as the speed of action on problems raised by foremen and on improvements in the effectiveness of meetings by training in systematic problem-analysis.

It is always difficult to make an accurate assessment of the savings which are directly attributable to a programme because of the many extraneous factors that affect performance. Preliminary reports showed that cost savings were running at a rate of over £15 000 per month, and that improvements of 10 to 20 per cent in key performance factors were being achieved. This experience confirms the results achieved by similar programmes in other parts of the company, and are sufficiently encouraging to suggest that the programme has overcome some of the limitations of conventional supervisory training methods, and made a start on the difficult task of improving organisation effectiveness. Similar experience have been reported by many other major companies, including the Westinghouse Managed Change Technique, ICI Productivity and Job Enrichment Programmes, and the 'task force' and 'trouble-shooting' techniques which are being widely applied in many industrial companies.

The sequence of events illustrated in Figure 6:3 is in marked contrast to the 'disconnected' phases of the conventional training course shown in Figure 6:2. To summarise, the characteristics of a unit development programme are that :

1 It is planned and led by senior managers
2 It is designed to solve real operational problems

Define goals	Analyse problems	Adapt structure and systems	Prepare action plans	Brief and train	Implement with on-the-job support	Evaluate and modify

Learning based on action and experience

Instruction in relevant skills and techniques

Figure 6:3   Unit development programme

'Education' in the sense that people are learning from each other, and from coaching by senior managers and specialist advisers, is taking place throughout the programme. In some circumstances, individual or group instruction in appropriate skills and techniques may be necessary.

3   It involves the whole management team and, in some circumstances, the whole workforce

4   Efforts are concentrated on the diagnosis of problems and on putting changes into effect. Managers learn by studying 'live problems' rather than by following a predetermined syllabus.

The potential pay-off comes not only from direct cost savings but from the intangible benefits of a healthy, more enthusiastic and adaptable organisation.

Developing an executive team

The second example of team development is based on a programme designed to prepare a group of department managers for promotion to executive positions in a medium-sized engineering company. The company, an independent subsidiary of a large engineering group, employs about 1000 people on the design, development and procurement of advanced engineering systems.

In 1970, the managing director was faced with a difficult situation. To quote his own statement, 'The problem that faced me was that due to an unplanned-for coincidence of moves of senior executives, the top management of the company, with the exception of two directors, had virtually no experience of working together and knowing each other's strengths and weaknesses.' As a result of the company's succession planning, a group of six young managers with considerable potential had already been identified. The urgency of the situation arose from the need for promotion at a much earlier stage than had originally been anticipated.

Apart from the practical difficulties of releasing six senior managers to attend outside courses, there were growing doubts both in industry and in some leading business schools about the value of the conventional 'executive course'. Senior executives from the company had, at this time, been taking part in informal discussions with the staff of these schools about alternative methods of executive training.

The urgency of the situation meant that training had to be carried out in a comparatively short space of time, without long periods of absence from the job; the new team had to learn to work effectively together, and to make an intensive study of the problems of managing a highly specialised business.

A plan was developed in collaboration with staff from the Manchester Business School. The essence of the plan was that the conventional method of sending executives to the Business School should be reversed, and that teaching staff from the Business School would act as tutors and advisers to a group responsible for directing its own programme of study.

The 'Group Six" project, as the experiment came to be called, was based on six two-day residential sessions which ran from October 1969 to May 1970. The early part of these sessions were spent in working out the aims and objectives of the group, in building up effective relationships and in planning a project based on the future development of the company's operations.

During the weekend sessions, staff from the Business School acted as tutors. Expert speakers from the Business School and from the company led discussions on specific topics. These topics included financial planning, capital budgeting, taxation, technological forecasting, marketing and product planning, organisation structure, company law and finance, staff relations, management control, organisation design and change. Formal sessions were supplemented by private readings and by a further 37 hours of informal group activities.

The project was planned in three phases:

1 Marketing study
2 Company formation
3 Company operation

The complete report was presented to a group of senior executives and Business School staff in June 1970.

Although they would want to make changes in any subsequent programmes, the majority of the group felt that the project had provided a valuable educational experience. They reported that it 'generated a team spirit amongst the members', that it provided an effective method of introducing a group who had 'a predominantly narrow range of experience, to the general problems of running a business' and 'helped significantly to develop the potentiality of our senior management team to work together in real-life company situations'. It also seems that the programme 'initiated a new management style in the company of working more as a team and less as an individual sector head'. 'The course had the advantages of a tutorial system. . . . The small numbers involved gave an opportunity for course members to engage in a frank exchange of views . . . and so to examine the basis for the various hypotheses put forward in a relatively short period of time.'

The main characteristics of this programme were:

1 The programme was designed to deal with a real and urgent situation.
2 It was designed and led jointly by the managing director of the company and by a senior Business School professor.
3 The members of the group played a major part in planning the content and structure of what was indeed 'their own programme'.
4 The company and Business School staff who provided tutorial support and instruction were used as 'resources' by the group, and were called in at their request.
5 The project was directly related to the future development of the business.
6 The members of the group were actually moving into 'executive' jobs during the period of the programme.

The members had difficulty in carrying out the project on a part-time basis, but there is no doubt from the reactions of the group, and from their subsequent performance, that the programme achieved a considerable measure of success. The costs of the programme compared favourably with those which would have been incurred in sending six executives on a conventional business-school programme. In any subsequent programmes, it is intended to provide additional tutorial and discussion sessions and to enable participants to devote more time to the project.

One member of the original group has since moved to a new appointment, but the remaining five have moved into senior executive positions in the company, and the managing director has no doubt that, if faced again with a need to train a new executive team, he would adopt the approach developed in the 'Group Six' experiment.

Summary

This chapter has briefly reviewed some common organisational problems and considered some of the ways in which they can be overcome. Two relatively simple ways of improving the productivity of a manufacturing unit and of developing a new executive team have been outlined.

The ideas can be summarised in the following way :

1   The structure, systems and style of an organisation combine to create a 'climate' which can help or hinder the achievement or strategy.
2   The work of most organisations is carried out, not by individuals working in isolation but by teams. The team, rather than the individual, is the most potent force for change and improvement.
3   Management, leadership and teamwork are applied skills which are best acquired through the study and practice of real situations.
4   This combination of team development and using a real situation as a basis for learning can be used to improve the performance of existing work, and to train new management and executive teams.
5   The success of a management development programme depends not only on competent administration, but on planned efforts to create an organisation in which men of appropriate ability can develop the skill, confidence and judgment needed for the difficult and demanding task of management.

Further reading

A simple introduction to recent devolpments in the behavioural sciences is given in :

Brown, Margaret, *The Manager's Guide to the Behavioural Sciences* (London, The Industrial Society, 1969). This booklet contains an excellent reading list.

Other relevant titles in the Industrial Society's 'Notes for Managers' series are :
The Manager as an Action-centred Leader
The Manager's Responsibility for Communication
The Manager's Guide to Setting Targets

The subject of organisation development is covered by a series of five books published by Addison-Wesley in 1969 :

Beckhard, Richard, *Organization Development: Strategies and Models*
Bennis, Warren G., *Organization Development: Its Nature, Origins and Prospects*
Blake, Robert R., and Mouton, Jane S., *Building a Dynamic Corporation through Grid Organization Development*
Schein, Edgar H., *Process Consultation: Its Role in Oganization Development*
Walton, Richard E., *Interpersonal Peacemaking: Confrontations and Third-party Consultation*

Other reading :

Bower, Marvin, *The Will to Manage* (New York, McGraw-Hill, 1966)
Burns, J., and Stalker, G. M., *The Management of Innovation* (London, Tavistock Publications, 1961)
Jaques, Elliott, *Work, Creativity, and Social Justice* (London, Heinemann, 1970).
Katz, D., and Kahn, R. L., *The Social Psychology of Organizations* (New York, Wiley, 1965)
Learned, Edmund P., Christensen, C. Roland, Andrew, Kenneth R., and Guth, William D., *Business Policy* (Homewood, Irwin, 1969)
Mant, Alistair, *The Experienced Manager: A Major Resource* (London, British Institute of Management, 1969)

Parker, Hugh, Bower, Marvin, Smith, E. Everett, and Morrison, J. Roger, *Effective Boardroom Management* (London, McKinsey & Co. Inc. and British Institute of Management, 1971).

Sofer, Cyril, *The Organization from Within* (London, Tavistock Publications, 1961).

(Interested readers should also study the works of E. Jacques and of A. K. Rice and E. L. Trist of the Tavistock Institute of Human Relations.)

Sutermeister, Robert A., *People and Productivity* (New York, McGraw-Hill, 1969)

Tannehill, Robert E., *Motivation and Management Development* (London, Butterworth, 1970)

Tannehill, Robert E., *The Management of Technological Change* (Manufacturing Engineering & Management, 1971)

The *Harvard Business Review* reprint service lists 49 recent articles on the subject of organisation development.

Comprehensive bibliographies are given in :

Hersey, Paul, and Blanchard, Kenneth H., *Management of Organizational Behavior* (Englewood Cliffs, Prentice-Hall, 1969), and in each volume of the Addison-Wesley series.

7

Union Membership and the Manager

Roger Lyons, National Officer, Association of Scientific, Technical and Managerial Staffs

At one time the unionisation of labourers was considered not only to be reprehensible, but as an offence punishable by transportation. During the nineteenth century this attitude changed, and by 1871, the Trades Union Act fully recognised unionisation both as legal and, by giving the unions financial and other protection, as a desirable activity for blue-collar employees in British industry.

The growth of white-collar unions

By the time of the First World War, trade unions were firmly established for most grades of blue-collar workers. During the war, and in the years immediately following, many unions were formed by white-collar staff in order that they could enjoy the benefits and protection of unionisation at a time of considerable change. Thus unions for civil servants, bank employees, supervisory and scientific staffs, insurance workers and others were inaugurated, and fairly rapid growth followed in a number of fields. The government recognised this development within its own area of employment, and Whitley Council machinery was established for staff within public service areas, enabling the unions concerned to hold national negotiating rights.

In the private sector, however, there was considerable resistance from the employers to the growth of white-collar unionisation, and even more to the granting of proper recognition and negotiating rights. Just as Combination Acts and transportation had been used against the union-isation of labourers a century before, some British employers used company-controlled staff associations, victimisation and even mass dismissal (as with General Accident Assurance in 1922) to try to hold back unionisation.

Independent white-collar unions in the private sector learned important lessons from the experience of the Bank Employees Union. This had rules which effectively prohibited industrial action. Despite this mild attitude the employers continued to refuse recognition and made greater efforts to destroy the union. Because of the mild attitude, workers were loth to join the union which, they thought, lacked the means to protect its members' interests.

In the engineering industry, the Association of Engineering and Shipbuilding Draughtsmen gained recognition from the Engineering Employers Federation (EEF) after a long struggle before the Second World War. However, the EEF refused to give the same negotiating rights to the Association of Supervisory Staffs, Executives and Technicians (ASSET) on the grounds that its members were 'managerial'. ASSET achieved recognition by using emergency wartime labour relations machinery, in 1944.

This breakthrough was most important to all managerial staff in the private sector of economy, for although the then 10,000 members of ASSET were mainly first- and second-line supervisors, rather than managerial-level staff, the resistance of the employers had been based upon their being 'managerial' in nature. The national procedural arrangements agreed then have since been extended in a wide range of engineering companies to cover true managerial grades of staff.

Present attitudes to managerial unions

The postwar Taft–Hartley labour legislation in the United States excluded all supervisory and managerial staffs from the right to use the new machinery for gaining recognition, thus stunting the development of both supervisory and managerial unions in that country. Without the 1944 breakthrough by ASSET, Britain might have adopted similar provisions against supervisory or managerial union recognition when using American labour laws as a basis for the 1971 Industrial Relations Act. Instead, the 1971 Act provides for the right of all employees, including managerial staff, to join a union, and to secure negotiating rights. The Code of Practice accompanying the Act states specifically in paragraph 5 (iii) that even when a union is not yet recognised for negotiating purposes, the company should 'make clear to employees that it respects their rights' to join a union 'and to take part in its activities, which include seeking recognition for negotiating purposes'. When the union is recognised for negotiating purposes, paragraph 4 (iii) states that the company should 'make clear to employees that it welcomes their membership of an appropriate recognised union and their participation in the union's activities'. The Code recommends (paragraph 84) employers to receive representations from the union official on behalf of any individual members in a category of employees for which the union has not yet secured bargaining rights.

It is true that most people do not know the extent of white-collar unionisation. One rarely thinks of doctors or ambassadors as union members. But tens of thousands of managers, already enjoying the benefits of collective bargaining through trade union membership, have made substantial progress in terms of enhanced salaries and conditions, career security and meaningful involvement in top-level decision-making. In order to illustrate what can be achieved in a very short time-span, one may point, for example, to the managerial grades of British European Airways and British Overseas Airways Corporation who are in membership of the Association of Scientific Technical and Managerial Staffs. Formal negotiating rights were secured as recently as late 1970, and initial negotiations obtained the establishment of agreed salary scales and increases in pay effective from January 1971. Increases in the order of £1000 a year were gained for managers in membership.

It is not only in the public corporations, such as BEA and BOAC, that managerial grades benefit from professional trade union bargaining, although it is still true that the greatest density of union membership is in the nationalised industries. In national and local government, various civil service unions and the National and Local Government Officers Association represent and negotiate for a wide range of managerial functions. Formal negotiating machinery has been in use for many decades at the highest levels, covering the interests of town clerks, the diplomatic service, permanent secretaries to ministries and many other highly specialised grades of senior staff within the public sector. Amongst the professions, collective bargaining and equivalent techniques for settling remuneration and other conditions are very prevalent. Lawyers have traditionally held a tight control over their rights to insist upon minimum scales for fees, as well as upon the maintenance of their 'pre-entry closed shop'.

Other professions such as dentists and doctors, bargain collectively over the salaries and conditions for the members. Thus the Medical Practitioners Union section of ASTMS, through it seats on the General Medical Services Committee, negotiates at national level. Similarly, negotiations take place at local level with hospital boards and local authorities.

The majority of managers in private industry and commerce are probably not yet fully aware of the extent of collective bargaining that takes place on behalf of professional groups in British society.

It is in the private sector of industry and commerce that managers are least unionised. However, the degree of unionisation varies widely from one industry to another and from one company to another. The relative size of the company is also a factor, although formal bargaining arrangements already exist in a range of companies from amongst the largest in the land down to medium and small-sized firms employing only a handful of managerial-level staff.

Reasons for joining a managerial union

The introduction of managerial unions into a company can act as a stimulus for a whole range of overdue and much-needed changes. The manager, however, when considering whether or not to join the union, does not usually have the advantage of a crystal ball in order to have precise knowledge of future developments. Managers are becoming unionised for a variety of reasons and the individual's motivation is usually based on a combination of the available reasons.

The most obvious factor is the promotion of supervisory, scientific, technical and administrative staff who are already in membership of a union. In years gone by it was customary for a newly appointed foreman to leave the trade union movement. Times changed, and this custom became very much the exception. In a similar way, newly promoted managers are more and more remaining union members. With the fast increasing density of unionisation in the more junior white-collar staff areas, there is a correspondingly larger proportion of newly promoted managers with a union membership card already inside their wallet.

Further union membership develops from the day-to-day contacts between managers already in membership and those who had never considered the proposition in personal terms. These contacts arise as easily from social intercourse between managers in different companies who meet in the pub or club, as from relationships in the senior staff dining-room of one particular company. This factor also leads to whole groups of managers joining the union, when news of developments in another company, or section of the same company, becomes widely known. Individual contacts may initiate interest, and even individual membership, but there is nothing as effective as well-publicised news of the successful example set by others in a comparable situation to start the unionisation bandwagon rolling. The only real limitation on interest elsewhere is the degree of publicity achieved in the mass communications media.

A second group of reasons for joining a managerial union can be summarised as feeling threatened by an exploitative (or at least inconsiderate) boss with a consequent need for the backing of an organisation with the capacity to negotiate on one's behalf—the classic reason for joining a union. As ASTMS stated in its detailed evidence on managerial salaries to the National Board for Prices and Incomes in 1969:

The British manager's security is limited, his contractual situation vague and his knowledge of the market forces affecting his own career and remuneration is extremely limited. The British manager finds himself bedevilled by the secrecy that surrounds salaries, the lack of coherence generally in private industry in settling them, his inability to run adequate checks on the market value of his job and the individual distortions as a result of mistakes and prejudice in given companies. Rational salary structures demand a rational theoretical approach. They demand the writing of descriptions, the settling of responsibilities and adequate evaluations. The point of our argument really is this: the manager belongs to the dwindling group in our society who are still treated as casual workers who can be treated with individuality. The growth of managerial trade unionism is still frail although growing. The impact of collective bargaining in this field—which has already been substantial in the public services—will be the most important single reforming factor on remuneration and security.

Some of the experiences that can contribute to a feeling of insecurity include :

1 Major technological change—particularly computerisation, which leads to replacement of labour-intensive organisational structures, changes in manpower and training requirements at all levels.
2 The sight of graduate trainees obscuring or blocking the promotional prospects of the man who has worked his way up without formal academic training.
3 Job evaluation carried out in a way that appears to impose a new salary structure without the individual manager's agreement.
4 The presence of consultants in circumstances that are not adequately explained.
5 Mergers with the consequent problems of reorganisation and re-dundancy.
6 Failure of a manager to gain directly from a productivity agreement that he has initiated, planned and implemented.
7 Increasing distance between the individual manager and the decision-makers at board level as companies get bigger by national and trans-national merger and acquisition.

For many managers, however, the two major prompters of the decision to join a union are pay and redundancy.

After a decade of increasingly sharp inflation, managerial grades have felt the effect of economic pressures on all fronts. Thus the rising cost of living combined with the absence of collective bargaining has com-pounded the accumulated neglect of many years, and economic pressures create a climate within which union membership becomes not just a more acceptable alternative to retaining the *status quo*, but in many cases a pressing necessity. Progressive deterioration of relationships is felt, whether in terms of loss of salary differentials *vis-à-vis* other employees, both blue- and white-collar, protected by union collective bargaining, or in the light of the steady movement towards equalisation of fringe benefits for all employees.

Faced with redundancy, the non-union manager feels that he is without professional advice, without the protection of a collective agreement and subject to the whim of the board. Turning to a solicitor or the equivalent will not secure the professional bargainer with detailed knowledge and experience of dealing with a redundancy situation, and indeed, of preventing involuntary redundancies in many cases.

In a redundancy situation, the manager will often find that his contract was no protection. Usually the period of notice is of a minimum nature, and the manager has to rely upon an *ex gratia* additional payment at the discretion of the board, rather than being able to enjoy a negotiated 'golden handshake'. ASTMS has been very much involved in advising managers on suitable forms of contract, and much time and effort has been spent in negotiating adequate safeguards for the managerial members concerned. However, it is vital to emphasise that whatever steps have been taken to draw up a suitable contract, any amount of careful drafting may be of little value unless its enforcement is guaranteed by union membership.

This question of enforceability is essential to a proper understanding of managerial unionisation, for there is an unequal balance between the employer and the employees in the managerial field which has increasingly disappeared from many other occupations. Whatever provisions are made for arbitration or other means for settling disputes between an employer and a manager, in practice the latter will not be able to invoke them except in the case of dismissal. In all other cases if he attempts to assert his rights in his personal capacity he is bound to provoke a conflict which will lead to the termination of his engagement. Even if it would not, the manager cannot afford to take the chance. On the other hand, even in cases where each individual manager has a separate tailor-made contract, if he is a union member, then that union can see that the conditions in his case are observed as part of their general policy and in a way which does not threaten the employment of the member. Thus the union can 'de-personalise' the potential conflict situation. Similarly the union can act institutionally in any legal case on behalf of the member, whether for inadequate notice, breach of contract, injury compensation or any other subject.

Most interestingly, the very fact that the manager is a union member acts as a check on unilateral or high-handed action from the top. Union membership becomes a form of insurance policy. Its existence acts as a deterrent, and often obviates the need for the manager to refer anything at all to the union offical. For managerial staff, union membership itself is a form of sanction, invariably leading to greater consideration of their grade interests by the board.

Managerial unionisation can really be to the advantage of a company, and my experience as a national officer of a major union has convinced me that the only companies actively opposed to managerial unions are those that do not yet recognise them. I call this syndrome, 'the virgin's fear of the unknown'. Once reality has been recognised the progressive company will quickly recognise the beneficial side of managerial union-isation. Advantages vary from company to company, and depend to an extent on the scale of the unit or the company as a whole. Especially in the larger companies, collective representation, negotiation, and com-munication is superior to any kind of alternative. Most important of all, most, if not all, of the frustrations facing the younger manager in modern British industry can be tackled openly with a view to a mutually acceptable solution.

Part 2

THE MANAGEMENT DEVELOPMENT ACTIVITY

'Yes, but what do we *do*?' was the blunt question at a recent seminar on managerial training, during which all the previous discussion had been about background problems and the training environment. Those attending conferences of this nature often feel that the overture takes three-quarters of the problem.

Now we try to answer the question of what are the particular components that can be used to make a programme of management development, and how the individual executive may carry out his personal responsibility.

8

Diagnosing Development Needs of Managers and Organisations

Hawdon Hague, Managing Partner, CONTEXT

The success or failure of a management development programme depends very largely on the way its starts.

Obviously the first step must be to find out what training and development needs exist and objectives must be set so that the success or otherwise of the programme can be measured. Less obvious, perhaps, is the fact that the tone and status of the programme are established in its early days and it is often impossible to recover from a bad start. A tentative and academic beginning will lead to an ineffective and academic outcome, while, if the exercise is to be high level, high powered and purposeful, this must be established from the very beginning.

It is important, therefore, not only to plan the development of managers but to plan the whole management development exercise and, in particular, how it is launched.

When management development schemes fail—and this is still the most common outcome—the reasons can often be traced either to a lack of planning in the early stages or, a more recent development, to an over-concern with the mechanics of planning at the expense of achieving any results. The early attempts at management training sent people off on courses without any particular consideration of what that manager needed and what he was supposed to get from that course.

If the early failures, then, were due to unplanned training, more recent failures have been due to overcompensating for this. A formula for 'training needs analysis' has been evolved which can take so long that no managers are ever developed. It is also my contention that this formula is unduly narrow in the training needs it produces and so I favour a new approach which is wider in concept, but somewhat rough and ready in its early stages, in order to achieve some quick and demonstrable results.

The theory of training needs analysis is thus in a state of flux. Nobody would defend attempting to train without a background plan and the formal approach of job descriptions and appraisals still has the majority of adherents. I will describe the formal approach and the wider, but still experimental, one.

I make no apology for being perhaps too black and white about the failures of management development. The development of managerial resources should be one of the three main activities in an organisation, but this stature is rarely achieved, and, without it, successes are partial and occasional. As Drucker says in *The Effective Executive,* the appraisal forms which are the cornerstone of most management development systems are not looked at when personnel decisions are to be made. In other words, management development is a paper exercise, a somewhat irritating one at that and in no way connected with the main activities and decisions of the firm. If this is the image, the best way to change it is to analyse the reasons for the failures to date and to put forward constructive alternatives.

Formal approach

The accepted sequence for defining training needs begins with a job description, which sets out what the manager is supposed to do, and goes on to an appraisal of how he is doing. The gap between the two is thus the training need for his present job. Potential appraisal, which considers how far he might ultimately go, gives his training need for future jobs. This is a logical sequence and avoids the early mistakes of sending managers on courses at random and thinking that all managers have the same development needs.

Management development grew out of the need to be more systematic, to consider when the firm would need managers, with what experience, and to provide recruitment and development plans accordingly. I will describe each of the standard diagnostic tools in turn and show the right and wrong way to go about them.

Job descriptions

The first stage in defining a manager's training needs is to set down an agreed statement of what he is supposed to be doing and what results he should be achieving. The size and scope of the job must be defined as well as the title, the relationships and the limits of authority.

Some parts of the job description are relatively easy; for example, who the manager reports to and how many staff he controls (although disputes are not unknown). The general purpose of the job is usually straightforward; for example, production to quantity, quality and cost standards and with the minimum number of operatives killed in the process. After that, however, it gets more difficult. How much money can the manager spend without consultation? Has he the power to fire or only to recommend? What are his precise relationships with people like the chief inspector and with the multifarious headquarters officials?

There are usually knotty points to clear up, points which have been established by an unwritten case law or which have never been established at all. It is often necessary to do some tidying up of the organisation structure where there are overlapping responsibilities or areas for which nobody volunteers.

It is important that a manager and his superior agree the job description and the recommended sequence is that the manager prepares the first draft and his superior prepares an independent one. These often differ considerably and it is a useful exercise for them to talk out the differences. The management development adviser should play as small a part as possible, although, for the sake of speed, it is always tempting to do the initial composition if not the whole job. Properly done, the preparation of job descriptions is a training exercise in itself and may tidy up the organisation structure as well.

Mistakes to avoid. The possible faults are being too loose and general or being too detailed and trying to do too much. Early job descriptions simply showed the purpose and scope of the job and listed the main

TITLE: Works Manager
Responsible to
The Managing Director

Responsible for
Timber Yard;
Soft and Hardwood Conversion;
Building Board, Plywood and
factored items;
Joinery Production

Duties and Responsibilities
Purchasing
Purchase softwood, hardwood and wood
derivatives at economic prices
Discuss forward shipment prices with agents

Stock Control
Ensure sufficient stock of all items are kept to meet
all foreseeable demands (as advised by sales
director)
Maintain a stock control system
Arrange stacking and re-stacking in the yard

Production
Prepare outline plans for the conversion production
on all items
Prepare an annual production budget based on sales
forecast and actual orders
In conjunction with the sales director, ensure that
delivery dates promised are kept as far as possible
Maintain quality standards in accordance with
customers' requirements
Consult daily with mill managers over the current
programme
Keep control of overhead costs in the production
departments
Keep machine time down to a minimum
Investigate new production techniques
Maintain an efficient machine layout and handling
system
Recommend any capital investment required

Maintenance
Arrange for a system of plant and machinery
maintenance
Ensure that health, safety and fire precautions are
obeyed, including machine guard standards, dust
direction systems, etc.

Staffing
Arrange for the efficient staffing of sawmills and
production departments
Select, appoint and discipline staff
Arrange training for staff
In consultation with the company secretary,
review pay scales

Figure 8:1   Job description for works manager

This is the same works manager as is described in Figure 8:3
Source: Furniture & Timber Industry Training Board

JOB DESCRIPTION

Broad Statement	Specific Statement
1 The broad statement of the purpose of the post: Title: Works Manager Relationships: *Responsible to:* Production Director *Directly supervising:* Machine Shop Superintendent Assembly Shop Superintendents (2) Works Maintenance Engineer Head of Progress Department Scope: Control of Manufacturing Departments located at ...; Works Engineering and Maintenance Department; Works Stores; Works Progress Department; Works Garage Resources: *Financial* — revenue expenditure as per agreed budget (£...) — capital expenditure, nil authority *Manning* — Works Staff... — Office Staff... Key Result Areas: **(i)** The manufacturing requirements agreed jointly with the Production Director to be met, i.e. in the quantities and types required, in accordance with specifications, to the delivery dates set and within budget **(ii)** Safety precautions in all factory operations **(iii)** Industrial relations	**2** The specific statement of the goals to be achieved: For the purpose of illustration, the specific statements relating to *two* years are given. The assumption is that appraisal of performance is being made at the end of, say, 1967 against the goals set for that year, and at the same time new goals are being considered for the year ahead. Hence training recommendations can be related to the needs identified by past performance and to the requirements arising from the new demands to be made Goals of the past year (1967): **(a)** To achieve the manufacturing targets (ref...) as agreed with the Production Director that is, in the quantities and types required, in accordance with the engineering specifications set and within the budget allocation (£...) **(b)** To ensure that proper safety precautions are taken in all factory operations so that the accident index does not exceed the level of last year **(c)** To deal promptly and effectively with industrial relation matters Additional goals for the year ahead (1968): **(i)** To prepare a report for submission to the Board on 1st July covering proposals for reducing machine maintenance costs by 10% **(ii)** To modify the present production control system so as to reduce the value of work in progress by 15%. Time period ten months

Figure 8:2   Job description for works manager
Source: Engineering Industry Training Board

duties and responsibilities involved in it. An example of this type is shown in Figure 8:1. This is better than nothing in that it lists the areas to which the works director concerned should give attention but it is little more than a breakdown of the obvious and an expression of pious hope. Worst of all, there are no quantified targets so, when the time comes to review performance, there is scope for infinite argument as to whether or not he has done well, and whether or not any bad results were his fault. A vague and generalised job description results in a vague and generalised —and probably resented—training need.

An example of a job description which, in my opinion, is too detailed is given in Figure 8:2. Is the division into broad statement and specific statement helpful and does the complete list of superintendents and workshops covered help to pinpoint training needs?

I suspect this wealth of factual detail may arise from a wish to make the exercise look more scientific than it is, or the fact that job descriptions are used for recruitment procedures and organisational structuring also leads to a temptation to produce an all-purpose job description. The result is often unwieldy and more suited to organisation analysis than specifying skills and abilities.

What to aim for. Better job descriptions incorporate management by objectives, and therefore they specify the key results of a manager— that is, those areas where the manager can have the greatest impact on the profitability of the firm. Whenever possible, specific targets are set so that there is no scope for argument about whether or not the manager has been successful. (The specific statement in Figure 8:2 is good in that four of the five targets are quantified.) This reduces the likelihood of emotion and temper entering into the appraisal and the discussion can be focused on whether any shortfalls were within the manager's control or not.

A better and more balanced job description is shown in Figure 8:3. This contains a minimum of verbiage, the performance standards are quantified and the method of measuring is shown. One can always criticise and, for example, one could ask whether the works director is responsible for setting the maintenance schedules, and, if so, how he is supposed to know the right balance between minimising total costs, maximising production and so forth. However, the job is concisely defined and the manager has a useful guide to setting his priorities and measuring his own progress.

TITLE: Works Manager
Responsible to: **Directly supervising:**
The Managing Director   Softwood Mill Manager;
                       Hardwood Manager;
                       Stock Controller;
                       Joinery Production Manager
Main Purpose of Job: To plan and control all production activities to the agreed standards

Key Task	Performance Standards	Review Information
1 Ensuring availability of timber at economic cost	1 (1) Not more than 5% of timber purchases are from landed stocks	Monthly list of purchases
	(2) Periods of stock turnover do not exceed: softwood 80 days, hardwood 125 days, wood derivatives 46 days	MD's periodic account (5-weekly)
2 Producing efficiently	2 (1) Overdue orders at the end of each week do not number more than 10% of the total	Weekly record of overdues
	(2) Material costs as a percentage of sales are: softwood 72%, hardwood 65%, building stores 80%, factored items 84%, joinery 40%	MD's periodic account
	(3) Number of complaints requiring credit does not exceed 10 per month	Complaints record
3 Controlling production costs	3 (1) Direct labour for softwood and hardwoods achieves 95% performance under the bonus scheme	Bonus sheet
	(2) Departmental and general works costs do not exceed the budget	MD's periodic report
4 Maintaining machinery and safety	4 (1) Maintenance schedules are met	Dated schedule
	(2) The legal requirements applicable for all plant and processes are being fully complied with	Accident records. Statutory registers. Comments by H.M.F.I.
5 Managing staff	5 (1) Training programmes are implemented for all staff requiring training	Training programmes
	(2) Labour turnover is kept below 20% p.a.	Personnel records

Figure 8:3   Job description for works manager

This is the same works manager as is described in Figure 8:1

Source: Furniture & Timber Industry Training Board

Areas requiring further research. There is another line of enquiry which should be pursued in relation to job descriptions. In *Managers and their Jobs,* Rosemary Stewart pointed out some very basic differences between different managers' jobs. She demonstrated that some jobs are much more fragmented than others. (For example, a production supervisor devotes on average only six minutes to one problem before being called to another.) She also analysed the types of decision they took by the kind of judgment required, the amount of information available, and whether the decisions were short or long term, continuous or discontinuous.

How much time is spent on the different aspects of the manager's work? What kind of contacts does the job involve and what form do they take? How much time does a manager spend in committees, how much with subordinates, and so forth? What sort of people does he deal with, in what sort of a relationship and under what sorts of pressures? These questions are very basic, but they are never answered in job descriptions although an analysis of job structure along the lines that Rosemary Stewart suggests would be more helpful for the trainer in pinpointing areas he could work on than a list of numbers supervised. This is a weakness in the art at present.

Performance appraisals

The second stage in the formal sequence is the appraisal of how a manager is doing, so that this can be compared with his objectives.

The theory of appraisals is that they are carried out by a man's immediate superior, generally using a form which makes him consider all aspects of performance. Without a form, few superiors would get beyond the two or three aspects which pleased or displeased them most strongly.

Appraisals are difficult, embarrassing and controversial. A DSIR study by Kay Rowe proved—as was long suspected—that appraisal interviews (that is, meetings at which a superior tells a subordinate what he put on the form) are almost universally ducked and even filling in the form is usually either ducked or else done so sloppily that it is useless. This reluctance is often rationalised as 'managers don't like to play God' but I think it is more accurate to say that managers don't like to be seen to play God. They do make and break men, and enjoy doing so, but they do so on criteria of who they like and dislike and they are aware that their lack of objectivity would be exposed if they completed an appraisal form accurately.

Of course appraisals always existed, even in the days before formal schemes. Whenever anyone said of a subordinate that he was 'a good chap' or 'not really up to it' he was appraising the subordinate and shaping his career to a considerable extent. Such appraisals, of course, were purely subjective and probably reflected whether or not the subordinate was industrious and respectful and behaved himself at the Christmas party but, in one form or another, appraisals are bound to take place.

Chapter 13 will discuss appraisals and counselling as part of the on-going management development process. My concern is with the initial appraisals to establish training needs, so I will not enter into the controversy further except to say that it is a basic human need to know how one is thought to be doing, and how one is being judged, and that there are no ethical objections providing agreed plans are made and carried out to help with shortcomings and to give greater scope for using strengths.

The subordinate is likely to view appraisals as a catalogue of his failings, to be put in some computer and used against him later, and he will lose this scepticism only when some resulting plan to develop him is put into operation. However, once he feels that the firm has his interests at heart and that the appraisal is a necessary part of making plans to help him, the whole procedure becomes a powerful motivating force.

Mistakes to avoid. As with job descriptions, the early appraisal forms were general and focused mainly on personality traits. The difficulty was that the judgments were subjective and led to arguments when discussed with the subordinate. Also, it was difficult to see how training or development could help a man who was rated low on 'endeavour', 'judgment' or 'leadership'. The potential embarrassment was then maximised and the purpose and justification largely lost.

The early forms tried to give managers some guide in their ratings by providing a five-point scale ranging from very good to very bad, and giving a short description of each category. The earnestness and futility of this process were beautifully parodied in the *Sunday Times* as shown in Figure 8:4.

Figure 8:5 is an example of a typical personality-biased form. Note how easy it is to give low ratings to someone you dislike because none

PERFORMANCE FACTORS	FAR EXCEEDS JOB REQUIREMENTS	EXCEEDS JOB REQUIREMENTS	MEETS JOB REQUIREMENTS	NEEDS SOME IMPROVEMENT	DOES NOT MEET REQUIREMENTS
QUALITY	Leaps tall buildings with a single bound	Must take running start to leap over tall buildings	Can only leap over a building with no spires	Crashes into buildings when attempting to jump	Cannot recognise buildings at all, much less jump
TIMELINESS	Is faster than a speeding bullet	Is as fast as a speeding bullet	Not as fast as a speeding bullet	Would you believe a slow bullet?	Wounds self with bullets
INITIATIVE	Is stronger than a locomotive	Is stronger than a bull elephant	Is stronger than a bull	Shoots the bull	Smells like a bull
ADAPTABILITY	Walks on water consistently	Walks on water in emergencies	Washes with water	Drinks water	Passes water in emergencies
COMMUNICATION	Talks with God	Talks with the angels	Talks to himself	Argues with himself	Loses those arguments

Figure 8:4   Guide to performance appraisal
Source: Sunday Times, 1 March 1970

DIAGNOSING DEVELOPMENT NEEDS OF MANAGERS

Department_____ Name_____

Section_____ Age at 1/4/70 _____Years

Position_____ Length of employment_____ *Months
_____ *Years

I   General assessment
(Tick as appropriate, any important
qualifications can be given in general remarks)

	Exceptional	Good	Adequate	Moderate	Poor
Accuracy					
Attendance record					
Energy and willingness shown					
Initiative shown					
Intelligence					
Interest in his job					
Knowledge of his job					
Output					
Performance in the job					
Personal appearance					
Punctuality					
Quality as a leader					
Relations with fellow employees					

2   How long has he/she been working for you?_____years_____months

3   Do you consider that he/she is fully and
properly employed in the work he/she
is doing ?   _____

If not, give reasons and state either :-
(a) whether you wish to retain him/her
on your staff ?   _____

OR

(b) whether you recommend that he/she :-
(i) be retained in the company's
employ in another capacity or   _____

(ii) should be encouraged to find a
job elsewhere ?   _____

Figure 8:5 Performance appraisal form

DIAGNOSING DEVELOPMENT NEEDS OF MANAGERS

JOB PERFORMANCE REVIEW

Date issued:
30 April 1970

For
A.N. Other

Agreed with:
General manager

Job title:
Mill manager

Reviewed by:
General manager

Item number	Standard		Reason for non achievement	Future action	Training needs
	Achieved	Not achieved			
Key task					
1					
2					
3					
4					
5					

Figure 8:6   Job performance review
Source: Furniture & Timber Industry Training Board

of the judgments need be backed with facts (except, of course, attendance and punctuality). Normally, however, play safe by putting one or two ticks under 'good' and the rest under 'adequate'. To be fair, this form was designed for junior managers and clerical staff but it is instructive to analyse why it is unhelpful to diagnosing development needs. Results could be comical if anyone was advised at appraisal interview to show more energy or more leadership quality, but it is hard to see what could be put on the form that would aid the training department in drawing up a plan. And the form is not untypical.

What to aim for. Appraisals are more objective if management by objectives is in operation. If targets are sets and results measured, the performance review form can be as simple as Figure 8:6. Given this type of appraisal, there is no embarrassment and the subordinate can

136

monitor his own performance. Normally, discussion can quickly proceed to 'future action' and the meetings can be short and purposeful.

A performance review form should ask both superior and subordinate to say what training or development they feel would help. Again, some general questions are legitimate, for example : What are the manager's strongest qualities? What could be changed so as to make better use of them? Has he any under-utilised abilities? Such questions are not the usual catalogue of weaknesses, but focus attention on strengths and may give the key to suggestions for development. The test of a good appraisal form is whether it produces agreed and usable suggestions for developing the manager, and helping him to help himself.

Potential appraisal

Performance appraisal shows up needs relating to the present job, but the other jobs a manager is likely to do must be considered in order to establish training needs for future jobs. Therefore, his potential must be assessed as well as the vacancies that might arise giving scope for promotion or transfer.

Potential appraisal is usually handled by additional questions on the performance appraisal form relating to qualities which are considered important in the higher levels. These often include judgment, decisiveness, willingness to delegate, acceptance as a leader and so forth. The list of qualities is subjective, and so is the assessment.

This can be acceptable in large firms. If there are a lot of grades (for example, there are sixteen grades in BP) and promotion is normally within the same function, it is reasonable to ask a man's boss to assess how many grades he might rise. The judgment called for is not too general and the superior does not feel that his own job is threatened if he recommends promotion.

Succession planning and potential appraisal are more difficult in smaller firms. The number of senior jobs is less and if A is being groomed for promotion this can only be at the expense of B, so the plans have to be kept secret.

Also, the type of promotion is very different, often involving much wider responsibilities. If promotion would entail control of marketing and finance by a man with experience only in production, the training needs are easy to diagnose, but testing his potential is far more difficult.

I would suggest a form as simple as Figure 8:7 which draws attention

POTENTIAL APPRAISAL			
Name:		Job title:	
UNDER-UTILISED ABILITIES	SHORT TERM What jobs could he do within a year	LONG TERM How far could he go	
			SELF ASSESSMENT
			SUPERIOR'S ASSESSMENT
			SUPERIOR'S JUSTIFICATION

Signature |
| | | | SECOND OPINION

Signature |
| | | | |

Figure 8:7   Potential appraisal form
Source: CONTEXT

specifically to under-utilised abilities and the manager's own assessment of his potential, but otherwise leaves it to the superior to give his views and justify them. A checklist of universal applicability is impossible, but a second opinion, even an outside opinion, could help.

Definition of training need

In the formal system, once job descriptions and appraisals are properly completed, the training needs are fairly readily apparent. Thus, if a production manager is failing to meet his targets because of numerous labour disputes and a high labour turnover, then obviously he needs coaching in human relations. If he is likely to be promoted to works director, then he needs experience to give him an appreciation of finance and marketing.

An example of the sort of training needs that emerge, and how easy this part of the sequence is, is shown in Figure 8:8. A medium-term external course is sensible for someone who is likely to move into a wider job, and the second and third suggestions would also give new and appropriate insights.

There is scope for interpretation and judgment in defining training needs. A shrewd assessor can spot that a particular manager might benefit from a change of boss or type of job. Appraisals tell as much about the appraiser as the appraised, and it is always worth while, when someone is not well regarded, to see if there is a simple explanation in terms of a personality clash. Equally, the man might be in the wrong type of job and a 'yogi' in a 'commissar' role, to use Antony Jay's distinction, will get bad reports that belie his ability.

It is important, therefore, to be sensitive to such possibilities when drawing out training needs from the job descriptions and appraisals, in order to compensate for possible errors in what is revealed.

Limitations of formal approach

I have tried to present the case for the formal approach as fairly as I can because it is widely used, but I have many reservations.

Job descriptions. Job descriptions are under attack from various directions: Rosemary Stewart says that at best they immortalise what was true at one point of time; Robert Townsend says that they cramp all

DIAGNOSING DEVELOPMENT NEEDS OF MANAGERS

APPRAISAL	PROPOSED TRAINING PROGRAMME
Job performance in relation to 1967 goals: (a) Mr———'s performance under this heading has been most satisfactory. Over the year, production targets have been met; delivery dates, specification requirements have been to the set programme; cost figures have been within 2% of the budget (b) Safety precautions have been effective; the accident index is down by nearly 7% and now shows a consistent improvement over the last three years (fi) There have been two major work stoppages, one of which might have been avoided if Mr ——— had acted more promptly Mr———is a strong candidate for promotion to the Board and a further review next year should conclude with a specific appointment	Arrangement to be made for Mr ——— to attend during the year an external course of substantial quality, probably lasting 6 to 8 weeks, when he can take the opportunity to develop his skill in decision taking (in particular long-term operations), and gain a wider understanding of the changing national and international environment, with its effect on policy-making in a business enterprise Mr ——— is to represent the Production Director on the Company's Forward Planning Committee Throughout the year, two or three opportunities will be taken for Mr ——— to accompany the Managing Director on selected business visits to customer establishments

Figure 8:8   Training needs analysis
This should be read in conjunction with Figure 8:2
Source: Engineering Industry Training Board

initiative. I indicated earlier my feeling that the information (on patterns of work and types of decision) which would be of use to the trainer is not usually given.

Even so, job descriptions take a long time to prepare, partly because of line managers' reluctance to lose their flexibility and partly because areas of organisational greyness are frequently discovered that one feels obliged to clear up before proceeding to the next stage. It is not uncommon for the job description stage to take a year, and this is not a dynamic beginning for the development programme.

Performance appraisals. The time factor is also significant in performance appraisals, which are resisted even more stubbornly by line managers. The first review cycle will meet with an inordinate delay and the first forms will be too sketchy to yield anything to the trainer—there

will be too many central ratings, boxes calling for analysis and recommendations will be left blank and the reasons for missing targets will be
so sweeping ('dock strike') as to give the trainer no help.

Performance appraisals are difficult and, even with MBO, it takes two
years' careful coaching to get satisfactory results.

Potential appraisal. Potential appraisal is by far the weakest link in the
chain, especially the principle of asking for a man to be rated by his
superior. An IQ of 130 cannot assess an IQ of 140, but the superior does
not write : 'This man is more intelligent than I, so I cannot rate him
accurately.' Parkinson quotes a manager, who is frightened of a subordinate more able than himself, as not saying, 'Mr Asterisk is too able'
but 'Mr Asterisk? Clever, perhaps—but is he sound? I incline to prefer
Mr Cypher.'

L. J. Peter, in *The Peter Principle*, talks, with more than a grain of
truth, of managers being promoted to one level beyond their competence,
and the reason is that promotions are still made on the basis of performance in present jobs. Everybody will tell you that the best salesman
does not necessarily make the best sales manager, but the fact remains
that the man who is performing well and giving little trouble is the most
likely to be promoted in selling or anywhere else.

Rosemary Stewart's classification of jobs shows that promotion can
often be to a qualitatively different job : a production manager who dealt
with shopfloor personnel and problems at six-minute intervals will need
an entirely different range of abilities if promoted to works director. To
assume that present performance will be repeated on promotion is thus
not enough. The man who was reliable at getting the accounts out is
likely to be the wrong choice as financial controller and a man who is
rebellious and unpopular may be a better choice if the job involves a
high degree of critical ability and original thought.

Not enough work has yet been done on defining the types of ability
that are important in different types and different levels of jobs : until
the specialists have done this, we cannot expect biased and harassed line
managers to make accurate assessments of potential.

Training needs analysis. The assumption of the formal approach is that
training needs are self-evident if job descriptions and appraisals are
available. In practice, this is sometimes just not the case. Often no
training needs emerge, but one cannot believe this is an accurate picture

even for managers not destined to reach the board, and probably not going to change jobs significantly.

When a clearly defined need for training emerges, there may be no indication of how to provide it. To take an absurd example, suppose a manager's objective is to lift 20 tons at a snatch and his performance appraisal showed that he was lifting only 18 tons, his training need is to lift the last two tons, but we do not know whether to send him to a muscle-builder or a psychiatrist.

Lack of sensitivity towards the psychological is the weakness of the formal approach. The sequence of Job Description — Appraisal = Training Need is mechanistic and tends to produce mechanistic needs, like a course in this technique or an appreciation course in that. These needs may be accurately diagnosed but most managers are limited not by ignorance of the latest management techniques but by factors for which 'psychological' is an unsatisfactory, but the only, description.

Summary. The formal sequence, although there is little wrong with its logic, has some major problems. It produces relatively unimportant needs and it gives little guidance on how to meet those needs. A course is always the likely prescription.

It can be three years before a new appointee develops any managers. Long before then, line managers have dismissed him as an academic producer of paper so he lacks the moral authority to carry his plans through, whenever—and it is the usual case—they are inconvenient.

As a corollary, management development can attract a breed of men who are resistant to this type of frustration; some are expert in preparing job descriptions (but nothing else) and others are content to follow the official procedures of their profession and to blame 'them' (that is, line managers) if they notice their own ineffectiveness.

Finally, the traditional sequence does not throw up company development needs, other than as the sum of individual needs. This is a serious omission as I shall explain in the next section.

Wider needs

Important management needs are often founded in the psychological rather than in management techniques, and a company has similar needs over and above the individual needs of its managers.

Individual psychological needs

Saying that managers are withholding intellectual effort or commitment for psychological reasons is not to accuse them of being in any way abnormal, quite the reverse. The word 'psychological' is used without any of the normal overtones of eccentricity or manic depression. Depression of a sort, however, is very common and the expression 'male menopause' is all too apt.

The average manager starts off with a generalised ambition, probably never articulated, that somewhere or somehow he wants to 'get to the top'. In time, he comes to realise he is not going to make it, possibly through a gradual realisation or possibly traumatic moments when somebody younger is promoted over him or a promised reorganisation does not take place. Such setbacks at work may well coincide with finding that he cannot last a ninety-minute football match and that his bonhomie to the girls in the office leads to muttered comments about 'dirty old men'.

Like everything else, the age of disillusion is falling, and if the 'menopause' occurs before 35, the manager has a further 30 years to work. If he has little to look for in the way of promotion, the best he can hope for is to maintain his status and employment and, not surprisingly, he becomes defensive. He works hard enough from 9 to 5 o'clock, but only in routine ways because he has much more to lose than to gain by doing anything new or adventurous. Robert Townsend estimates that managers use 20 to 25 per cent of their intellect at work : this could be an explanation.

There are other psychological restraints. Many a manager stops putting forward suggestions because he meets nothing but cold water. Worse still, somebody else makes the same suggestions two years later (often a consultant) and is praised to the skies. A personality clash with his boss, a feeling that there is little scope for job development, or that extra effort would not be welcomed, even if it was noticed, all these factors cause managers to switch off, and 'psychological' is the best word to describe them.

There is no need to dwell on the amount of time and nervous energy devoted to political intrigue, personal animosities or trying to 'beat the system'. A major constraint is disbelief in the possibility of change. Frequently managers agree with a new suggestion but feel that 'the old man would never accept it' so they see no point in getting excited or even in making experiments. For varying reasons, most managers feel themselves to be prisoners of their situation—the situation being the organisation spirit, the boss or inflexible colleagues—and they have stopped trying to change it.

Can anything be done about psychological problems or is it impossible on the grounds that a man's personality cannot be changed? In many cases something can be achieved. When a manager is limited by his view of his situation, either his view or the situation can be changed. If he is in a rut then, at the very least, he can be picked up and dropped in a different one. Alternatively, a thoughtful gesture showing that he has not been written off can help, and being put on a project team which makes him relate his work to the rest of the company can bolster morale and stimulate new thinking.

If a group of managers can be shown that they can influence their situation, that may be all the help they need and they may develop themselves immeasurably thereafter. However, it may well be necessary to tackle the organisational climate at the same time or even earlier.

There are no universal answers to psychological questions because the problems differ in each case, but this is an argument, not for funking the issue (still less for using standard courses) but for individual diagnosis and action. It is easy to ignore such problems and to pretend that middle-age disappointments are not your business. If a man is removed from his familiar routines and friends, there is a chance that he will leave. This will involve the trouble and expense of replacing him, but is 25 years of gradually diminishing performance really the better alternative?

Some examples

New entrants to management. New entrants to management are either trainees or promoted supervisors. In either case, they need the whole range of management skills and techniques and, for the first eighteen months at any rate, they are willing to learn. (Report has it that this is now dropping to nine or ten months in the case of graduates.)

A promoted supervisor, however, has psychological problems, especially if he is promoted over former colleagues, and he may well need a sympathetic discussion or help on the job. The trainee has a strong desire to contribute in an area where his results can be measured, so he needs stretching and possibly quite tough assignments. Classroom exercises, then, should be only a small part of the development plans in either case.

The high flyer. The high flyer is frequently sent on courses and is probably bright enough to abstract something from them. Also, he changes jobs so quickly that he never stops learning—the only danger being that he might rotate so quickly that his mistakes never catch up with him.

The high flyer's needs are technical, then, but just as long as he is flying high. Once he feels he is not being stretched, he becomes an able but frustrated manager with psychological problems in plenty.

Top managers. Today's top managers frequently received no planned training and have little understanding of functions other than their own. Many have a fear that if they took part in training exercises they would show up as less able than their juniors. If the fear is justified, management development has one problem; if the fear is unjustified, the problem can be one of building up confidence in the seniors.

The basic problem, however, is to get senior managers to do some new thinking, in terms of looking at their own jobs afresh and of looking outside it. With success as well as years under their belt, and the feeling that their own careers disprove the need for 'any of this fancy training', it is difficult to make them realise their need to do anything differently. This 'unfreezing' of top managers is the most difficult, and the most critical, task of management development, because unless they are willing to experiment, all plans for lower managers will gradually come to nothing.

Other experienced managers. Many long-serving managers stay in the same function all their careers and in the same job for large slices of it. The Mant Report drew attention to their development needs but the sheer size of the problem still discourages any serious action. Such managers need to keep abreast of changing technology but they also have the greatest temptations to switch off, so they must be kept mentally alert by whatever changes of scene and problems they can cope with, and encouraged to exchange their experience with each other.

Company development needs

A company has development needs which are not just the sum of the needs of the individual managers. It may be short of numbers in some categories or weak in, say, marketing awareness. It may want to diversify and not have the management to do so. It may be a question of numbers or abilities or, on occasion, a particular management technique that is needed, as, for example, in a construction firm that was innocent of network analysis.

More common, however, are needs to change the organisation structure or philosophy because they are cramping the growth of managers and hence of profits. For example, some organisations are over-defensive and all managers stick to the rules and retreat behind their rank when confronted by suggestions for change. An autocrat may have died and his son may want to be more democratic, but the former yes-men find it hard to be either critical or participative. Some organisations seem unwilling and incapable of reaching any decisions at all.

The organisation structure can be unhelpful. It might have lots of staff officials and coordinators of this and that, all inviting internal power games. The structure may date back to a time when marketing was no problem or when the firm centred round one man with an unusual combination of abilities. A more modern disease is the firm which changes its structure so often that nobody knows what he is doing or believes anything to be permanent.

Some organisations lack middle-management talent and therefore have no next generation of top managers. Some organisations have too much talent and their able men sit in needless committees wasting each other's time. The need in the last case is for some to be taken off their present jobs and told to launch a new division. The question of whether there are the right number of jobs, sufficiently stretching and at the right levels, to provide opportunity for managerial growth is an important one.

The organisation's structure and spirit largely determine how much effort its managers will put into developing themselves and it seems axiomatic that a company is developed by developing its senior managers. It is still most common, however, to find that management development is performed by someone relatively low in the hierarchy while anything touching on the organisation structure is handled by a prominent firm of American consultants. It is far better if one agent steers the development of the organisation and the managers, partly for coordination and also because changes in organisation, with (hopefully) discussions before and after, are the best of all subjects for training projects, being of interest and concern to all levels. It is a pity if only American consultants benefit from the learning opportunities involved.

The development of the organisation is acknowledged—in firms which do it deliberately—to be a top-level matter and central to the firm's activities. Management development, on my definition, is part of the same process and should be similarly regarded.

Diagnosing the wider needs

There is no established method of diagnosing the wider company and individual development needs as these are areas of current experiment-ation. The method I shall describe is a self-assessment form followed by a confidential interview. Whoever does the interviewing gets a quick and sufficiently accurate view of the development needs of the company and its managers and can quickly set up some development exercises in line with what the managers want. The arguments in favour of this approach are speed, cooperation and the fact that self-assessment is an unfreezing and a teaching device in its own right. More accurate training needs can be defined later, and the projects, or whatever is set up, will be much better than any appraisal form at revealing potential, or the lack of it.

Self-assessment

The idea of self-assessment may seem naive but in fact a form such as the one shown in Figure 8:9 gets perfectly sensible results. The managers are asked to define their own training and development needs but not before they have been taken through a series of thought-provoking questions.

The first questions are on key tasks, which the manager may be able to complete from his files. Even so, it is worth making him think how much time he spends on his key results areas. The questions in the next group probe the pattern of the job and the types of decision taken.

It is sometimes painful to state what has been accomplished in the last twelve months, but the next three questions are more enjoyable and allow the manager to make constructive suggestions. He is then asked to consider his career pattern and whether he or the firm has a plan for him—a sequence of thought which surprisingly few managers have followed through.

Questions are asked about how far the manager feels he wants to go, and could go, and these produce surprises in both directions; some have high and possibly illusory ambitions while others who are highly regarded

SELF ASSESSMENT

Please answer the following questions. There is no pressure to reveal anything you do not wish to, so answers can be long or short, and typed or hand-written. Anything you wish to be kept confidential will remain so. (Put a 'c' beside the appropriate answers.)

1. What is your job? It will suffice if you indicate its main purpose, the main people dealt with, and the limits of authority.

2. What are your Key Results Areas? In other words, which are the five or six things which, if done well, will have the most beneficial results for the company?

3. Roughly, how do you think your time is allocated between:
   - (a) Key Result Areas
   - (b) Other Areas, but still necessary
   - (c) Areas of doubtful necessity

   How do you think your time is allocated between:
   - (d) Travelling
   - (e) Being alone
   - (f) Being with one other
   - (g) Being with more than one other

4. What percentage of your time is spent dealing with personnel matters?

5. What would be the typical length of time you get to devote to any one thing?

6. What types of decision do you take, individually and with others, and how often?

7. What are your strong points in the job?

8. What have you accomplished of particular note during the last 12 months?

9. Are there any changes which would enable you to accomplish more during the next 12 months?

10. Is there anything you would like your superior to clarify?

11. Are there any circumstances which frustrate you and make you less effective than you would otherwise be?

12. Have you any skills and aptitudes which are not fully utilised in your present job?

13. What qualifications have you for your present job? Did you get it as part of a wider plan, either of your own or of the company's?

14. Is your present job in line with the sort of career pattern that suits you? Give reasons in either case, and show the pattern you would like to see with an indication of time spans.

15. Would you appreciate the type of career pattern which would give you a change from time to time, even if no promotion was involved?

16. Are there any other points about your work, ambitions or interests which affect the course your career might take?

17. What other (or larger) job could you do?
   - (a) Now?
   - (b) Within a year?
   - (c) Within 5 years?

18. What training and development would you welcome from the point of view of:
   - (a) General interest?
   - (b) Your present job?
   - (c) Possible future jobs?

Figure 8:9   Self-assessment form

Source: CONTEXT

have no ambition. Under-utilised abilities are asked for and, finally, training and development needs.

Having gone through this exercise very few managers put down that they could be managing director immediately or that they have no training needs. Things commonly asked for are an understanding of finance and marketing, coaching in group effectiveness and an appreciation of the interrelation of functions. Training in advanced techniques in the manager's own function is rarely asked for, but this is probably an accurate reflection of the real needs. Self-diagnosed needs are unlikely to be wrong and they are rarely as trivial as one might expect.

Interviews. As the next stage, somebody has a one- to two-hour discussion with each manager centred around his questionnaire. The somebody can be an outside consultant or an internal man, providing he is not thought of as part of the establishment or as a Red Guard in a 'cultural revolution'.

The interview is necessary to amplify the questionnaire, as some managers put down guarded answers while others find it hard to make the necessary abstractions. A good interviewer, however, will learn a lot about the manager's job and career needs, and in particular about any frustrations or apprehensions that are limiting his performance. The more intelligent the manager, the more absorbing he will find the questionnaire. Everybody enjoys the interview, as it centres on him, and, once he sees the point of the exercise, he joins in wholeheartedly and thereby starts his own development process.

The interviewer gets a picture of the individual's psychological needs; if there is a basic quarrel with his boss or a feeling that being adventurous would be punished, this will emerge. In one sense, it does not matter whether the feeling is correct or not; it is affecting that manager's contribution and it must come into the open before anything can be done about it.

The interviewer will also get a picture of the company's needs. A similar picture often emerges from different managers and it is not uncommon for several managers to make the same recommendations for organisational change although they have never made the suggestions to each other.

If the boss takes part in the exercise, the participants will feel that it is 'for real' and it is important that managers feel free to talk about whatever concerns them. If, on the other hand, discussion of the organisation or the top managers is barred, there will be few constructive proposals that the managers can put forward and the exercise will be just another list of their shortcomings.

Diary.   Another crude but effective tool is the keeping of a diary, say for a week. This too is diagnostic and self-teaching. The ideal timing for this is after filling in the questionnaires as the managers would be able to compare how they actually spent their time with what they thought to be the case. Self-awareness can be taken a stage further by asking colleagues (as suggested by Drucker): 'What do I do that wastes your time?' and by group discussions on steps to improve mutual use of time.

Continuous diagnosis.   Some of the suggested exercises are part diagnostic and part treatment. For example, a group discussion on use of time by managers who have recently kept diaries can produce immediate results (such as agreements not to interrupt each other casually, or not to use the internal telephone between 10 a.m. and 12 noon), but the discussion also makes the managers think about their own self-organisation and about how they could improve. This is good; diagnosis of needs and learning are both continuous processes, and it is not the case that one has to finish before the other begins.

This is particularly true of uncovering potential. If managers are put on projects which make them consider the long term or something far-reaching in its implications, this will show up their own potential to look at things from a company-wide as opposed to a departmental viewpoint. If a manager puts himself on the succession charts in this way, this automatically gives him further training needs.

It follows that the role of the interviewer, or catalyst, must also be continuous. He is not trying to define needs at one point in time but to set the process in motion and thereafter to keep diagnosis and action proceeding simultaneously.

Tactics and sequence

I have described the formal approach to the definition of training needs, expressed some reservations and outlined the latest developments. Which approach will work in a particular company? Can the formal and new approaches be combined? The answers to these questions depend on whether the formal systems are more or less established or whether the company is starting from scratch.

Starting from scratch

Someone, either a line manager interested in management development or a new appointee charged with setting up the function, who is starting from scratch, should adopt the self-assessment and interview approach. He should get some development activities under way by the second month, and if managers feel some benefit by the third month, the most difficult part of his task will be accomplished.

The self-assessed needs are approximations, but the job description and appraisal exercises can be done later, partly for completeness and because they will produce additional needs, but they are also training exercises in themselves. Job descriptions could be introduced 'to see how things stand at present' and any anomalies thrown up could be discussed. Appraisals always need careful coaching even though potential appraisal is not as difficult when managers are engaged on projects.

This approach brings the benefits of a thorough-going analysis of training needs, and the difficulties involved can help the teaching process instead of holding it up.

Established departments

In an established department where job descriptions and appraisals are in existence, it would be foolish not to make use of them. The chances are, however, that there will be gaps in the existing system and that the appraisals will not be completed satisfactorily. The appropriate sections of this chapter should help to make the paperwork more purposeful.

To put new impetus into management development, self-assessment with the higher-level managers might be attempted, prefaced with the comment : 'I don't think the normal methods of assessment apply to you, would you like to take part in a special exercise?' This can be done independently of the formal system, and, in the case of very senior managers, it might be worth the expense of an outsider observing each of them for two or three days. This is the only effective way to analyse whether they are organising their own time well, taking decisions properly, being effective in committees, and so forth. The purpose of this exercise is again self-awareness, but this is harder to provoke in top managers who can say : 'We've done our duty by management development, we've set up a department.'

To make some further impact in an existing department, either the running system can be tidied up, and there is always scope for redesign and coaching, or one of the new techniques can be introduced and run in parallel.

Use of outsiders

There is much less of a tradition of using outsiders at the diagnostic stage than in the provision of training, and a new appointee might feel open to ridicule if his first action was to bring in a consultant. In many ways, however, the diagnostic stage is the most difficult and any ground lost can be irretrievable.

The catalyst needs to be a management specialist, rather than a management development specialist, to draw the most out of the interviews and to monitor any subsequent projects. Alistair Mant made the point that management teachers need consulting skills and experience rather than lecturing skills, and, although it is important that they could 'do the job themselves' if necessary, they should work mainly by catalysing—that is, by suggesting and prodding and leaving as much of the initiative as possible with the managers. This sort of ability and basic credibility are not often found internally.

Apart from his specialised expertise, an outsider is likely to get more honest answers to the questionnaire and he may be in a better position to raise questions of organisation structure. Use of a consultant might help dispel the 'disbelief in the possibility of change' and he need not step so gingerly as a new appointee in his first few months. So, for several reasons, an outsider can speed things up.

On the other hand, the management development adviser may prefer to be the catalyst himself and, if his experience and status are right, he can learn a lot about the firm and make his influence felt very quickly using these methods.

Advantages of the self-assessment approach

The advantages of the self-assessment and interview method of defining training needs are speed, impetus, unfreezing and importance.

The process is far quicker than the formal sequence and does not run into the same delays or hostility. Because managers take part in assessing the needs, and because they have a genuine interest in the resulting projects, they are more committed than if somebody else, or a process, defines their needs. If they feel benefits for themselves in the second month of operation, they will then provide the impetus themselves.

All training schemes fail, no matter how good their material and presentation, if managers do not see that the lessons apply to them. Internal activities are preferable from this point of view, as managers can experiment as ideas strike them, and this is the basis of learning. The questionnaire and the diary, of course, are unfreezing devices in themselves.

Finally, the needs diagnosed include psychological and personality factors as well as technical deficiencies, while weaknesses in the organis-ation structure or spirit are shown up. Not all such needs can be remedied, but only by this approach are they defined at all.

Status

When management development schemes fail it is usually because of the status and management ability of the people administering them. If the management development adviser takes several months or is too academic going through the formal sequences, he will lose stature long before his first plan goes into operation. As most plans involve taking somebody off his job, for some time at least, a fairly naked battle is usually fought when the times comes and the management development adviser must be strong enough not to have to yield to the short-term convenience of line managers.

Developing senior managers and their successors ought to be one of the two or three most important concerns of an organisation; I would put it second only to staying solvent. To a considerable extent, the status given to the function is the status it assumes during its early days, hence the importance of making an impact and of achieving some demonstrable successes.

The adviser must establish that he is there to develop all managers, not just those who earn less than himself, that he has the authority to pass comment on the organisation structure and spirit, and that no one and no policy is above criticism. If he sets his sights on finding suitable courses for lower levels of managers, he will quickly number among the ineffectives in management development. If he sets his sights as I have suggested, he will improve the managers and the management of his firm.

References

Drucker, P., *The Effective Executive* (New York, Harper & Row; London, Heinemann, 1967).

Jay, A., *Management and Machiavelli* (London, Hodder and Stoughton, 1967).

Mant, A., *The Experienced Manager* (London, British Institute of Management, 1969).

Parkinson, C. N., *Parkinson's Law* (London, Murray, 1958).

Peter, L. J. and Hall, Raymond, *The Peter Principle* (London, Souvenir Press, 1969).

Rowe, K. M., 'Research into Appraisals', DSIR project 1966.

Townsend, R., Address to The Industrial Society, 22 June 1971.

Stewart, R., *Managers and their Jobs* (London, Macmillan, 1967).

9

The Body of Knowledge

D. F. Sutton, Management Consultant, Action Learning Projects International

When considered as a sphere of academic learning, management suffers from there being no single formal body of knowledge which can be considered as the background to the study. The practising chemist needs a knowledge of chemistry, the engineer a knowledge of engineering, the mathematician a knowledge of mathematics: the manager must draw his knowledge from a wide range of disciplines. Moreover these disciplines, such as economics, sociology, law and mathematics, are each recognisable fields of study, capable of being pursued to considerable depth, and not obviously interrelated in the generally accepted academic sense. It is impossible for any manager to be thoroughly conversant with every aspect of all the academic disciplines with which he or she is likely to be involved and it is necessary to select as the body of knowledge relevant to a managerial education, those topics or items which are of value in studying the practice of management.

First stages

The earlier attempts to analyse the component elements in the managerial job were by such writers as F. W. Taylor[1] and Henri Fayol,[2] both of whom wrote in the earlier years of this century. They described the management activity in terms of the tasks of management and applied scientific method to an examination of these tasks. Taylor sought to produce a methodology from this analysis which would increase management efficiency. Fayol looked for a conceptual framework upon which managers could base their activities of forecasting and planning, organising, commanding, coordinating and controlling. Both saw management as a practical activity, capable of analysis in its own terms and not calling upon a body of knowledge from supporting disciplines as a prerequisite for effective managerial performance. A further step in this thinking was work such as that of J. S. Lewis[3] and E. T. Elbourne[4] in developing techniques of costing, stock control, production planning and other such administrative activities which emphasised the technical content of the management task.

As John Child points out in *British Management Thought*,[5] there is a 'three-fold distinction of management as a technical function, a social group and a system of authority'. The Cadburys, the Rowntrees and the Renolds recognised this peculiarity of management when they allied the teachings of Taylor's 'scientific management' with their own principles involving a sympathetic view of the workers.

Management had been taught as a technical subject at Wharton as early as the late nineteenth century, but the first formal training courses and conferences in the United Kingdom were held immediately after the First World War when, in 1919, the Manchester Technical College began teaching industrial administration, Seebohm Rowntree organised the first of the 'Oxford' management conferences and a school of management was run at Cambridge under C. S. Myers.

The British approach to the study of management in the 1920s is probably best described in a book by John Lee[6] where he called for 'a trained body of administrators' and said that the universities should instruct suitable recruits to the managerial ranks in a 'synthesis of sciences' that comprised management knowledge and the ethics needed to safeguard the proper use of managerial authority. He recognised the value of Taylor's scientific management but said that 'human nature is too complex for the crude scientific management'. The subjects in which he thought a manager should be trained ranged from psychology to accountancy together with the study of a model of organisation and of human relations. His book, which prefaced the work of Mary Parker Follett[7] and Elton Mayo's Hawthorne Experiments,[8] saw management as a closed system. It has been the contribution of the sociologist and the specialist in organisations and behaviour in organisations to widen the approach and orient the manager towards his whole environment. This concept has, of course, affected the entire body of knowledge, not only by including in it a study of those social sciences which have themselves examined the management activity but also by extending the general body of knowledge in the fields of economics, law, finance and human behaviour outside the confines of the manager's own factory or office.

Teaching management

The teaching arising from this general approach to the task of management was initially based upon the professional management institutions each of which represented a particular body of knowledge (Institution of Works Managers, Institute of Personnel Management, Institute of Marketing and Sales Management, and so on). These institutions saw management teaching as comprising the study of their own specialism combined with the relevant body of law, an introduction to economics, psychology, accounting and varying amounts of quantitative techniques plus the all-embracing title of 'principles and practice of management'.

In the United States and, more recently, in Great Britain management has been recognised as a field of human activity in its own right and from the rather crude beginnings which are associated with Taylor's work, an attempt has been made to formalise a curriculum suitable for teaching 'management' *per se* and not management as it relates to any particular area.

Fundamentally there have been two approaches to the problem, both of which are described in T. M. Mosson's book, *Teaching the Process of Management*,[9] in which he summarises admirably the proceedings of the IUC (Inter University Contact for Management Education) Seminar at Amersfoot in June and July 1964. The objective of the seminar was to study the management process and from this derive the requisite knowledge content. As Mosson says in his introduction, 'the decision-making approach demands a knowledge of the functional fields if it is to be anything more than an academic exercise, an elegant manipulation of symbols divorced from the confusion and the constraints of the real world'. This philosophy is examined in different ways. Professor Bela

Gold of the School of Business Administration of the University of Pittsburgh based his curriculum on two simple concepts:[10]

1 Top-management decisions centre around the internal integration of the various functional fields and also around integrating the firm with the surrounding environment.
2 Each of the functional fields encompasses an array of problems which can be dealt with most effectively by the application of the concepts, theories and tools of economics, the behavioural sciences, and a complex of mathematics, statistics and accounting.

The resultant curriculum produced a three-term programme. The first term included managerial economics, psychology and sociology in business, analytical methods (including computer programming) and accounting concepts and controls. The second term concentrated on functional fields—production, marketing, finance and the management of human resources. In the third term primary emphasis was on 'integrated decision-making' and 'business and society'. The only element of difference in student programmes being some research and advanced study in the third term.

The second approach referred to by P. L. Smith[11] is analytical, based on the four basic fields of study: systems analysis and statistics, industrial psychology and sociology, environmental studies and business policy. In this approach the firm is seen as an economic socio-technical system within which the management process operates and which exists within a wider environment. This approach depends largely upon research-based methods of analysis of the management job.

The first systematic approach to research was that undertaken in the Hawthorne Experiments[12] and, since this work in the late 1920s, a series of research programmes have been carried out in both the United States and the UK which have changed the pattern of management training. The application of rigorous research methodology to the investigations into the management process has developed a conceptual stringency in the design of education and development programmes. This strict approach has led to research-based, action-based programmes such as the joint development activities designed by Professor J. F. Morris at Manchester Business School and the action-centred training developed by Professor R. W. Revans at the Fondation Industrie-Université in Brussels, in Egypt and elsewhere.[13] Other schools have developed flexible systems using either research-based electives or a particular teaching methodology—for example, case studies at Harvard Business School—which have to some extent pre-empted the curriculum design and syllabus content.

Integration of studies

Speaking at a seminar held by the Foundation for Management Education in September 1968,[14] Professor R. J. Ball of the London Graduate School of Business Studies suggested that the business schools should teach what is best taught in a business school, be selective in their approach and not aim at a course to produce the complete manager. He saw a need to cross disciplinary boundaries and for the integration of the disciplines under the headings of resource allocation, organisational behaviour, information and control, and the environment. Service courses would produce the required level of skill in mathematics and statistics. In this approach disciplines *qua* disciplines disappear and the economist, the operational research worker and the accountant would, for example, join in developing a programme in resource allocation. Professor Ball also saw the need to study in the functional areas and for the study of at least one elective in depth and some training in research and research methods. This latter training is not intended to deepen knowledge but is of importance as a method of self-learning, a means for claiming authority in some area, and as a training in research and research methods.

In the summer of 1966 the Foundation for Management Education arranged a UK/US Management Seminar in the course of which working groups considered the problems of curriculum design for management education. The reports of these working groups[15] provide a valuable background to curriculum design but, because they see it from an academic viewpoint, do not completely cover the field as it will be seen by the management development manager. The programmes suggested are fundamentally educative in nature and are concerned with educating in management rather than with training a man to be a manager in one particular post at one particular moment in time. The management development manager is faced with the education/training dichotomy at every stage and must therefore decide not only which broad category encompasses the trainee but also the training needs of a specific individual operating in a known post.

As the working group say in their report, it is the concern of the course organiser 'to establish whether there are typical patterns of progression through a manager's career in management' and 'to discover what job problems managers have and how management training might help them to their development'. They also differentiated between the general needs of :

1 Postgraduate degree students, with highly diverse academic backgrounds
2 Junior executives already working as managers
3 Senior managers
4 Undergraduate students of management sciences or business studies.

Since 1968 a fifth category has come into prominence : the technological undergraduate (usually at a polytechnic or a technological university). The course, like those for the CNAA degrees in applied chemistry or biological sciences at Manchester Polytechnic, includes a programme of management training designed not to train the student as a manager, but to give him some understanding of the ways in which managers make their decisions. The assumption is that in the early stages of his industrial career the trainee will be mainly involved in work of a technological nature and, without introductory management training, may not fully comprehend, and may therefore resent, some of the management decisions which affect his technological work.

Curriculum content

In considering the knowledge content of the training required by a manager we must, first of all, consider the forms of input which can be envisaged and then relate these inputs to the needs of the actual situation. Inputs can come under the general headings of :

1 'Technological' knowledge—that is, knowledge of the technology which must be mastered if a manager is to have a complete grasp of his work situation and that of his immediate subordinates. This 'technology' may be engineering, banking, vehicle maintenance or

any of a host of alternatives appropriate to the manager's industrial or commercial background.
2   Background academic knowledge of a general nature of economics, the law, general social patterns, politics and ethics.
3   Academic knowledge in the field of psychology, sociology, economics, accounting and law as they relate specifically to the manager's immediate situation.

A simple example of the difference between the general and the specific academic knowledge would be in law. Any manager needs to have a working knowledge of the principles of English law and such general legislation as the main clauses of the Industrial Training Act and the Industrial Relations Act. The works manager needs a comprehensive, detailed understanding of the Factories Act and the chemical works manager has an even more specific piece of legislation in the Alkali Act with which he must be familiar.

4   Knowledge developed from research into managerial behaviour which has been formalised into certain subject areas. These subjects form the core of what is generally accepted as being the body of purely management knowledge :
(a) The theory of organisations and organisational behaviour, which should help the manager 'to determine the optimum degree of control necessary to operate efficiently'.[16]
(b) Business policy:which B. W. Denning says should develop a conceptual framework appropriate for a top manager, develop habits of systematic analysis, place other business studies in the perspective of top management and develop an entrepreneurial attitude.[17]
(c) The principles of management, which 'are concerned with the method of subdividing and allocating to individuals all the various activities, duties and responsibilities essential to the purpose contemplated, the correlation of these activities and the continuous control of the work of individuals so as to secure the most economical and the most effective realisation of the purpose'.[18]
5   The 'tool' subjects necessary if the manager is to study in a numerate manner the problems of economics, the proofs of psychological theories or the models derived from the techniques areas under the

generic title of operational research. In the training of production managers, these 'tools'—mathematics and statistics—should be supplemented by a further study, work study, which is so fundamental that, for them, it can be considered to be a tool rather than a technique because of its applicability to so many practical management problems.

6 Management techniques.
7 Management skills.

Techniques and skills require a background of knowledge but are dealt with very fully in the next chapter.

A systems approach

The manager can be considered as being in control of a system, that is, 'a set of interdependent parts which together form a unitary whole that performs some function'.[19] This system comprises the resources with which the manager is supplied or which he has the responsibility to acquire and it is this system which he must operate in order to achieve his stated objectives. This system operates, however, inside an environment and a further function of the manager is to ensure that the successful attainment of his system's objectives is accomplished in a manner compatible with the environmental demands and the smooth integration of his system with the environment to which it relates. Any system is in itself a subsystem of a larger system which will form at least part of its environment. The environment may be such that both environment and system fall within the same overall commercial or industrial organisation or there may be some aspects of their two environments which they do not share. For example, a company within a conglomerate will have as part of its environment suppliers and customers who may not be shared with any other company coming under the conglomerate umbrella. Alternatively the system which forms a machine shop within an engineering works may be completely encapsulated by its supersystem as environment.

If we accept the role of the manager as being that of operating the system and also taking responsibility for the relationship of the system to its environment, it can be seen that the knowledge he requires is that which enables him to diagnose problem areas, analyse situations, recognise opportunities and synthesise solutions in order to optimise the return, as expressed by the output/input ratio from his system or resource area, and also to control the interactions between his resource area and the environment.

Inside his resource area the manager tries to optimise the returns from his resources—fixed and variable capital, human resources and financial resources. In his contact with the environment he must appreciate the general effect of the nature of the environment, recognise opportunities, anticipate and prepare for change and understand the nature of the communication processes at the interface between system and environment.

To understand and define the precise areas of study, the manager must consider both the macro and the micro aspects of resource definition, procurement, allocation, utilisation, control and disposal and also of the interaction with the environment. In optimising his return on resources, the manager in the macro sense, forecasts requirements, coordinates activities, organises and communicates. In the micro sense, he plans, motivates and controls. In his relationship with the environment he is, in the micro sense, concerned with his day-to-day contact with legal, social, economic, political, organisational, financial and human matters and, in the macro sense, with the same matters on a longer time-scale. This longer time-scale means that they have to be anticipated and planned for rather than experienced and handled. To deal with any of these problems, internal or external, micro or macro, the manager may need to call not only upon his knowledge but also upon managerial techniques and skills—the knowledge, the techniques and the skills requiring a command of the 'tool' subjects if their validity is to be adequately used and meaningfully tested.

In order to decide upon the knowledge content of any management training and development programme, one must consider both the nature of the resource area and its attendant resources and also the nature of the environment within which the resource area operates. Normally the parameters of the system and of its environment will also determine the depth and complexity of the decisions with which the manager is faced. If we accept H. A. Simon's 'mild liberties with the English language'[20] and use 'decision-making' as though it were synonymous with 'managing' we can see the possibility of arriving at both the requisite knowledge content and its practical implications by an examination of the system and the environment in relation to which the manager operates. Simon's analysis of 'decision-making' involved what he called the whole process of decision in three principal phases: finding occasions for making a decision, finding possible courses of action and choosing among courses of action. In the context of any manager's task these steps are occasioned in general and in specific detail by the nature of his resource-area system and its environment.

The incumbents of some posts in commerce and industry can be involved in making decisions which 'manage' the activities of the entire enterprise while having little responsibility for staff, little involvement in other branches of activity and contact with only a limited environment. A life assurance actuary has little to optimise in the way of resources other than his personal skills and is involved with only a limited range of environmental factors—medical statistics, population statistics, rates of interest. A colleague seeking to calculate a premium for a 'loss of profits' policy will have many more environmental factors—social, legal, economic and political—to take into account. In further contrast, the owner/manager of a ten-man firm of sheet-metal workers may have the full range of problem possibilities both inside his resource-area system and in the contact with his work and varying environment. Nevertheless, the intellectual demands made upon him are much less extreme because he is dealing with matters of much less complexity. The above examples were all of situations in which the technological content of the manager's job was extremely high because he is 'close to the coal face, near to the actual operations which he is managing' to use Jean Lawrence's words.[21] At the other extreme, Alfred Sloan[22] speaks of the responsibility of central management at General Motors as being that of determining which decisions can be made more effectively and efficiently by the central office and which by the divisions.

Matching needs with knowledge content

In seeking to match the knowledge needs of his managers with the knowledge content of a management development programme the management development manager must, therefore, take into account not only the areas for consideration but also the depth that is required in each subject area. Any subject can be taught at the depth suitable to the job situation, although there are limitations to the value of surface appreciations of the 'tool' subjects—indeed work study is one subject where a little knowledge is a dangerous thing. Even business policy, usually considered to be the crowning subject of a course for senior management, can be taught at appreciation level in order 'to develop an understanding of business practice' as described by H. S. Corlett.[23] Corlett's article brings one to consider the third variable to be taken into consideration when essaying a match between needs and inputs— the method.

The importance of the method in a more formal type of course than the purely project-based action-centred programme is underlined by David Marples in his account of the Churchill College course.[24] He says 'the subject matter was largely determined by the experimental nature of the course, which was to explore the feasibility and value of fieldwork projects as a teaching device in management education.' Using as his model the training of engineers through laboratory and practical work, Marples and his colleagues treated the body of knowledge as arising from and being supportive of the fieldwork exercises. Much of the input was provided by the students and industrial speakers and the whole approach was oriented towards the management task as expressed in terms of the exercises undertaken and the actual management functions carried out.

The body of knowledge must therefore be categorised in three ways— subject matter, depth and teaching method and this content must be matched as accurately as possible to the needs of the student body. Needs will differ from one individual to the next in such a way as to suggest that individual tuition is essential. Economic factors expressed in terms of teachers and teaching facilities and also the educational benefits arising from a group learning experience require teaching in groups and there- fore a certain homogeneity of content and approach. This does not, of course, mean that the individual is less well treated. Indeed it is generally accepted that in any management training the learning process arising between the students is at least equal in value to that existing between teacher and student. In the extreme form of action-centred management training the learning is predominantly between the student and his peers (other students or members of the group within which he is undertaking his training) and, as Professor Revans points out,[25] the academic staff are used as an information bank upon which the students can draw and an advisory body whose services are called upon less and less as the training proceeds and the students develop a greater capacity to use the resources which are immediately available.

Assessing the need

The problem facing the management development manager is of assessing, in the face of the theories being expounded and the opportunities offered, the need inside his organisation and then matching the need by devising a company-wide management development programme. In the case of the individual this is practicable but in approaching the organisation-wide scene he must adopt a general analytical model seeing the managers as groups and using a typology of management development practices which will meet the needs of each of these groups. One such typology has been suggested by Douglas Garbutt.[26] In his article in *Management Education and Development*, Garbutt differentiates between general and specialist managers—that is, those concerned with the general direction of the work of others and people highly qualified in specialist fields and generally responsible for managing specialist groups. The typology then appears as:

General management	—	informational
General management	—	operational
Specialist management	—	developmental
Specialist management	—	supplementative
Specialist management	—	informational

Informational training for general management is a means of increasing the manager's knowledge of his own organisation. Operational training involves the manager in corporate decision-making activities. Developmental training for a specialist reflects a need for training in specific new techniques for managerial specialists in their own field. Supplementative training is designed to augment the training of the specialist and to broaden his skills into fields normally regarded as within the competence of other specialists. Informational training for specialists can be external in order to improve managers' knowledge of the customers' industry or internal in order to study the contribution of other specialist departments.

Meeting the need

On the supply side of management education many of the business schools, universities, polytechnics and colleges of technology have accepted the analysis of the system as the approach to be adopted and developed their own methods, with differing accents on the amount of action-centred analytical learning and of knowledge input. The 'weighting' of each type of learning and the sophistication of the method has depended upon the sophistication and academic capability of both staff and students.

The body of knowledge required for management education is that arising from the needs explicit in carrying out the management task. This body of knowledge can in general terms be summarised as the broad educational knowledge needed to comprehend the general environment, the 'tool' subjects needed for model-building and specific knowledge areas revealed by an analysis of the perceived management situation. Not only the academic institutions but also many in-company schemes use a broad educational base upon which they build from an analysis of the real situation to reveal the body of knowledge, the techniques and the skills that are needed. The day of the pontificating teacher is over and good teaching now rests with the teacher who is analyst, creator, interpreter and possessor of interpersonal skills—in short the teacher who possesses the abilities of the good manager which are used for the development of other managers as another man might develop a service or a product; always seeking to optimise an output/input ratio in the resource area while retaining compatibility with a changing environment.

References

1   Taylor, F. W., *Scientific Management* (Harper, 1947).
2   Fayol, H., *General and Industrial Management* (Pitman, 1949).
3   Lewis, J. S., *The Commercial Organisation of Factories* (Spon, 1896).
4   Elbourne, E. T., *Factory Administration and Accounts* (Library Press, 1914).
5   Child, John, *British Management Thought* (Allen and Unwin, 1969).
6   Lee, J., *A Study of Industrial Organisation* (Pitman, 1921).
7   Follett, M. P., in *Dynamic Administration: the collected papers of Mary Parker Follett*, ed. H. C. Metcalfe and L. Urwick (Pitman, 1941).

8 Roethlisberger, F. J., and Dickson, W. J., *Management and the Worker* (Harvard University Press, 1939).
9 Mosson, T. M. (ed.), *Teaching the Process of Management* (Harrap, 1967).
10 Mosson, *Teaching the Process of Management.*
11 Mosson, *Teaching the Process of Management.*
12 Roethlisberger and Dickson, *Management and the Worker.*
13 Revans, R. W., *Developing Effective Managers* (Longmans, 1971). Ashwamy, S., and Revans, R. W., *The Nile Project* (a monograph published for the 1972 Conference of the Association of Teachers of Management).
14 Ball, R. J., 'Some problems of curriculum design in business schools', *ATM Bulletin* Vol. 8 No. 4 (December, 1968).
15 'Working Party Reports from UK/US Management Education Seminar', *ATM Bulletin* Vol. 7 Nos. 1 and 2 (January and March 1967).
16 Pugh, D. S., introduction to *Organisation Theory*, ed. D. S. Pugh (Penguin, 1967).
17 Denning, B. W., 'Conceptual Frameworks for the Teaching of Business Policy', *ATM Bulletin* Vol. 9 No. 4 (January 1970).
18 Urwick, L., 'Organisation as a Technical Problem' reprinted in *Papers on the Science of Administration,* ed. L. Gulick and L. Urwick (Columbia University Press, 1937).
19 O'Shaughnessy, J., *Business Organisation* (Allen and Unwin, 1969).
20 Simon, H. A., *The New Science of Management Decision* (Harper and Row, 1960).
21 Lawrence, J. K., 'Project Management—a Relevant Option in Business Schools', *Management Education and Development* Vol. 3 part 1 (May 1972).
22 Sloan, A. P., Jnr, *My Years with General Motors* (Doubleday, 1964).
23 Corlett, H. S., 'Alternative Methods of Teaching Business Policy', *Management Education and Development* Vol. 2 part 2 (October 1971).
24 Marples, D., 'The Churchill College Course', *ATM Bulletin* Vol. 9 No. 2 (July 1969).
25 Revans, R. W., *Developing Effective Managers* (Longmans, 1971).
26 Garbutt, D., 'Management Training Needs—a Typology', *Management Education and Development*, Vol. 2 part 3 (January 1972).

10

Management Training: Techniques and Skills

Jean K. Lawrence, Senior Tutor, Manchester Business School

In the previous chapter, the knowledge which a manager needs and the ways in which he can acquire his knowledge have been described. The manager also needs techniques and skills. In this chapter, methods of developing a manager's effectiveness in using management techniques and ways of increasing his management skills are discussed. First, however, the techniques and skills involved in managing an enterprise must be determined. By analysing the nature of the management of a task the techniques involved in the activity can be distinguished from the skills; several research studies of the content of the manager's job are available and can be used to assess the relative importance to the manager of the various known techniques and of the groups of skills which have been identified.

Recent work in the field of management development has increased the variety of training methods available to improve managerial effectiveness in using techniques and to develop management skills. It seems likely that those responsible for facilitating the development of managers may, in future, be less involved with management courses and more concerned with management growth through management action.

Management of a task

It must be clear that the techniques and skills employed in the management of a task are distinguishable from those employed in performing the task itself. To accomplish the task, the operator requires certain techniques and skills; where the task is diverse and complex, the work of the operators must be managed, and this management activity demands its own techniques and skills. The skill of defining the task initially is a management skill. As complexity increases this whole management activity must itself be managed by more senior managers.

Many authorities have distinguished several stages in the process of management; here it is sufficient to note that the manager is involved in deciding objectives, analysing situations, planning, deciding action, organising and motivating others, evaluating performance and assessing the results of his own decisions. The task being accomplished may be in the hands of typists, computer programmers, fitters, bank clerks or shop girls; their techniques involve using keyboards, languages and programmes, spanners, tills or mechandise and their skills include working with speed and accuracy, translation, first-time balances, maintenance problem-solving or customer relations.

What is the work of the manager? Professor Revans has said that management is essentially concerned with asking the right questions, analysing situations and taking control.[1] What skills does the manager require to do his job? What techniques does he employ in his job? How can he acquire these skills and techniques and make it possible, and easy, for others to acquire them? These questions are central to this chapter.

The manager's effectiveness is based on knowledge as discussed in the previous chapter. He must know the broad objectives and policies of the organisation. He must know the environmental background within which he has to operate, the technology, the legal, economic and social framework. He must know the extent and the complexity of the system for which he is responsible. He must know what concepts have been found useful in successfully handling similar sets of activities at other times and in other environments—in other words, he must be familiar with management theory.

In a study of sixty-six middle managers carried out in 1965,[2] in which they tried to define the knowledge and skills required for effective management, Horne and Lupton used a four-part categorisation of management activity: formulating, organising, unifying and regulating. They found that a manager 'needs technical and commercial knowledge of his own firm, and an understanding of relationships there'.

Techniques and skills in the management of a task

Against this background of knowledge, the manager has to be able to understand clearly his particular situation at any one time—to identify his problems and to recognise his opportunities. He must have, at his command, a set of tools to exploit his opportunities, to analyse problems and to develop appropriate plans of action to meet or to avoid them. He must be skilled in the use of these techniques so that, like the fitter, he can not only select an appropriate tool and use it properly but can understand his entire problem so well that he can solve it as a whole, quickly and effectively. He must use tools in the right order, change tools, with economy, at the right moment, continuously re-evaluating the state of his work as he performs it, until he reaches the chosen solution and learns from this solution how better to tackle a slightly different problem in future. The more skilled the fitter the more flexible he can be in his use of all the techniques at his command. Where necessary, he can go back in the cycle and, after re-assessing his problem, change his method of approach. He is aware of many alternatives at each decision point in the cycle and uses each tool in the best possible way. One can say that he is managing his work (by using management skills) and producing a skilled performance.

In the same way, the manager needs both techniques and skills; he needs techniques which enable him to develop alternative hypotheses and strategies and he needs skills in the identification of opportunities, in choice of alternatives (judgment) and in evaluation of his decisions. These techniques and skills used together help the manager to tackle management tasks such as those of deciding objectives, analysing, model simulation, selection of hypotheses, decision-making, and evaluating results. In these activities the manager has, on the Revans model, asked the right questions and analysed the situation, and he has made a judgment. To 'take control' further skills are needed: the skill to 'get others to act', the skill to translate his decision into action—action which involves others—and the skill to devise systems which keep him informed of actions and outcomes. The successful manager will eventually manage managers. He will achieve progress towards an agreed objective through managers, supervisors, skilled craftsmen, clerks and computer operators. For this he needs skills. The identification of these skills and methods of developing them in others is one of the most difficult problems facing the management development specialist—and provides his greatest challenge. The Owen Report (1971)[3] makes it clear that some top managers do not believe that the business schools develop the skill of 'achieving results through people'. If this is the case, there is a need to explore new directions in management development.

The manager's job

So far, management of a task has been discussed in theoretical terms. The job of managing has been broken into stages of the management process. In this section the total job of the manager is considered to see what importance should be given to each part of the manager's job when considering the techniques and skills needed to carry through his job.

In the study referred to above, Horne and Lupton emphasise the need for skills in face-to-face communication—influencing, persuading and facilitating. This seems to be a generally agreed stance and is supported by later studies by Rosemary Stewart[4] and by an earlier study in the US by Hemphill.[5] Each study, however, also indicates that the *type* of job the manager has is a very important influence on the balance of his activities. Diana Pheysey, in a recent study of 96 middle managers,[6] selects what were seen in previous studies to be the important activities of managers and tests them in action. These include trouble-shooting, forward planning, briefing subordinates, conducting meetings, reviewing subordinates' progress and being interested in personal problems. She finds that the first three activities are very important to these managers and the last three less so.

Rosemary Stewart, in her extensive study of the manager's job,[4] based on diaries kept by 160 managers over four weeks, categorises the manager's main activities as discussions, committee meetings, paper work, inspection and travelling. The range of activities recorded by the managers requires the use of a range of techniques and skills. Elsewhere, Rosemary Stewart[7] has defined management as 'deciding what should be done and then getting other people to do it'. At first sight, it might seem that managers in the action situation use techniques to help them to decide and skills to get other people to do what has been decided. It is clear from these studies that a great deal of the manager's time is spent with people, getting them to do what must be done, and that some of his use of techniques and some of his analysis takes place while he is interacting with other people. Certainly managers spend relatively small amounts of time alone, thinking, analysing, planning, deciding, evaluating; these management activities often involve two or more persons. According to Rosemary Stewart, the average manager spends two-thirds of his time with others. Also, the studies show that for any one manager in any given period, the person with whom he is involved may change frequently. One must conclude from this that his thinking, analysing, planning, deciding and evaluating is often done while he is also communicating and taking action.

It may, therefore, be too simple to say that techniques are needed to help to decide what to do and skills to get other people to do what is decided. We may have to look very carefully to decide what techniques and what skills are needed in carrying through the manager's job, but it is already clear that skills in relating to people are absolutely essential to the manager.

Management techniques

Techniques are those parcels of knowledge formulated to solve specific problems sets or, according to Argenti,[8] management techniques are 'recognised methods of analysing and solving a recognised type of management problem in a detailed, systematic way'. Formulated, organised, recognised, systematic—all these words indicate a group of management problems which are well structured, clear and neat, well defined. Techniques are a necessary set of tools available to the manager to help him to clear his mental desk. Each part of a problem, each well-structured recognisable 'bit', can be analysed and exposed and, sometimes, solved— in that an answer is obtained—by the use of a technique. This kind of problem Professor Revans has called 'puzzles'; a puzzle is a problem to which there is a known answer, in which we know that by using a specified path, we shall come to a conclusion. With these 'puzzles' solved, the manager can turn his attention to the problems which lie at the limits of his understanding of the present situation. His puzzles out of the way, he can turn to what are the real problems, the undefined and disorganised, unstructured, untidy problems which seem more frequently to occupy his time and for which he needs skills as well as knowledge and techniques. Simon[9] includes in his taxonomy of management techniques 'heuristic problem-solving techniques' and Argenti talks of 'heuristic models'; both are recognising that perceived and assimilated experience can be made to pay dividends in situations where repetition is likely. Techniques can thus become of themselves learning systems and solutions to our problems can be developed by using previous experience of similar problems which have been analysed so that these particular problems can be brought nearer to becoming puzzles. Argenti lists over 100 techniques which he relates to thirty types of 'problems'.

Some of the techniques he selects and labels E for essential—essential to the management of any organisation. He postulates that not only are these techniques highly effective but that almost every organisation will meet the problems for which the technique is appropriate; these techniques include marginal costing, contribution analysis, job description, productivity bargaining, method study. All the techniques are also categorised, O, A or S—ordinary, advanced or specialist—indicating approximately the educational level required by the practitioner. Job evaluation is in the O category, network analysis in is A and queuing theory is in S.

Argenti was, in 1969, recording the techniques in existence at that time. We have to ask ourselves not only what techniques already exist but what techniques are appropriate to the manager's job under consideration. We can assume that some, at least, of the techniques listed have been found to be relevant in certain circumstances and Argenti comments on each one individually. He shows some to have been less useful than their 'inventors' hoped.

Argenti suggests that to find a way through the maze of 100 techniques, a manager should examine his own area of work and identify the two or three *types* of problems occurring in his job and then decide which of these is the most important to him and concentrate on that one. Argenti recognises that this process of identification of problems is difficult and gives some indication of how to approach it. Having analysed his own situation, the manager should scan the appropriate sections of the list of 30 problem descriptions. If he is, for instance, a sales manager he should look through a section on general problems and one on company problems and then turn to sales and marketing problems. If he decides that his most important problem is best described in terms of product design, he should select the techniques appropriate to this problem. He will find, under 'product design',

EO Value analysis
ES Market research
O   Brainstorming
A   Variety reduction
S   Technological forecasting
S   Ergonomics

Each technique is described and he will find that ergonomics is included because 'product design' can include products (such as machines) where an operator will *use* the product being designed, and man-machine coordination will be important. In this case costs are said to be high, and the comments indicate a growing conviction that the technique does have important and useful effects, though the difficulties in evaluating the technique are also mentioned.

Argenti, in this book, attempts for the first time to categorise management 'problems', and the techniques useful in their solution, and he exposes the variety of techniques available to any one functional manager.

The key question for the management development manager when considering the competence of his management in using techniques is —how much does the manager need to know about the techniques? Is it sufficient for him to know that they exist and in what general area they are useful, or does he need to know much more, perhaps to become personally competent in their use? Senior managers are concerned with problem recognition rather than with the process of working out problem solutions. Senior managers, therefore, need to understand how the technique is useful—indeed, how it has been used—and what its limitations are in terms of both the problems to which it can be usefully applied and the results which can be obtained. They must also understand and appreciate the cost of applying the technique in terms of staff and computers and possible disturbance, etc., and the associated benefits arising from the development of the individual staff and project teams involved. There may also be spin-off benefits for the general system of the firm. It is of no use for the manager to know that linear programming exists and is concerned with optimising the allocation of resources within certain constraints, unless he is also aware of the generally high order of requirements in skills and time to use the technique effectively, the limitation of its use to linear relationships and the expectation that the solution will need to be updated fairly frequently as, for example, market demands, traffic flows or distribution needs change.

The programming and manipulation of the data involved in any technique can safely be left to specialists but the senior manager must be able to discuss the principles of the application and be able to evaluate the results. There is a tendency with more advanced techniques, particularly quantitative techniques, not to be aware that the results are, in some cases, only true within certain limits. A senior manager should be able to apply his basic statistical knowledge to understanding the significance of a concept like a 95 per cent confidence limit, so that he does not expect that every piece leaving his factory will meet specification because statistical quality control has been installed; it is *his* job and *not* the specialist's to judge the appropriate level of risk to be run in accepting that some material will go out below specification.

Queuing theory can tell the cinema manager how long, on average, his patron must wait in line to buy tickets on Saturday night when a James Bond film is showing, but only the manager can decide whether this is an acceptable level of service, taking into account the changed data supplied to him were he to employ another cashier. Equally, he can be told what will then happen to the crush at the sweet kiosk, and take into account the possibility of lost sales. The difficult decision he has to make is to set the tolerable level of delay for his patrons at either point. The optimum arrangement of staff and service points can then be proposed and subsidiary questions of expense of installation, flexibility of arrangements with varying flows of patrons, etc., faced, so that a good decision can be reached. Managerial skills will be demonstrated in the ability to understand and balance the pressures of the market, the trade unions and the various abilities of staff, in coming to a decision which can be successfully implemented and which takes into account rapidly changing conditions—the James Bond film may not be showing next week!

Some managers, operating in a specialist field, who take direct responsibility for the solution of a particular group of problems, may need to master a technique completely, as an engineer needs to master his formulae. In this event, the manager must develop a high degree of competence, in operating and implementing the technique himself and may be required to train others in its use.

Management skills

It is more difficult to arrive at a useful definition of skills. Mere competence in using a technique (or a tool) does not constitute skill. A carpenter is not skilled because he uses a screwdriver competently; a driver is not skilled because he changes gear quietly and at the right rate of engine revolutions; a manager is not skilled because he can manipulate a stopwatch in producing a standard time for an operation—nor because be can carry through a pairs test in market research.

It might be said that a skilled manager is one who can use techniques well in a simple natural way. In everyday life, he can do many 'technical' things—drive his car, tie his shoe-laces, operate his intercom system, use his telephone. He is so familiar with these activities that he does not need to analyse them, and can take them into account automatically when they occur as an element in a decision—such as the need to drive his car from A to B in a given time to order to keep an appointment upon which he has decided.

'Skills' and 'techniques' can be clearly distinguished when we consider the skilled craftsman. The teapot caster in a pottery is highly skilled—he understands that the way in which he attaches a particular spout to a particular teapot body will be affected by the entire shape of the body. His techniques—of 'sticking together with slip', of 'pouring slip into a mould' or 'taking out' (gently taking the soft spout from the still damp mould)—are second nature to him. He decides just how long to let that piece dry before he attaches it—too long a time and it will crack away, too short a time and it may be mis-shapen. His skill is in putting together into a series of interrelated decisions all the technical elements in his job to produce a unified whole directed towards his original objective—a complete teapot ready for firing. In his daily activities, he knows that he must face some balancing losses as he makes his decisions—should he take a little longer trimming these pots or take that extra time to put into use the new set of moulds which is perhaps not quite dry? Or can he do something else altogether thus giving the moulds time to dry? And what effect will bringing forward the work on the 'something else' have upon the total pattern of his work? It is easily seen that, in these circumstances, the skilled man, like the fitter, is managing his own work. The concept of the skilled worker thus includes the ability to exercise, in an unsophisticated way, management skills in planning, choosing, evaluating and getting things done. The worker, however, is managing only his own activities and possibly the work of a mate, such as a girl fettler of teapots. Essentially his 'work'—his primary task—is his activity in making the pots. The manager's 'work' is organising the whole activity and managing the work of others.

Management skills involve the use of techniques in a natural simple way. An early stage in the process of management is deciding what is to be done—using the relevant techniques in coming to a decision which allows the manager to take a further step towards his desired final objective. At this stage the manager is working towards a very distant objective which can only be achieved if he can determine at each decision point the most advantageous approach and thus the pattern of his subsequently decision-making. Only when the manager is skilled enough to interpret the information resulting from the use of various carefully selected techniques, and to build on these interpretations using all his knowledge of the situation, can he achieve success in selecting the right path to follow.

Skills of analysis and judgment

Skills of analysis and judgment are involved in decision-making. An examination of these skills necessitates a breakdown of the stages of the decision-making process.

Initially, a situation is analysed. Many techniques are to hand—those under the general headings of operations research, management accounting, economics, are obvious choices. A *skilled* process of analysis is one where the problem situation is broken down (and later restructured) and the elements are analysed and regrouped—synthesised—in a more positive and fruitful way. When analysing a productivity problem it will be helpful and constructive to examine in turn the methods, rates of pay, incentive schemes, labour turnover, layout, industrial relations, cost breakdowns and inventory system, using the many techniques available. The skilled manager will, however, make a preliminary analysis designed to expose the relationships between these elements and then structure his investigations to show quickly the main problem areas, so that the time and money spent on the investigation can be budgeted more expertly. He will use the techniques skilfully, directing his effort towards his objective from the outset; as Revans said : asking the right questions.

Thus, even in the technique-dominated area of analysis, the manager can be seen to be exercising skills.

At the further stages in the decision-making process—producing hypotheses, and selecting solutions or making judgments—skills are even more apparent. Techniques of brainstorming, sensitivity analysis, cost-benefit analysis, have their place but the skill of the manager is shown in the way in which these techniques are applied and in the approach used to assess the information they generate, and its validity in the particular situation.

The decision-making process described above began with analysis of a given situation in terms of a desired objective, and has proceeded to reaching a decision, showing how the information resulting from the use of techniques can improve our judgment. The skill in handling this process is exercised in the progressive balancing of conflicting information and the validation of results, until, at that moment of decision, a single course is seen to be optimal.

Skill is even more important in the initial stage of problem recognition (or the more positive approach of opportunity recognition) and in the final vital stage which determines management effectiveness—implementation.

Very little is known about the skills involved in problem recognition. Livingston, in the 'Myth of the well-educated manager',[10] points out that formal education programmes emphasise problem-solving and give little attention to the 'development of skills required to find the problems that need to be solved'. He points out that the skills required for these two activities are quite different and suggests that the 'problem-finding' skills can only be developed by doing. He points out that Mackworth[11] showed a lack of correlation between scholastic achievement and proven problem-finding ability. Opportunity-finding skills have similar characteristics and are not adequately taught. Though help towards useful techniques can be given in the classroom, these skills can only be developed on the job, by practice, in the business situation. What must be developed is a 'nose' for a problem or an opportunity, so that, for example, a manager picks up early cues from the environment when changes are on the way—and this requires something more than analytical skills. It is likely that those managers who undertake 'real-life' project work gain some practice in opportunity- and problem-finding and may develop some skills.

It is a great deal easier, so far, to say how these skills might be developed, than to say what they are. Our inability to identify them may have increased the speed of adoption of the case study method in management development. Analytical skills are applied to a whole situation (the case) in the belief that the basic problem in the situation will be diagnosed, exposed and treated. The student is encouraged to examine the presenting symptoms in the situation but also to explore fully the total case before proposing any treatment. This 'problem-recognition' learning may be transferable; certainly, skills of analysis seem to be developed by this method. It is, nevertheless, questionable whether, in studying the 'whole' case problem, students have tasted more than a suspicion of the flavour of the complex dynamic environment of a real-life situation, where analysis can hardly keep pace with changing parameters, and problem recognition seems to be much more intuitive than many management teachers care to admit.

In the area of implementation, a little more is known. Programmes such as management by objectives are designed to free managers to 'do their own thing', but at the same time to recognise the 'things' the organisation is doing, and to relate their efforts to organisational objectives in an effective way. Job analysis, job description, job specification and so on, are a range of associated techniques which help managers to help others to perform well. They are a means by which the real-life uncertainty about exactly where one job ends and another begins, can be reduced. Having defined the task as exactly as possible, the qualifications, training and abilities which are most suitable for the task can be assessed, to give a useful formula, resulting from the application of 'a recognised method of analysing and solving a recognised type of management problem in a detailed systematic way'. If a manager knows and agrees exactly what is required of him, and his performance is evaluated, he has the opportunity and the understanding to work towards the agreed objectives. Organisationally, it is assumed that there exist structured relations within which it is possible for each manager to do his own useful piece of work, and that his work will be successfully coordinated with the work of his colleagues.

It may still be found that the manager is working ineffectively and, though motivated, he has not the necessary skills to perform his task. The difficulty may be that in his part of the organisation managers are not working well together—they do not 'get on well'. Difficulties frequently occur, managers stand on protocol, new ideas are squashed and their inventors 'put down'. Coordination, though it is achieved, occurs through hard and painful work. These managers may need to develop improved social skills—interactive skills—so that relationships within the group may be permanently improved.

Interactive skills

Every manager needs interactive skills—skills in relating to others—and the extent to which he masters these skills is often a measure of his success as a manager. He works with others as he discusses and decides, 'trouble-shoots', formulates plans, gives instructions, interviews new staff. Remembering that Rosemary Stewart showed that little of his time is spent alone, his performance as a manager must depend to a large extent on the level of skill he has been able to develop in this area. No manager will 'implement', 'perform', 'act well' in a managerial capacity unless he has found an effective way of relating to others—superordinates, subordinates, peers, specialists and generalists—in the organisation and outside. Rackham, Henry and Colbert[12] call these skills 'interactive skills' —but one may also use the terms 'social skills' or 'interpersonal skills'.

Any definition of skills must include the concept of a pattern of behaviour appropriate to a specific situation. An improvement in the interactive skills of managers would mean that when they relate to others their behaviour will be more appropriate to the situation and will lead to purposive activity in the situation—resulting in the achievement of agreed objectives. The manager's personal make-up (his personality) and his understanding of the situation (knowledge) have an effect upon his behaviour, but there is another alterable factor in this complex situation : the manager's skill in dealing with other people. Since a manager spends two-thirds of his time with other people, those responsible for his development should be particularly concerned with developing 'interactive skills'.

As in other skill areas, techniques underlie the skilled performance. In this case they are social techniques, like asking questions, shaking hands, developing conversation, cracking jokes. Skill here is shown in the ability to put all these simple known behaviours, and others of a more complex nature, into a pattern, to produce appropriate behaviour in *this* situation directed towards *this* objective.

Even at the techniques level of interpersonal relationships, talking about the behaviour is not sufficient for the achievement of improvement. Talking about how to shake hands, how to kiss, how to smile, is an ineffective way of learning. 'Knowing' how to do it is not enough, though knowledge also underlies skill. Changing behaviour is difficult and complex and the methods used to achieve the change will also be complex. At this simple level, if we know how to shake hands and practise the technique we become competent. Interactive skills develop when the techniques are practised *and* when the situation in which the skills are exercised is as near to reality as possible—or, though artificial (say a 'laboratory'), allows maximum flexibility of experience. Behaviour change —undertaken here by adding a new social technique to the repertoire— is based on knowledge of the technique and practice in its performance. Research findings support this direct approach showing that behaviour can be changed by directly practising changed behaviour. Changing behaviour in a training situation *can* produce lasting results, because attitudes can be affected by the observation of the successful results of the new behaviour, and familiarity (practice) may bring acceptance of the changed behaviour as natural and comfortable. The steps in the learning process are to examine present behaviour, to experiment with new behaviours, to observe the results and to practise changed behaviours shown to be successful. It is not so certain that the other approach— changing attitudes in order that behaviour change will follow—is also effective. When attitudes are changed by training (for example, when the trainee is convinced that a more democratic or participative management style is more effective), it has not been shown that consistent behaviour change in the desired direction necessarily follows.

In his decision-making activities the manager exercises his analytical skills, but he is also building on and developing hypotheses using his own and others' abilities to use management techniques. His skill is seen in making a good decision—one that moves his part of the organisation towards agreed goals. He uses his skills to draw from the group a solution which rises above his or their own thinking, as a conductor draws a performance from an orchestra which transcends the level of performance of himself or any one of his players.

A good decision, however, is not enough. The manager also needs skills of interaction if he is to implement the decision. Interactive skills have played a part in analysis, judgment and synthesis but, in implementation, in working towards a changed situation, there is a paramount need for skills of interaction. Many management tasks which occur in implementation, such as interviewing, persuading, counselling, appraising, instructing, communicating, listening and understanding, encouraging and approving, require interactive skills and, without effective action in these areas, no process of management will have identifiable results.

How can all these skills and techniques be learned?

Methods of teaching

Management techniques and skills can be learned in many ways. The training methods described here are accepted as validated and are in general use or, if they are new, are soundly based in theory. Methods appropriate to the particular purpose which the trainer has in mind must be selected. The skilled craftsman/manager selects the appropriate technique and uses it, often in relation to another, to help him solve a particular problem. This approach applies as surely to the management trainer. With skill the trainer becomes flexible in his approach and adapts to the demands of each particular situation.

If techniques have to be learned, it is possible in the early stages to use highly structured methods. Short formal courses arranged for *specific* levels or areas of management where a particular level of understanding and expertise in certain techniques is needed can result in the managers acquiring a useful cluster of techniques ready for use—'recognised methods of analysing and solving a recognised type of management problem in a detailed systematic way'.

A combination of information-giving, by lectures and the written word, and practice on simulated problems gives a basic understanding and allows the learner to recognise the value of the techniques in similar highly-structured situations. Further development of the understanding of the appropriateness of the technique to business situations can be achieved through involvement in more complex simulations such as business games—where the selection of the technique appropriate to a particular problem may also be practised. Competence can be much increased by the use of the project method in which students solve 'real' problems in the real world using these techniques. The learners can move to less structured, less recognisable problems in this way, becoming aware of some of the subtleties and some of the limitations of the techniques, and thus move further into the area of 'skilled' performance.

In teaching techniques, case-study teaching can play a large part. Cases can sometimes be used at an early stage to demonstrate to the student—through his own discovery process—that a problem exists to which he does not yet have a simple structured approach, and that there is a known approach to the solution of this problem : a technique. The technique can then be taught while it is seen to be relevant to a problem already appreciated by the student. Cases are also often used to provide a situational framework for a particular technique which has already been taught. For example, the student has learned by lecturing and practice about discounted cash flow; now a company is to decide in which of several projects it will choose to invest. At a more advanced stage, cases can also be used to give practice in recognising the appropriate situation in which to apply the technique and to afford opportunities for practice in using the technique in different circumstances, on each occasion comparing its use with other possible methods of solution and selecting and using the most appropriate method.

The teacher can also use a case study, late in a course, to raise the 'technique understanding' level to the 'skill' level. The technique then becomes just one of several known ways of approaching a particular problem and the manager can use it and build upon it in relation to all the others in his repertoire when dealing with a messy unstructured real situation. Work on real-life projects will include this experience and the greater the complexity of the choices to be made in the cases and projects the more useful the experience of the selection and the use of appropriate techniques and the more skilled the manager may be said to have become if he successfully meets his objectives in the case or the project. He will then be skilled in using those techniques to 'solve' cases or projects.

'Action' learning—on the job, with responsibility—will be required to ensure that the transfer of learning has been accomplished. Here the learner can prove to himself that he has grasped the techniques, has made appropriate use of his understanding of them (has become skilled in their use), and that his results have improved. His learning has been 'transferred' from the case or project to the action-centred, job-oriented, normal situation. He has learned; he is skilled as a manager.

In the traditional approach to management development—sending people on courses—this 'transfer of learning' from course to job situation is an essential late stage in the learning process. It is often, however, only sketchily carried out, through haphazard job experience, on the manager's return to his organisation. The manager is experiencing the re-entry problem at this time—the difficulty of adjusting to the unchanged perceptions of his colleagues, though *he* knows that he has changed while he has been away. The temptation to revert to his previous self—which fitted so well into the organisation—is strong. Much course learning concerned with attitude and behaviour change is negated in this way, and even development, through practice and application, of his understanding of techniques to the level of skill may not take place. In more recent developments, the 'action' learning *is* the course—the learning takes place *in* the job situation and the transfer problem is eliminated.

Consideration of the effectiveness of methods of teaching management techniques and of raising the level of competence in the technical activity to a level of skill in their use involves examination of the way in which the manager's performance *on the job*, rather than in the training situation, is improved. This is the world of 'skills'. Neither knowledge, in terms of the previous chapter, nor knowledge of techniques, nor even competence in performance in case studies will produce results in the balance sheet— or in the service offered by the organisation.

As soon at the discussion moves to skills rather than techniques, real-life projects and action-centred learning feature prominently in the mix of training methods. In one sense, the book of the case, like the book of techniques, has been written. The book of the project, the learning through action, the experiential learning situation, like the book of management skills, has still to go to press. The outcomes and progress of the experiential learning cannot be predicted—even the 'lessons' to be learned are, in a very real sense, unknown at the beginning.

More traditional teaching methods can be used to convey to the learner an understanding of the process of management. The management task can be broken down, analysed, taught and integrated so that a deep understanding of interrelated functions and disciplines can be acquired. Something, however, is lacking in this approach and every experienced manager on a traditional course recognises it. There is an air of unreality—a load of commitment and responsibility is lifted from his shoulders. Though he can participate enthusiastically in an analysis of the management task, his job is not involved. His brain may be exercised, perhaps overexercised, but the manager, even at the height of excitement in decision-making in a business game when a mythical £50 000 is at stake, is somehow outside the action.

It is possible that institutions of management education should return to one of the old saws about management—that the exercise of authority and the acceptance of responsibility are cardinal features of a manager's activities and in them lies the heart of the manager's job.

One of the strengths of the various forms of experiential learning is that the learner is put in a position where his authority is visible to others (and often explicit in its smallness but also in its reality) and that he has to accept responsibility for his own actions, and often for the actions of others. Because, in a well-designed activity, the learner has moments to withdraw from the situation and to examine the process as its develops, he also has the opportunity to examine his own and others' authority—how it is exercised, legitimised, defined—and how he and others take, accept and share responsibility for the action. The Tavistock model for the conferences on authority and organisation,[13] in particular, makes these tasks explicit within the experiential learning activity.

There are strong arguments for adopting this experiential approach to management learning if the learning objective goes beyond the accumulation of knowledge and the development of competence in a full repertoire of techniques. Where management skills are to be developed, the learner must *feel* the reality of the situation. This direct approach to changing managers' behaviour, described earlier in discussing interactive skills, can, perhaps be readily accepted in considering skills in this area. But, as will be seen later, involvement in real and compelling management situations gives opportunities for the development of other management skills— analytical skills, decision-making skills, problem recognition and definition, opportunity exploitation, planning and evaluation—in addition to personal and social skills. The ability to examine and to learn from one's own experience in action may be an essential management skill which can be developed—though it could be said that this skill is essential in all of life and not only in management.

There are various established methods of experiential learning designed to develop interactive skills. They are based on small-group methods of training and are often referred to generally as sensitivity training. There are now many variants, but one, the T-group, emerging from the National Training Laboratories (NTL) at Bethel, began to be known in the early 1950s in the USA and is now the best-known form of small-group training. The objectives of T-groups, as stated by P. B. Smith, are 'to achieve increases in trainees' sensitivity, diagnostic ability and action skill'.[14] There are informative papers on the methods and uses of T-groups and criticism of their use in management training and of their results in an ATM publication,[15] edited by Galvin Whitaker. Here, it is only possible to mention sources of further study and to comment that, after more than twenty years, controversy still surrounds the use of these methods for managers and it is difficult to find agreement about learning objectives, structure or lack of it, use of stranger, peer or 'diagonal slice' groups, what has been learned or how much has been learned. The weight of evidence, however, is that these forms of learning do produce results and sometimes the effects are lasting. Well-known variants of the pure T-group—activities which can be included in 'sensitivity training'—are Coverdale, Managerial Grid, team training and 'instrumented' or 'measured' groups ('organic skill training'[16]) like the programme put forward by Rackham *et al.*, whose recent book[12] begins with Terry Morgan's discussion of these methods. Richard Hacon[16] has gathered together many fine contributions on these development methods and emphasises their connection with organisation development. In his introduction, he quotes the recent North American survey[17] of 302 companies which showed that 35 per cent of these companies actually use experiential learning activities conducted by the NTL and many more are interested in these methods.

In all of these programmes the theoretical essentials of learning through behaviour change exist—the opportunity to observe one's own and others' behaviour, the development of the ability to give and to receive feedback on the behaviours observed, and the opportunity to modify those behaviours and to test again.

Real-life project-based activities are undertaken in many learning institutions (technical colleges, staff colleges, consultancy organisations, etc.) in which managers are placed in roles where they need the skills and abilities listed in Smith's objectives of T-groups. Managers in these roles affect the implementation—the final results—of their projects immediately they arrive in the 'real-life' situation in the firm. They affect the relationships within the organisation and begin to build new relationships themselves. They behave in ways appropriate to or inimical to the success of their project and/or their learning immediately they, as strangers (or, at the least, in a strange role), make the first tentative contacts with the people in the organisation. It is, therefore, important that they should focus upon the effect of their behaviour. If they are aware of their impact on others, sensitive to others' reactions, able to pick up quickly the ways in which the organisations' staffs relate to one another, and able to choose to behave in a manner which is likely to affect the host organisation in ways selected by the managers themselves, then the project is more likely to succeed.

Recently, the Revans programme in Brussels, Cairo[18] and other places, and the joint development activities at Manchester Business School[19] have attracted a great deal of interest. In both these programmes major long-term action-learning activities are being undertaken and senior managers are required to maintain this intervention role for nine months to a year. Senior managers tackle problems in their own or in other companies, individually or with colleagues. In each programme the manager lives with the task from the beginning to the end, drawing upon the skills of his mentors in learning institutions as he needs their help. Tutors are continuously concerned with the projects and act as brokers when necessary, organising resources to meet the various demands for references, seminars, tuition or consultation as the managers make them. Projects take place in organisations, not in business schools. They produce changed activity, changed attitudes, changed perceptions and changed behaviour in both the recipient organisation and in the learner but the precise degree and direction of these changes cannot be predicted at the start. Some attempt is being made to find means of assessing these changes after the event but much work remains to be done in this thorny area of evaluation. At present, we must rely mainly on the opinions of nominators to the programmes, learners and host organisations, and many of these show great enthusiasm for what has been achieved.

In both programmes, before the work on the project in the organisation begins, there is a preliminary stage particularly concerned with the development of interactive skills. Much of the activity in this first period is directed towards personal and organisational commitment to the projects, personal awareness and team building.

Often in the more established project programmes the element of 'practice' in techniques is important, the approach being to some extent 'bottom up'. The student is taught techniques, practises them, then faces real-life experience (the project) in which to gain further practice and to learn to select and to apply techniques appropriately—thus developing, to the level of skill, his use of the new techniques. In some of these programmes, in contrast to those above, too little attention is paid to the role of the manager in the activity and he is not adequately helped to analyse what is happening to him and to the organisation while the project is being carried through. A rather rare learning opportunity may be wasted if there is no opportunity for him to develop his interactive skills in a 'training' situation before or during the project.

This discussion of the methods employed in developing managers in appropriate techniques and skills shows that there is a close relationship between what is to be learned and the preferred method of teaching.

As we move from the more defined area of techniques, through the selection of appropriate techniques and familiarisation with their results and limitations, towards skilled performance, we can see a progression in training methods from exposition, exercises and evaluation, to case studies, and business games. When we reach the messy, difficult, but essential area of interactive skills, we have moved to experiential learning and we can employ one of the small-group methods of development. Or we can carefully design 'project' training to reinforce technique training, to develop skills of analysis and judgment and to enhance interactive skills; or we can combine these two approaches in relation to the same work situation.

The two major programmes mentioned perhaps stand alone at present because in these long-term projects there are opportunities to learn all that has been discussed in this chapter. The manager demands the resources he needs as he perceives the need. He meets a problem which is, in fact, a 'puzzle', and he is introduced to a new technique. He has to take decisions and make judgments about the development of the project and its content, and he has to build fruitful relationships with members of the organisation, with academics, and with other managers concerned in the programme. He can discuss his ideas and difficulties at all times, drawing upon the expertise of the staff of the institutions—and also the knowledge and experience of his colleagues.

This kind of programme is likely to change the demands on teaching staff and a new kind of management teacher/trainer is beginning to appear. In this change of role, teachers in institutions will need active and sensitive help from practising management development managers—and, frequently, from their chief executives. If suitable incumbents of these roles can be found or developed, and their role is fully understood, accepted and exploited, the benefits for organisations, chief executives, individual managers *and* management development managers could be enormous.

References

1   Revans, R. W., 'The Manager's Job' in *The Theory and Practice of Management* (London : Macdonald & Co., 1966).

2 Horne, J. H. and Lupton, Tom, 'The Work Activities of Middle Managers—an Exploratory Study', *Journal of Management Studies* (February 1965), pp. 14–33.

3 'The Owen Report' Business School Programmes—the Requirements of British Manufacturing Industry, CBI/BIM, 1971.

4 Stewart, Rosemary, *Managers and their Jobs* (London: Macmillan, 1967).

5 Hemphill, J. K., *Dimensions of Executive Positions* (Columbus: Ohio State University College of Administrative Science, 1960).

6 Pheysey, D. C., 'Activities of Middle Managers—A Training Guide', *Journal of Management Studies* (May 1972).

7 Stewart, Rosemary, *Reality of Management* (London: Pan Piper, 1969).

8 Argenti, John, *Management Techniques: A Practical Guide* (London: George Allen & Unwin, 1969).

9 Simon, Herbert A., *The New Science of Management Decision* (New York: Harper & Row, 1960), p. 8.

10 Livingston, Sterling, 'Myth of the Well Educated Manager', *Harvard Business Review* (January/February 1971).

11 Mackworth, Norman H., *Originality in the Discovery of Talent* (Harvard University Press, 1969), p. 242.

12 Rackham, Honey and Colbert, *Developing Interactive Skills* (Wellens Publishing, 1971).

13 Rice, A. K., *Learning for Leadership: Interpersonal and Intergroup Relations* (London: Tavistock Publications, 1965).

14 Smith, P. B., *Improving Skills in Working with People: The T-Group* (DEP Training Information Paper 4) (London: HMSO, 1969), p. 3.

15 Whitaker, Galvin (Ed.), *T-Group Training: Group dynamics in Management Education* (ATM Occasional Paper 2) (Oxford: Blackwell, 1965).

16 Honey, Peter and Hacon, Richard, 'Organic Skill Training'— chapter 9 in *Personal and Organizational Effectiveness* (London: McGraw-Hill, 1972).

17 'National Industries Conference Board'. Behavioural Science Concepts and Management Application Studies in Personal Policy. No. 216, 1969.

18 Ashmawy, Saad and Revans, R. W., 'The Nile Project', Paper for the Association of Teachers of Management Conference, 1972.

19 Morris, J. F., 'Note on Joint Development Activities', Paper presented to the Association of Teachers of Management Conference, 1972.

11

The Individual Development Programme Plan

G. B. Ticehurst, Adviser to Ford Motor Company on Organisation Development and Management Education

The emphasis in this chapter will be on the development of the performance and potential of in-post managers: those members of management staff at all levels and in all functions who have managerial aspects to their jobs but who may or may not have managerial accountability. The chapter will, therefore, discuss the situation of the very large majority of people whose daily round and common task is in the management firing line, helping to earn today's bread and butter, but whose response to today's challenges will, to no small extent, determine how tomorrow's bread and butter is to be earned.

Whatever pipe dreams we may have of managers of the future, and of managements and organisations of the future, today's mass of bread-and-butter earners in management are also tomorrow's, and it is to their needs that we need to address much more of our effort and to which this contribution is directed. The reader should not expect, therefore, to be enlightened on development programmes for identified young high fliers, nor for those whose careers envisage elements of business school or other advanced education. Nor will there be more than reference to the role of the set-piece programmes like MBO, Grid, teamwork or leadership.

The manager's job situation

The situation of many of today's managers in the firing line is almost as circumscribed in terms of time as Wilfred Brown's description of the foreman—an off-the-machine direct producer of the product.[1] His job exists in its own right, whether he is there or not; but if he is not there the chances are that problems won't get attended to, decisions will be made without his influence, events will have developed and changed without his participation in them. Whatever time he finds available to him after dealing with immediate crises, he must use in preventive planning and improvement planning, and, of course, in trying to fit in his increasing holiday allowance.

The manager himself

He is a man of very varied education, less rather than more likely to have a degree; more rather than less likely to have some technical or commercial qualification. He is highly knowledgeable about his job and has learnt how to handle it. He will live, along with his colleagues, without much certainty of promotion, although promotable, and with career prospects foreshortened in time and narrowed by specialisation. He identifies himself closely with his company and, to some discerning eyes outside, betrays characteristics that identify him, if not with his company, quite clearly with his industry. He is Mant's 'experienced manager';[2] he is Owen's 'post-experienced manager';[3] at 40 he is every insurance company's security risk, both in terms of life span and of income growth.

Programme characteristics

What, therefore, are the constraints that affect the objective of a development programme for such a man? His needs are as unique as his job or possible future jobs, and his ability to do his job or possible future jobs; so that his programme must be unique, albeit containing common modules.

The time he can devote to his programme off the job is minimal, so it must not only be confined to essentials but must be of very high quality in terms of relevance to needs.

The end result must be his own responsibility, so that he will be motivated to achieving the result. This means that he is closely concerned with the objectives, design and process of the programme. The content must relate closely to the job, either for improvement in his own, or in preparation for a possible future one. But in the latter case, such are the facts of management life, there is no guarantee that it will be he who is selected.

He will need counselling assistance from a person or persons of credibility in his eyes, and he will require that the programme be supervised so that he can experience the pressure of being kept up to the mark, as well as the incentive of working for someone's approval other than his own.

Programme development: job analysis*

Whether or not there exists a job specification for the job he is in, in which he is required to improve, or for the job for which his programme is a means of developing him, the manager will need to determine just what that job, in its own right, exists to do.

What results are expected of this management job, today and every day, regardless of the current job holder and his ability? There will probably be up to eight or nine such main or key results that constitute the total job. When these results have been determined, and some standards of performance for each result have been established, the job needs looking at in relation to other management jobs which serve it or which it serves. The manager will then need to determine the sorts of decision authority and influence levels that are required to enable each result to be achieved to the standard established; and to determine the sorts of communicating links required for each result to be achieved, described by their direction, extent and nature.

As a result of carrying out this sort of analysis, the manager already knows a great deal more about the job, whether his own or another, than he did before, and he knows the job from a more objective organisational

* I am indebted to J. Bernard Windle of J. Bernard Windle and Associates Limited for the concepts described in this section and the next.

standpoint than the subjective personal view he may have previously held. Then, and only then, should it be logical for him to determine what knowledge, information, skills, experience and even attitude or style are required, or are appropriate, in the job holder to achieve each result.

Programme development: job-holder analysis

The manager can now look at the job holder or job holder to be, that is himself, and compare his abilities, experience, skills and attitudes with those that have been objectively determined, drawing up an inventory of pluses and minuses. The minuses will indicate need for the appropriate form of experience development, counsel or education and training action; the pluses will indicate areas where he can help others with corresponding minuses.

The manager himself will know his strengths and weaknesses. What remains is to negotiate any further needs the organisation may have and may require him to meet, so that personal and organisational needs can be reconciled.[4]

Whether any further action is taken or not, he will already have added two dimensions to the potential of the organisation—an improved job analysis and an improved job-holder analysis. Action, by means of a formal programme to fill his minus gaps and use his plus resources, that is coordinated with other managers' programmes, represents the gear-changing mechanism by means of which today's level of performance is lifted to tomorrow's, a process that is continuous, satisfying and profitable.

Experience development, education and training action

The data which have been analysed about the job and its job holder, together with the personal needs of the current or prospective job holder that have been deduced, form the basis on which the manager can, with specialist help, draw up a programme to suit his circumstances. An example of such a programme, with guide notes, evolved as a result of analysis, is shown in the appendix. The manager, the head of a large technical department concerned with manufacture, equipment and processes, had been identified to become manager of a plant of around 5000 employees. He himself was totally responsible for the conduct of the programme, assisted by tutorial counselling and advice from his manager, his colleagues, his consultant and the training specialist. The programme was developed some four years ago, thus dating some of the specifications, particularly those concerned with seminars and with prescribed reading. Nevertheless, the flexibility of the programme and its relevance and attention to other criteria mentioned earlier is evident.

Given a population of managers carrying out at different times individual improvement projects to achieve selected development objectives, based on this sort of analysis and description, it is not difficult to ensure a measurable improvement in the level of performance of both management jobs and of job holders which, when related in the organisation structure, amounts to continuous improvement in the level of results achieved, and in development of the organisation from today's situation into tomorrow's.[5]

References

1   Brown, Wilfred, *Exploration in Management* (Heinemann, 1960), p. 191.
2   Mant, Alistair, 'The Experienced Manager—a major resource', British Institute of Management Publication (1969), Section 2, p. 7.
3   CIME report on the requirements of British manufacturing industry, British Institute of Management Publication (1971), Section 3.
4   'The Need and Demand for Management Education in the UK', Institute of Manpower Studies (1972), Chapter VIII.
5   Second NEDO Management Education, Training and Development Committee report (1971), Section 3, paragraphs 19, 20, 23.

Appendix: Example of a Management Development Plan

1. *Objective* By the end of the training period (15 months) the trainee will be able respect of both labour and management.

	Forward Plans	*Plant Operations*
2. *Purpose*	To inform himself on forward plans so that he can contribute to decisions affecting the manufacturing plans and operations of the Plant	To examine the objectives, procedures and problems of manufacturing staff and services in order to form balanced judgment and reach correct decisions affecting Plant objectives.
3. *Assignments*	Car marketing plans Car product engineering Process and equipment engineering plans Labour Relations plans P. & O. plans Finance Project Control	Supply—Purchase, Parts Control Quality Control Production Services Labour Programming and Scheduling Operator Training Maintenance Operational Research Financial Control
4. *Visits*	Related industries' plants including those of selected suppliers	Company and competitor assembly plants
5. *Senior Management Conferences*	As required by Group, Operations and Plant Managers	As required by Operations and Plant Managers, and as needed by trainees
6. *Projects*	The improvement of labour effectiveness	The formulation of specific objectives for achievement by Plant Staffs and Services that will help to achieve Plant objectives more effectively
7. *Courses*	Donovan Report seminar Entrepreneur in Business	Company 'P' Course—Finance Company 'O' Course—OR Network Analysis seminar Linear Programming seminar Management by Objectives seminar
8. *Reading*	*Handbook of Management Technology*—Wills and Yearsley	*Improving Business Results*—Humble
9. *External Consultant*	As required by trainee to help him achieve the purpose of the training	As required by trainee to help him achieve the purpose of the training

to manage the plant when called upon to do so with no loss of its efficiency and with the

Control	Leadership	Education	Remarks
To determine what control information he needs for command and control of current and forward operations	To determine the most appropriate and effective method, or styles, of leadership for the Plant and its management team and to learn how to adapt to it personally	To update and broaden knowledge and concepts and to sharpen personal skills, so that he can fill the role of Plant Manager	
As required to plant staffs, and also to Sales Service and Warranty	—	Included under columns 1, 2 and 3	
As required internally	—	Written reports on visits indicated under columns 1, 2 and 3	
Functional conferences as needed by trainee	Included under columns 1, 2 and 3	Included under columns 1, 2 and 3	
The organisation of control information on current and forward operations to meet his personal needs for command and control	—	Appraisal of written reports as indicated under columns 1, 2 and 3c	
Interfirm comparison and management ratio seminar	Louis B Allen seminar Attendance and participation at supervisor and shop steward conferences	Senior Management Course, Problem Solving and Decision Making Course, Effective Speaking Course, Chairmanship Course	
Business Charts— Rose	*Exploration in Management—* W. Brown *The Professional Manager—*McGregor *The Social Psychology of Industry—* J C Brown	*Introduction to Capital Expense—*Garbutt *Business Budgets and Accounts—*Edey *The Effective Executive—*Drucker	
As required by trainee to help him achieve the purpose of the training	As required by trainee to help him achieve the purpose of the training	As required by trainee to help him achieve the purpose of the training	

THE INDIVIDUAL DEVELOPMENT PROGRAMME PLAN

Guide notes for trainee

1 *Objective.* This states the situation which should obtain at the end of the training period. It represents what the trainee should have achieved, and forms the standard against which the effectiveness of the programme can be measured once the trainee is acting in the job.

2 *Planned Purposes.* These, in each of the five identified areas of training need, form a guide to the knowledge and information for which the trainee should be searching. They should inform his thinking in each area so that his concentration is channelled and his learning time spent economically.

3 *Assignments.* Prior to visiting any staffs, the trainee should think out his needs, draw up a list of information requirements, problems, etc., and communicate these to the staff member concerned so that minimum time is wasted on tuition. He should maintain a diary or log of his assignments and their results.

The trainee should make his own arrangements to meet staff members, and it is not envisaged that such meetings, if properly prepared, should take up more than two hours each.

4 *Visits.* The trainee should seek a clear brief from his line supervisors on the purpose and scope of each visit. He should subsequently write a report to specific terms of reference, and this report should be subject to tutorial critique and discussion as to its layout and style, etc.

5 *Senior Management Conferences.* The main purpose for attending these is for the trainee to become accustomed to thinking in the wider perspective and the longer term. Attendance will also provide a guide to the norms, values, standards and expectations of more senior managers, will help the trainee to establish a relationship and will indicate to him when fundamental misunderstandings can arise between different functions which directly affect his own operations.

Briefing and debriefing discussions with his line supervisor will assist in this process of learning.

6 *Projects.* The trainee is given the opportunity to think through for himself his own approach to some of the problems of efficiency and morale which will become his overall responsibility to advise on and direct. For each project the trainee can call upon the counsel of a tutor —who will be a Company specialist of high performance and potential— against whom he can test his thinking and his ideas.

7 *Courses.* These can be attended at any time convenient throughout the training period, the purpose of attending each being linked with the overall purpose of that area of development under which the course has been designated.

8 *Reading.* The trainee should so programme his time as to be able to assimilate the prescribed material, or any other he chooses, over the total period. Reading should form part of his thinking when considering fresh ideas and approaches to the job of managing.

9 *External Consultant.* The services of a professional consultant may be used in order to let the trainee discuss aspects of his learning and of his future responsibilities that he may not wish to discuss with Company staff, and to clarify areas of knowledge, techniques and management problems that are better discussed with a person with consultancy experience.

The trainee should make his own arrangements to meet, realising that a full day with a consultant costs about £–; a half-day being proportionate.

10 *Administration.* The trainee is ultimately responsible for his own development which will be measured by subsequent performance in the job. The training plan allows this development to be engineered by the trainee on his own initiative and by his own effort, assisted by tutorial counselling and advice from his own managers, his colleagues, tutors and consultant.

It is recommended, therefore, that the trainee manages his own programme based on this plan, with administration and coordinating assistance from Training, and that its conduct be supervised by his immediate line supervisor.

Examples of application

Assignment. Within such a programme, a manager on an assignment, to, say, Supply, would ensure that his needs for information were met through the despatch of an agenda sheet to the manager of the department concerned, who would be asked to divide and allocate parts of the agenda among his subordinate managers as appropriate. Disregarding such details as timing and location arrangements which the trainee is also responsible for arranging, here is a typical list of questions for which the trainee may be searching for answers. In sum, of course, they represent the job of the Supply Manager. He may not himself have realised it until asked these searching questions by an outsider:

What are the main purposes of the job?
What are the essential requirements of the job to enable it to function?
How are these requirements made available to the job?
To what extent does the job 'make or buy' the services which it exists to provide?
How are the services checked to ensure that they meet specifications?
How are the services potential and capability retained in readiness until required?
How are the services applied where needed?
How are they used?
How are their operations maintained in effective order?
How are they put right if and when they break down or go wrong?
How are the services improved?
How are costs recovered?
How are the services evaluated?

The pressure these questions exert on the responder forces real thinking so that two managers are educated for the price of one.

External Consultant   A typical use of a consultant half-day would be for the manager to make his personal arrangements for a visit by the consultant, probably before, over and after lunch, and probably at a neutral location, during which he, the manager, can express to the consultant his problems—technical, administrative, managerial, personal— in a way that it would not be possible for him to do with, say, a colleague.

There is not only the advantage of confidentiality; there is also the opportunity to test out ideas, possibly even ideals; to receive a stimulus to his thinking outside the conventions of the job or the company; to establish a relationship with a resource of professional information and experience which can be of future use, personally or in the job.

This use of a consultant is a purely private arrangement and is not in any way a commitment by the organisation to his services for any project. It represents the procurement of best and most appropriate advice and service according to the individual manager's needs.

Internal Course

A typical in-company course syllabus and programme detail would be as shown. Such internal courses, by being kept under continual review and modification, are always as relevant to company needs as it is possible for any 'course' type development action to be.

Course G—Operations Planning and Control
Supervisors—5 days for 15 staff
Managers—5 days for 15 staff
In each case there will be part of 1 day follow-up on the job.

Aim of the Course
1 To enable participants to practise techniques for increasing productivity through logical planning.
2 To study linkages in the flow of a work system and organisational roles within it.
3 To study appropriate techniques of determining and illustrating control information in order to take control decisions.

By the end of this course a participant will be able to analyse critically the content of work, to plan the logical sequence of doing it, to determine the critical points of operations that need to be controlled to meet objectives, and to devise means of illustrating control information.

Outline Syllabus
The importance of the logic in planning
Exercise in the construction of networks and calculations of the critical path
The allocation of resources
Some associated statistical and analytical techniques
Determination of nature and level of subordinate decision function
Recognition of the operating characteristics of a system
Information gathering and evaluation
Assessment of anticipated problems
Measurement and appraisal of departmental work
Computer applications and future trends
Review of performance, control data and objectives

Note on method of conduct. After each main subject area has been explained and discussed, an exercise will be done in the associated techniques. Tutoring will be done individually throughout, according to need.

THE INDIVIDUAL DEVELOPMENT PROGRAMME PLAN

Pre-Course Reading
Course Manual, F.M.C.
Critical Path Analysis, F.M.C.

Supplementary Reading
Network Analysis for Planning & Scheduling, A. Battersby (Macmillan).
The Theory & Management of Systems, Johnson Kast Rosenzweig (McGraw-Hill).
The Practice of Management, Peter Drucker (Mercury Press).

Coaching and Leadership

D. F. Sutton, Management Consultant, Action Learning Projects International

Learning to manage

Management is a 'job-specific' learning activity. Any skill or knowledge acquired in the formal learning situation is only of value in so far as it can be applied in the working situation—a working situation which can never be fully replicated in training. Fortunately the working situation can itself be used as an infinitely variable learning experience, and only needs to be approached thoughtfully and systematically for the developing manager to benefit.

The key figure in this pattern is the *boss* of the developing manager. The management development activity can be seen as an 'eternal triangle' involving manager, boss and consultant/trainer with, hopefully, two-way communication between all three as in Figure 12:1.

One can safely assume that manager and trainer are committed to the successful development of the former as a manager; the limits of their success are determined by their own personal effectiveness and the constraints put upon them by the environment within which the manager must operate. The boss is not only a member of the triangle, he also forms one of the constraints and controls a great many other limitations

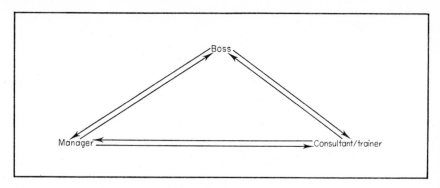

Figure 12:1 Pattern of management development

—financial resources, development opportunities, contacts inside and out-side the organisation. Regrettably there are instances in which the boss is not noticeably committed to furthering the development prospects of his subordinates. The short-sightedness of this approach is inferred by Professor J. F. Morris when he refers to management development as an area in the personnel field marked by a sense of *opportunity* rather than of *problems* and *breakdowns*. How often are the *problems* of subordinates seen as problem areas or sources of breakdown rather than the *opportunities* for learning which they truly comprise?

The work which has been undertaken in Belgium and Egypt by Professor R. W. Revans and at Manchester Business School by Professor Morris has sought to remedy this situation by employing the concept of action-centred training for management in which the learning process is developed in the working environment. Training in an alien work environment (that is some other environment than that in which the manager normally operates, whether in his own organisation or another company) sharpens experience and concentrates the mind on important factors, such as the role of the subordinate and the value of group activity in decision-making, which are often ignored in traditional training methods. Additionally, problem-solving in the real and living situation and exposure to the dynamic atmosphere of the management workshop force the learner to stretch his mental faculties and to accept a degree of responsibility comparable with the responsibility carried in the manage-ment job. To this extent the Morris/Revans action-centred approach to management training has a greater input than training in the routine job situation, by removing the manager from the familiar situation, thus quickening the training and reinforcing its impact. Nevertheless only the day-by-day management activity contains the vital elements of completely realistic action and personal involvement which are essential to the ultimate concept of action-centred management training—a goal to which many teachers of management are now committed. Even the more conservative teacher of management accepts the need for his theories and his training to be validated by job performance and evaluates his training methods by some system of job appraisal in the 'back-home' situation.

Role of the boss

In short, practical involvement in the working situation can be seen as: an extension of other forms of training, a training method in its own right, a reinforcement of formal theory and knowledge presentation, or a system of appraisal. These are all admissions in varying degree of the importance of training based on the practical management job. On-the-job training *for* managers *by* managers has a particular significance arising from the dual role of boss as trainer. Few bosses realise how important they are to their subordinates. Because they are the channel of communication, the mediator, the source of instruction, the provider of resources, the maker of decisions, they loom large in the eyes of their subordinates and have one great advantage over professional trainers— they are usually given attention. What is even less often realised is that in many cases a learning situation not unlike the parent/child situation exists between boss and subordinate. To the man one rung further down the ladder the boss represents success and is very often accorded respect for this reason. However sophisticated the company, its systems and procedures, the value which we put on our own humanity makes us identify with an individual rather than with a system. We identify with an individual whom we respect and who is seen to be successful and show our learning from him in the most obvious way—by imitation. The imitative activity is often unconscious but can be so deep-seated that it is reflected in a very personal manner—copying a turn of phrase, affecting a mannerism, echoing a line of thought—even adopting a characteristic opening to a conversation. Intensely personal, habitual responses to the effect of another man's personality.

With an acceptance of the importance of on-the-job training for managers and with a realisation of the power of his own position, no manager can ignore the need for coaching his staff as part of his contribution to the company programme of management development.

Not only is the superordinate in a position of power, he is also in a position of exposure. No one else in the organisaional unit is subject to as much criticism as the boss. Because his activities (and even worse, his inactivities) have a profound effect on the success of the unit and upon the working lives and concerns of his staff, his every action is subjected by that staff to criticism and examination. This criticism relates to his work as it is seen or thought to affect the way in which the unit operates and also to the effect he is seen to have upon the personal lives and ambitions of the individuals for whose work he is responsible. If he is to play his full part in the programme of management development by effective coaching, the boss must be capable of the type of leadership that engenders confidence, loyalty and a willingness to respond to guidance and instruction.

Acceptance of the importance of his role as coach and leader in management development is, for the boss, only the first stage in making an effective contribution. There is a need for conscious planning, preset objectives, imaginative procedures, careful decision-making with control of results and an acceptance of the human and organisational factors in the situation. In particular, the boss must cultivate an awareness of the relationships between himself and his staff and accept that there is always liable to be a conflict in the working situation between the material content of a job and the personal objectives of the participants in the activity.

If the boss accepts the need to involve himself fully in the management development programme, he must also accept the necessity to think through his own role in relation to his staff. In preparing himself to undertake this combined role of teacher and leader, he is committing himself to carry out in the staff development programme the full range of activities undertaken by the teacher in the more formalised learning situation :

1   An assessment of the objectives of the programme as it relates to each member of staff; with an associated timetable
2   An evaluation of the present standing and future potential of each member of the team
3   An accurate measurement of the learning needed to progress the

learner in such a way that the objectives of both organisation and learner are achieved and the potential of the individual is realised

4 A selection from the learning media available of the most effective means whereby learning can take place

5 A learning programme in which the tutor takes an active part

6 A system of assessment or evaluation whereby the success of the programme can be judged.

This task can be lightened for the boss if the company employs specialists in management development, uses sophisticated methods for examining performance and potential, has an accepted management development programme and has a reward system which recognises increased managerial effectiveness. Even in such circumstances, however, the role of the superordinate is vital. The only change is that he switches from being the programme administrator seeking specialist advice to that of the adviser with local knowledge to whom the organiser of the specialist programme turns for assistance. The boss has the invaluable detailed knowledge of the workplace situation and the opportunity to observe performance under the stresses and variations of the working environment which are not permitted to the staff training specialist.

The management development programme

If the boss has no specialist assistance in preparing the management development programme, he should undertake the following procedure methodically, referring to it continually and using it as a criterion for assessment :

1 A management manpower plan for present and future needs should be drawn up and projected forward at least five years. This plan must be based upon realistic job descriptions and personal specifications.

2 The current ability and future potential of each member of the management team must be assessed and compared with the requirements of the manpower plan.

3 A programme must be formulated for each member of the management team designed to improve his 'fit' in terms of the requirements of the plan. This programme must be fully discussed with the manager and the boss must gain acceptance of the concepts by his subordinate.

4   The most effective means (in cost-benefit terms) of implementing each individual programme must be determined by examining and evaluating the media available—the national education system, resources inside the company, consultancy services, industrial training board services.
5   The boss must determine and fully undertake his own part in the training programme.
6   A system of continuous measurement, feedback, evaluation and up-dating must be instituted. This may be in the nature of a highly formalised scheme such as management by objectives or may be of a more informal nature. Whatever the form, the core of this section of the programme will be some version of the appraisal interview.

Just as the teacher must fit himself for his role in the classroom the boss must fit himself for his role in the management development programme :

1   By committing himself to the programme's objectives
2   By acquainting himself fully with the philosophy and concepts of his organisation's management development programme
3   By acquainting himself with the administrative procedures necessary for the programme to operate
4   By learning how to act as teacher and coach as an extension of his leadership activity.

The boss has to develop his ability to act as a teacher/coach by using his knowledge of the development required of his subordinate, translating this necessary development into knowledge, techniques and skills areas and devising an individual learning programme, the effectiveness of which is monitored by assessing the on-the-job performance. As a first step the roles to be played by the developing manager, the boss and the training consultant must be assessed—whether the training consultant be a company management development officer, a management consultant or a member of a professional or academic institution. For both effectiveness of learning and reduction of cost, the optimum use must be made of whatever resources are available. If training staff exist within the organisation they are obviously fitted to give advice in this field. If the line manager has the responsibility, he must build up a range of contacts as carefully and systematically as he would in the case of raw material suppliers—examining the suppliers available, deciding upon which supplier to use by weighing anticipated benefits against costs and continually reappraising the situation. Some of the best facilities may exist within the organisation; their effectiveness is increased by familiarity with the work situation, and confidence in the knowledge and ability of the participants on the part of the developing managers. Outside the organisation, contacts should be made with the business schools, the industrial training boards and local colleges. These institutions can provide not only services in the form of trainers, facilities and organisation but also an information service as to what is available on an industry, a regional or a national basis. The work of independent training and management development agencies (mainly provided by management consultants) can also be of value. Although the cost may be higher, the benefits arising from the provision of tailor-made services may offset the increased cost.

The manager as coach

The most important aspect for the manager is the part which he must play directly in the development of his subordinate based on an acceptance of the importance of management development as a major objective in the basic philosophy of management by objectives. If this importance is accepted, the manager must fully involve himself in coaching, by acting as a 'special tutor' : the 'specialism' being the job situation and its relationship to the development of the subordinate.

By acquainting himself in detail with the programme of training, the boss can integrate the knowledge or skill gained into the job situation by providing opportunities for the knowledge and skills to be exercised (delegation), by pointing to practical situations in which the knowledge or skills have been or could have been used to advantage (constructive criticism) and by regularly and continually assessing the effectiveness of the subordinate and advising him or her in the light of the superordinate's knowledge, skill, experience and ability to see the wider picture (appraisal and counselling). The boss must also carry out his own duties in such a way that he guides, encourages and inspires the subordinate, setting standards by way of precept and example and earning respect for the way in which he carries out his duties (leadership).

Coaching encompasses the first three activities of the superordinate—delegation, constructive criticism and appraisal and counselling. Counselling and performance appraisal are covered in detail elsewhere in this book. Delegation is the act of giving, to a member of one's staff, a task for which he or she is completely responsible to the delegator and vesting him or her with the authority necessary for its satisfactory completion.

If delegation is to be exercised effectively in terms of both satisfactory results and meaningful training, certain criteria must be observed. The objectives, terms of reference and boundaries of the authority and responsibility delegated must be accurately and clearly defined. Standards must be set and both objectives and standards assessed in terms of results required, preferably in a quantified form. Controls of either a systematic institutional or personal nature must be designed and standards of performance assessed against the desired objectives.

Delegation provides positions of adequate nature, scope and range in which an individual can apply his specific skills within the appropriate setting using the requisite tools in order to contribute effectively to the objectives of the enterprise. In this setting the subordinate is perfectly placed to contribute to his own development and at the same time to monitor his own performance with the help of his superior as a sounding board and assessor of performance. The delegatee is appointed largely because of the specific skills which he is expected to employ. It is therefore practicable for his superior to use the situation to isolate the management content of the post and to concentrate his coaching on the managerial section of his subordinate's efforts. In doing this he will demonstrate how the purely management skills can be used to take full advantage of the technical abilities (in the broadest sense) of the delegatee. The delegatee should, from his knowledge of the technical elements of the situation, be helped to appreciate the way in which effective management can be built upon technical skills.

It is in the delegation situation that the boss can most clearly exercise his ability as a coach. The essence of coaching is the exercise of knowledge and experience to inform the person coached of deficiencies in his performance, and to advise him of ways in which these deficiencies can be made good. The coach must have a sound basic understanding of the principles which make for good performance (he should be a trained and experienced manager himself), must have the analytical ability which helps him to determine the basic reasons for inadequate performance, must command the respect and confidence of his pupil and must have the capacity to explain and illustrate the required improvements.

When delegating, the coach, having predetermined standards against which his pupil is to be judged, should be able to isolate the management content of the task, determine the areas in which his subordinate is failing to perform adequately and then help him by working through the problems which are being mishandled. Action should always be in the hands of the subordinate—the coach confining himself to analysis, criticism and suggestion, and encouraging in the subordinate the most effective form of criticism—self-criticism. The skill of the coach lies in timing his interventions (too few and the pupil makes mistakes which undermine confidence, too many and he leans on his coach as a prop), analysing accurately and suggesting alternative practicable courses of action without doing the actual problem solving for the pupil.

It is impossible to lay down rule-of-thumb criteria for these coaching activities (they will change with every situation and every subordinate) but the experienced manager by training himself to consider human behaviour and to analyse critically the actions of his subordinates can improve his performance as a coach and can certainly be more effective than a coach who is removed from the workplace situation. The rowing coach who never appears on the towpath, the cricket coach who eschews the nets and the football coach who will not don his track-suit are never among the leaders of their calling. Management coaching is a workplace activity for the manager's boss, not a function of the head office or the business school.

The manager as critic

At the feedback stage of delegation it is necessary to develop healthy constructive criticism which will lead the way to acceptable counselling and appraisal. To be of value, criticism must be acceptable to the person being criticised and, therefore, must be seen to be fair and objective, to be based on facts rather than opinions, to be aimed at positive constructive improvement and not lead in any way to denigration of the person criticised. Criticism should uplift and inspire by testing results against objectives, praising where praise is due, correcting errors by consultation and improving performance by setting new standards.

One role of the critic is to hold up a mirror in which the performer can see the details of his performance in an objective way that will enable him to analyse his activities in the light of what he was hoping to achieve. The critic must, however, seek to do more. He must interpret the standards anticipated in such a way that the performer can carry out a critical analysis which will compare his performance with the standard expected of him and thus enable him to set his sights on improvement.

Three things the critic must not do :

1　He must not distort, although he has a responsibility to highlight the important areas. The manager/critic who concentrates on his subordinate's deficiency in some trivial areas (such as actual misinterpretation of some legal information) which can be amended by a little knowledge training, but fails to mention some area of importance (such as unsatisfactory working relationships with colleagues) is doing the organisation a disservice by directing attention, and thus resources, into an area which does not justify this attention.

2　He must not instruct. The relationship that the criticism is intended to improve is that between the performer and the standards expected of him in performing his management task. The superordinate as a critic can suggest, advise, compare; it is the function of the subordinate to take this criticism, interpret it and apply the lessons learned in such a way that performance will be improved.

3　He must not indulge in criticism intended to destroy. Criticism that is to be useful must also be constructive. Constructiveness can be achieved by :

(a) Pointing to areas of strength, analysing the factors from which this strength arises and showing how these strong points can be used to remedy weaknesses. For example, if a manager communicates well in writing but badly in verbal confrontations, an analysis may reveal that he has adequate ability in perceiving, analysing, and constructing a communication and in timing its use even though he lacks the ability to communicate face to face. These strong points can be used as a basis for improving his verbal communications by giving him training to help him to overcome his weakness.

(b) Analysing weaknesses objectively and using the phrase 'I suggest that you should consider this course' rather than 'You are wrong to do that'. One of the earliest surprises in the career of the management teacher is that his students welcome criticism. This is a realisation of the tremendous drive for self-improvement on the part of most managers and the desire to benefit in some way from what they see can be a creative and self-accelerating process.

The only times when such criticism is resented is when it is seen as being unsound, emotive, defensive, aimed to 'cut down to size' or unfairly excessive.

The manager as leader

The emphasis in delegation, criticism and appraisal and counselling is on the cooperative, two-way aspect of the relationship between superordinate and subordinate and similarly, by what may seem to be a paradoxical interpretation of the literal meaning of leadership, the emphasis in a study of leadership is on an integrated relationship between the two men in the roles of leader and led. The function of the leader is to provide the subordinate with the information upon which he can determine his objectives and make his decisions, the resources necessary for him to fulfil the task satisfactorily and the guidance which will enable him to make correct decisions and implement them successfully. This relationship is, in a successful organisation, mirrored by similar relationships up and down the chain of command. It rests upon a mutual respect and confidence, engendered as a natural by-product of succesful joint participation in the learning process. In fact the joint nature of this participation provides another paradoxical situation which further emphasises the benefit of positive involvement by the superordinate in the career development of the subordinate.

Any competent and successful teacher will admit to learning from his pupils. In the field of management teaching the teacher/pupil relationship relies greatly upon pupil contribution and feedback. Both teacher and pupil derive benefit from the learning activity and this leads to a positive development of managerial ability within the organisation.

A relationship of this nature depends for its success upon mutual confidence and respect and upon leadership based upon acknowledged ability. The authority structure whilst assuming a hierarchical form in order to implement the policies of the organisation, actually rests upon a degree of interdependence and the free interchange of information. In the hospital service frequent use is made of the phrase 'sapiential authority' (that is, authority based upon knowledge) and this should be the foundation of a manager/leader's approach to the superordinate–subordinate relationship. To this sapiental authority must be added authority flowing from an ability to act positively and accurately and a willingness to encourage and accept criticism if it can be seen to lead to an improvement in performance.

In the management development field perhaps the most important characteristics of the boss are the ability to assess potential in his subordinates and the capacity for not standing in the way of his staff when he sees them develop and justify advancement. 'I was still addressing envelopes at your age, my lad' is never an excuse for not promoting a capable young executive.

Having established the need for the boss to be involved, having accepted the need to construct a framework of learning in the job situation and having dwelt upon the nature of coaching and leadership it may be appropriate to give a checklist of do's and don'ts which can be borne in mind by the boss.

DO look upon your staff as 'resource centres'. See in them areas for development.

DO see each member of staff in two lights: as a member of the organisation and as a whole personality. Each person has only so much total ability, skill and energy to offer to the world. You can persuade him to offer a large proportion of his talents to the organisational task, equip him to exercise these talents and show him the opportunities which exist, but you cannot make the choice for him.

DO recognise that with a new incumbent a job needs a new job description. Each manager brings to a position personal skills, specific knowledge and past experience which mean that he may be better or worse at the job than his predecessor. Make allowances for these variations in deciding what you expect of him and in designing the training which you see as necessary for his development.

DO remember that the final pay-off (or send-up) for his training will be in the job situation. A mismatch between the job situation and the training activity may not only be wasteful, it may be dangerous. It is obviously foolish to send a man on the world's best operational research course if you know that he will never work as an OR specialist and would have been better suited by a two-day appreciation course.

DO acknowledge that the greatest aid to learning is student motivation. Let your subordinate know that the training will benefit him directly and above all let him see that the training is relevant to his needs.

DO discuss the subordinate's training with him. The most receptive student is the man who has asked to go on a course and discussed his training needs with his boss.

DO use the job situation as the foundation for all training. Learning by doing is not confined to the five-year-olds. The junior manager learns more and his learning is better and quicker by doing a job and having a part in monitoring his own learning from his job performance in collaboration with an interested and informed coach—yourself. Additionally you cannot fail to benefit and develop personally and will find that your management development activity is the most rewarding part of your work.

DO work hard and thoughtfully in your coaching job. Your own results depend upon how good you can make your staff. Develop good managers and you can let most of your worries be taken care of my your subordinates' commitment and effectiveness.

DO think of the best teacher you ever knew and analyse the reasons why he achieved results. He almost certainly had firm discipline without bullying. He would surely have mastered his subject and be completely involved in it. He would cooperate in the learning process without ever abrogating the leadership. He would believe in the value of the work which you were doing together. He would be interested in you (and in every other member of the class) as an individual. Use him as a model.

DO analyse your own experience, failures as well as successes, and attempt to condense and crystallise the lessons which you should have learned so that others may benefit from concepts drawn from a thoughtful interpretation of real experience.

DO work at your own job in such a way that you are effective and can be seen to be effective in the eyes of your staff. The respect and confidence necessary for successful coaching/leadership will not be forthcoming if you are seen to be incompetent.

DO build your staff into a training team whose learning will complement and expand the experience of each member of the team by using each other's knowledge and experience. The effect will be learning of a highly acceptable nature—learning from one's own peers who are currently experiencing the same problems at the same level of commitment, involvement and responsibility.

DON'T forget the position which you occupy and the way in which you will appear to your subordinates. To them you are the difference between success and failure by the way in which you provide them with resources, appraise and report on their performance and guide them through their career development.

DON'T forget the existence of the management development industry. You would never consider building your own manufacturing plant although you would be greatly concerned in the design, attend to the commissioning and to the running-in and would then put the plant into operation. In the same way you are greatly concerned that your management development programme should operate effectively and you are greatly involved in its operation, but should take full advantage of services offered by specialists in the field—always providing that they offer the right product at the right quality and the right price.

DON'T impose pressure for the sake of pressure as part of your coaching and teaching. The art of pacing a learning programme lies in keeping the learner fully stretched but not over stretched.

DON'T use the management development programme as a substitute for management. The final responsibility is still to achieve results and cannot be abrogated by saying that 'it was run as a training exercise; things can go wrong and anyway look at all the learning that took place'.

DON'T adopt the same training strategy for every manager.

DON'T assume that because one training programme in one particular situation is unsuccessful the manager in question is untrainable.

Finally, remember that in twenty years' time you may be relying on the men you are training today to provide you with a pension.

13

Performance Appraisal and Counselling

Rex Adams, Director of Studies, Ashorne Hill

Organisations carry out management development so that they will have a sufficient supply of managers adequately prepared to meet their predicted needs. In a changing world this involves improving the performance of all managers in their present jobs and preparing at least some of them for the posts they are likely to hold later in their careers. To do these things effectively requires formal judgments about managers' present successfulness and their future potential, and some or all of the conclusions to be conveyed to them so that they can take steps towards doing better in the future.

There is less than complete agreement as to how appraisal and counselling can best be effected, but the usual steps in one cycle may be listed. They are discussed in this chapter, together with certain other significant points. In Figure 13:1 the steps are shown in rather greater detail in diagrammatic form, which brings out better the cyclical nature of the process and the key role of the superior at various points in the cycle.

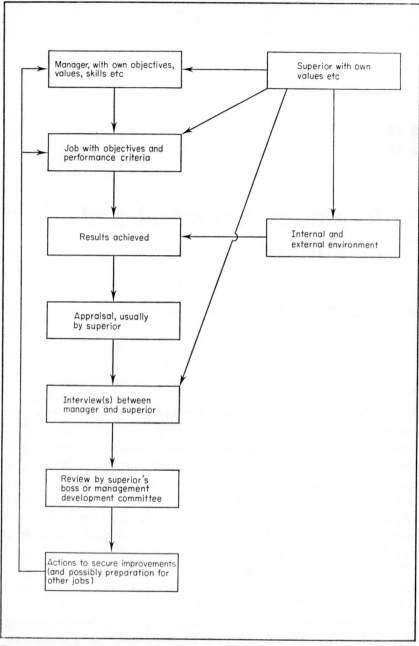

Figure 13:1   The appraisal and counselling process

The extent of the superior's involvement is understated in the figure, since he is usually the second most important factor in the achievement of results

1 The performance of a manager in his job is judged by his superior (or others) by observation and interpretation of data with reference to established criteria.

2 The manager's potential is also judged.

3 A form is filled in (and possibly completed after step 4).

4 The results of steps 1 and sometimes 2 are discussed by the manager and his superior, and the manager is counselled.

5 The form, and possibly a report on the interview, is considered by the superior's boss, and/or reviewing body, and the manager is compared with others.

6 Actions by the manager and others in the organisation follow in line with the aims of the particular scheme.

If we look at appraisal from the viewpoint of the person being assessed, his contribution to the organisation and his abilities are being judged, if not the personal characteristics which contribute to his performance. Criticism is probably an attack on his self-esteem, so he is probably extremely sensitive about the whole idea of appraisal and counselling. Not infrequently, superiors are untrained in interviewing or treat the whole process as a chore that they have to do. As a result the manager may, even nowadays, be advised to be 'less shy', or to 'concentrate more on the big things', or told that he has done very well, but not well enough to justify a salary increase.

A poor or inappropriate appraisal scheme, or one that is badly operated, can have serious consequences, not least for the motivation of managers. In a high technology company recently, a new scheme led to widespread discouragement, numerous cases of declining individual performance and a distant relationship between managers and professional engineers. In another instance in a similar company, the scheme led to most of the engineers who left being men with above-average ratings because those with low ratings had apparently lost confidence in themselves, and were reluctant to risk moving.[1]

This chapter, assuming some sort of average manager, explores many of the issues in appraisal and counselling by examining the available experience and drawing conclusions from it. Although a certain amount of research has been conducted in this area,[2] it is less than is desirable if appraisal schemes are to yield their full potential. However, there is a very wide gap between current practice in many firms and the developments in knowledge of the appraisal process, especially during the past decade. There is much that can be done now to get better results, both in Britain and the USA, on the basis of existing, reasonably established knowledge, as well as by experimentation within organisations.

Why appraisal?

Judgments and choices about people have to be made within all organisations, and for the sake of everyone involved it is desirable that they should be made on the basis of systematic evaluation rather than casually, and known to be made in a way which is as fair and acceptable as possible.

Management appraisal is most widespread in large businesses of all kinds, presumably because managers are usually in competitive situations and they are concerned to improve their performance, and are aware that good management is crucial to improved performance. Since it is almost impossible for the senior manager to know personally all his juniors, there must be procedures. Organisations of all kinds have, therefore, visualised many possible benefits from appraisal schemes. Those most frequently mentioned are:

1 The assessment of past performance:
   (a) to improve performance in the present job, for example, by setting objectives, indicating training or resource needs or desirable job changes;
   (b) to allocate salary increases in relation to achievements;
   (c) to indicate any need to change the job incumbent;
   (d) to uncover particular talent of any sort;
   (e) to evaluate selection procedures and possibly training schemes.
2 The encouragement of the deliberate managing of subordinates, including the conscious observation of their work, coaching and development.
3 The assessment of potential for promotion or transfer, especially in relation to the company's management succession schemes and manpower planning generally, and the identification of consequent developmental needs.
4 The improvement of managerial motivation by:
   (a) letting the men know how the company considers they are progressing, and their prospects;

(b) allowing men to express their own career interests;

(c) the encouragement of two-way discussions between man and boss on whatever either wishes;

(d) showing that salary increases, promotion, etc. are made on as objective a basis as possible;

(e) showing that the organisation is concerned about people.

If appraisal and counselling schemes can contribute usefully to all or many of these objectives, they are of the utmost significance. In fact few firms treat them as having that degree of importance, presumably because they are not getting sufficient benefit from their current practices. Several possible reasons for this will emerge later, but lack of clarity about objectives is often the first weakness, and a basic one. In particular, there is always a temptation to try to do everything by means of one scheme. In this chapter the emphasis will be on the achievement of improved performance in the present job, and the assessment of potential.

Some of the purposes listed above concern the immediate superior, others the latter's boss, and some a management development or salary committee, and perhaps a central personnel department. Some require an appraisal scheme to be organised in different ways to others. Some objectives are much more readily achieved by one mode of assessment than by another, and this sets practical limits to what can be achieved by any appraisal form of a length and complexity which managers will be prepared to complete conscientiously.

There is controversy about the linking of some objectives: several managers and writers wish to avoid any connection between appraisal and salary increases, a startling suggestion at least until one has examined some of the problems of making assessments and of the factors other than personal performance which influence and may determine decisions on salary increases. It is also suggested sometimes that the whole process of critical review is resented by both appraiser and appraised as 'partaking of surveillance' and out of accord with the democratic values of society.[3] This is most often expressed in the USA, but certainly a reluctance to appraise has been noted in this country, too.

Finally, it would seem sensible that any company's prime objectives should be stated somewhere in the literature about its scheme, so that the appraisers and those appraised, at whatever level, and including newcomers to the organisation, are aware of what they are trying to do. Not every company does this,[4] and even in four companies where it was done, 'the purpose of appraisal schemes was not clearly understood by most line managers'.[5] Under these circumstances acceptance and commitment are unlikely, and a scheme becomes just another chore, to be carried out mechanically if there is sufficient pressure behind it, but otherwise allowed to fade away.

Factors in job performance

This is no place to review the determinants of managerial effectiveness, especially as the task has recently been undertaken,[6] but the performance of a manager in his job is the first element in most modern appraisal schemes and requires some comment since it is less simple than it might appear.

Performance results on their own are not necessarily either the best or the only criteria of a manager's effectiveness, however well measured and appropriate the standards. For example, his sales results may have been due to a change in tariffs, or in fashion, or his competitors' policies, uninfluenced by his efforts. Indeed, should he not have done still better under the prevailing conditions? And what part did the advertising campaign, the publicity at the exhibition, or the revised price schedule play? What of the internal climate under which the manager operated? How far did the moratorium on recruitment, or the delays on the computer, or the constraints on holding finished stock and spare parts, or his boss's other policy decisions affect the results? Was he lucky? Or unlucky?

How far were the results due to the one manager, how far to his unit or to other units who contributed by more rapid distribution or product improvements? Even connecting a manager's actions causally with his own unit's performance is often not easy in the short run. Job performance is the resultant of a person, his or her job behaviour, the superior, and an organisational and external environment. Typically, the superior is, after the manager himself, the most significant influence on performance. All must be evaluated together if the result is to come near a meaningful appraisal of what has occurred. After that, what has the individual contributed?

Clearly this raises several difficulties, such as how the boss can appraise satisfactorily if he is a party to the results, a matter taken up below in the section, 'Who Should Judge?'. Leaving this problem aside, the complexity of many—but not all—situations is such that the first appraisal of a manager's performance in any job may not be very reliable. If the process is carried out on several occasions, and by more than one person, confidence in the outcome is greatly increased.

The problem of distinguishing the connection between a manager's actions and the short-run performance of his unit has been mentioned. In fact the whole question of time scales is of considerable significance in all management appraisals, because in general the more senior the manager, the longer the time span desirable to evaluate his decisions. Even then subsequent decisions to meet changing environmental and internal conditions 'make the relation between action and results . . . often hard to identify'.[7]

The judgmental process

Judging someone's performance involves several theoretically discrete steps, particularly observation of the person's behaviour and the scrutiny of available results, recall and interpretation. The organisational position of the judge or judges also affects the evaluation, and similarly their predispositions.

Observation, or perception, is highly selective, so that we tend to notice these things relevant to our own needs, interests and goals, or evidence that confirms existing beliefs, rather than contradictory facts.[8] A large dramatic event may capture the attention at the expense of minor, continuing items. Something said by an important person looms large. The experiences that we can evaluate in terms of our pre-existing values or categories are more likely to be appreciated than those that do not fit. The evidence heard casually in a working environment may often be hearsay, incomplete and one-sided, whether or not deliberately slanted. And it is impossible for us to identify all the factors on which our judgments are based.

Social relationships are highly influential in reaching conclusions. For example, the higher the rate of interaction between two or more people, the more positive their sentiments towards each other tend to be. Since an interaction system cannot function smoothly if it contains impediments, subordinates' ability to interact smoothly with their superiors will be important to the latters' view of them. Superiors will also attach importance to those characteristics of their subordinates' performance which are related to their own personal needs, and they will tend to see the subordinates' results in terms of their own perception of the quality of the relationship. Agreement between superior and subordinate on the dimensions of the latter's job leads to more favourable evaluations than where agreement is low. It is also the case that, other things being equal, superiors can judge men with a similar background to their own more accurately (and so probably with greater confidence) than other people.[9]

Retention and recall are equally subject to the forces outlined, and are highly selective, with the dramatic and pleasant being better remembered than the reverse. However, experiments have shown that most people are unable to recall a few hours afterwards even a small proportion of events they have experienced. Appraisers tend to remember best the more recent behaviour, which may not be representative of the whole period being reviewed, particularly, perhaps, if the subordinate knows the appraisal date. The difficulty of recalling demonstrable facts is illustrated by the experience of a personnel manager who was testing a proposed selection form on experienced supervisors. He included 'attendance' and 'output', two verifiable items, and found that the ratings were only randomly related to actual performance and attendance. The supervisors' judgments turned out to be related to their liking for the operators they were judging.[10]

The interpretation process starts from an individual's tendency to be lenient or severe, that is to hold particular standards, so that in appraising, one manager tends to regard all his geese as swans, while another adopts the opposite viewpoint. However, training in judging filmed behaviour and other data simultaneously with other appraisers, and then comparing ratings, goes some way to resolve this difficulty, which can anyway be allowed for by a reviewing superior or management development committee.

A superior's judgments may also be influenced by the expectation that he will have to defend his view to his own boss, and, to a greater or lesser extent, to the subordinate. As a result some superiors indulge in the 'error of central tendency', that is, 'play it safe', placing everyone close to centre of the scale or ratings they are using. Other managers perpetrate the 'error of leniency' where most people are placed at the high end of the scale. Kay Rowe found that in five out of six firms, ratings of 'more than adequate' and 'satisfactory' totalled 84 per cent of those given, and in one firm 98 per cent. There was no instance of more than 5 per cent of those graded being categorised as 'barely adequate' or worse.[11] The US Navy was recently in the position of having 98.5 per cent of its officers graded 'outstanding' or 'excellent', and just 1 per cent 'average'.[12]

The 'halo effect' is a further problem requiring mention. Not only does the quality of personal relationships influence overall ratings on unrelated matters, but there is a strong tendency, especially for appraisers dealing with traits of personality, to rate each unit very largely as reflections of a general factor (or 'halo') such as overall merit. To give an instance, Elliott found that 83 per cent of a rating on organising ability was determined by a general factor, 1 per cent by a factor common to five of the qualities, and only 16 per cent by the factor supposedly being evaluated.[13] Obviously this greatly reduces the value of such ratings in determining training needs or suitability for particular jobs. It has been argued that the halo effect reflects consistency of values in an appraiser, or, using the term rather loosely, between different managers assessing the same subordinate, and so is valuable as reflecting an overall measure of a person.[14] Certainly it would seem to reflect an assessor's view of his ability to work with, or get on with, the subordinate, and should not, therefore, be ignored. As Elliott noted, the worker who believes that his rating depends on whether his face fits may not be far wide of the mark.

Both the organisational climate and the personality of a manager will influence the appraisals he makes. Emotionally well-adjusted people tend to be good judges.[15] Younger appraisers tend to be tough. Insecure managers probably try to 'play it safe' by giving ratings around 'average'. Heavy pressure on a manager may lead to undue criticism of subordinates, while organisational distance tends to reduce the effectiveness of judgment.[16] Instances have been recorded of a change of manager leading to almost complete reversals of gradings, such as a man considered 'unsatisfactory' by one director being promoted second-in-command by the latter's successor eighteen months later.[17]

Who should judge?

It is customary for appraisals to be made by a man's immediate superior, and this has an obvious rationale. The superior has a wider view of the organisation's objectives than his subordinate, and is responsible for a performance which incorporates the latter's achievements. In addition, it is often the case that the superior has done the subordinate's job, or one similar to it, earlier in his career, and he is apparently the person best placed to judge how well his junior has done, and help him to do better. If the first objective of appraisal is to improve present performance, including the setting of appropriate objectives for the future, this seems a logical arrangement in a hierarchical organisation.

Against this is the point demonstrated in Figure 13:1 : the superior is invariably a significant determiner of his subordinate's performance. This being so, the superior is not only judging his junior, but also how far he has carried out his own responsibilities towards his subordinate. In the scientific sense, his judgments are contaminated, a fact which draws attention both to other possible appraisal methods, and certainly to the need for satisfactory review procedures.

The US military forces have experimented with peer (or 'buddy') ratings, especially in officer cadet units, as a supplement to appraisal by the superior. Certainly peers see much behaviour that is unknown to anyone at a higher level. E. P. Hollander, the social psychologist, reviewed the earlier research in this area and concluded that on some occasions peer ratings were a better indicator of leadership performance than ratings by superiors, and that generally they were of good reliability and validity.[18] A more recent study concluded that 'the peer rating paradigm is the most consistently effective predictor of military officer behaviour and is also an effective predictor in two industrial situations where it has been tried'.[19] Although very little is known of personnel practices in companies in Britain other than some of the larger 'household name' organisations, it is unlikely that much experimentation is being done in this area. However, one does hear instances of some smaller companies successfully allocating management bonuses in this way. Peer ratings might appeal to younger managers in the future, and be acceptable to senior management because of the value of the additional viewing point they provide, and the removal of some of the emotional problems of judging subordinates.

Almost certainly most managers would reject appraisal by their subordinates with as much intensity as university teachers reacted against the suggestion that their teaching skill should be judged by students. But apart from this 'threat to discipline' problem, subordinate rating is liable to all the problems of bias in judging discussed already. In addition subordinates are typically quite ignorant of many aspects of their bosses' job, including the sorts of viewpoint appropriate to the position, so that they could probably only comment on some parts of the total task, inevitably the ones most concerning themselves. Professor Harry Levinson of Harvard has recently proposed that this is exactly what subordinates should do—appraise how their superior has helped them to do their job and develop them. He argues that such feedback on the superior's performance would allow the latter to defend himself or change his behaviour.[20] Obviously any rating by subordinates could only occur in situations where the climate is very open, and under defined procedures. It is analogous to Drucker's recommendation that senior managers enquire of their juniors what they should be doing to help them, and certainly, if managers could systematically listen to their subordinates' views, evaluate them, and act on the appropriate ones, considerable benefits could ensue.

Self-appraisal, as one preliminary to an interview with a superior, is probably getting increasingly frequent as a side-effect of management by objective schemes, and the often-quoted 'reluctance of appraisers to appraise'. Under self-appraisal, the subordinate usually completes the appraisal form and gives it to his boss, and they then seek agreed conclusions wherever possible, or at least understanding of where and why they differ, especially on matters of the standards each holds. It is also possible for both subordinate and superior each to complete an appraisal form separately as the basis for the interview, a process known as 'joint appraisal', although it is only joint appraisal of the subordinate.

As a way of minimising the subjectivity in a single manager's judgment of his subordinate, appraisal is sometimes done by a group of senior managers who all have dealings with the subordinate. Experience confirms both that many additional items of information can be brought to bear on a judgment, and that the consensus view often differs from that of the immediate superior. Obviously this method is very expensive in terms of managerial time and, unless such sessions are highly valued in the system and managers are not under great pressure, there may be considerable delays in getting such groups of superiors together. This arrangement does provide several of the advantages of the review of an individual appraisal, so that the apparent loss in time is less than it appears.

A strong case has been made out for using ratings on several factors, by peers, subordinates and superiors, both for research and for personnel decisions. The matter is important, and the argument convincing, but it is too remote from practicability to be more than mentioned here.[21]

In practice most organisations will continue to have bosses appraise their subordinates, and this does have the merit of keeping the boss responsible for his subordinates' performance and development. There is a need for an adequate review system, however, and there are possible problems in the assessment of potential. Both of these are looked at below.

Finally, almost all managers have more work to do than they can readily accomplish in the time available. In such a situation priority is given to those things which are the subject of pressures or rewards. Whoever assesses, they are more likely to do the job well if there is 'something in it' for them. That is why the way subordinates are appraised is often a factor on which superiors are assessed.

Criteria for judging: traits

Suitable criteria are a prerequisite of effective appraisal, and it is in changed ideas about criteria that most has been done to increase the value of appraisal systems in recent years. Until about a decade ago, most company schemes rated their managers against various criteria of personal qualities, or traits, and general characteristics of their work. Some companies still work on this basis,[22] while others have mixed schemes, bringing in traits alongside other factors. Yet a person is not a loosely tied bundle of separate qualities, but a complex organised system.

Typically a trait-rating system would list a dozen or so personal characteristics, such as 'leadership ability', 'cooperativeness', 'judgment', 'inventiveness', 'industriousness', 'personality' and so on, and the appraiser selected some grade on a scale ranging from, say, 'outstanding' to 'unacceptable'. Often, job performance or particularly relevant skills got little or no mention on the forms used, although obviously some of the traits, such as ability to work with other people, are of some general relevance.

Several fundamental objections have been levelled against appraisals on this basis. Generally appraisers are reluctant to 'play God' in McGregor's phrase and appraise in the way the forms suggest,[23] or when they do so, do not do it very well.[24] Considering how subjective such judgments must be, this is hardly surprising. How does one decide whether a manager is using 'common sense' or 'intelligence', is 'self-confident' or 'aggressive', 'stubborn' or 'tenacious'? Indeed the traits that an individual displays are likely to vary from one situation to another, depending on the other people involved, the task and other factors.

There is also the basic question of relevance. What is the connection between 'punctuality' (which was rated in some schemes of this kind) or having a 'good personality' and performance, and getting results? In fact almost any trait may be advantageous in some situations, but dysfunctional in others. Indeed, one of the classic stories about appraisal is of the salesmen in one company who scored high in 'integrity' and 'honesty' being unsuccessful (in terms of results) whereas those who scored low in these qualities turned in good sales figures.

The same point may be made another way. As Kenneth Andrews has said, 'There is no one model of a model modern manager';[25] in other words, very different managers can get equally good results through quite different methods, although they may possess totally different combinations of personality traits.

Finally, there is a moral problem: what right has a manager to comment upon non-job-related characteristics of a subordinate? What has it to do with the company, providing the manager being appraised is performing his job satisfactorily? As McGregor asks, does not the traits approach constitute 'something dangerously close to a violation of the personality'?

Criteria for judging: performance

With powerful practical and moral arguments against them, it is not surprising that appraisal schemes based on rating traits have been strongly attacked. At about the same time alternative bases for appraisal were established by research, for example, in the General Electric Company of America with its Work Planning and Review System, and, more empirically, in the concept of management by objectives. Indeed Drucker, the 'father' of MBO, and Humble, one of its strongest proponents, both saw the connection with appraisal from the beginning. Essentially appraisal has become focused on what an individual manager contributes to the organisation's results. Professor Harold Koontz has recently argued persuasively for the need to add a specific assessment of a manager's skill in managing to appraisal against objectives,[26] but, with this addition, performance-based assessment is the present accepted wisdom.

Among the advantages of judging a manager on how he has managed, and not on his personality, is that appraisal (and more generally management development) ceases to be some separate task carried out once a year, but becomes an integral part of normal manageral activity. This is particularly relevant in terms of appraisal interviewing and counselling. Second, the relationship between superior and subordinate is shifted towards greater acknowledgement of interdependence, with the manager either proposing his own targets as a contribution to his boss's goals, or at least agreeing the targets his superior proposes, after they have both looked at any resources, training or organisational changes needed. Third, the system, properly done, provides suitably challenging goals for each individual, so that appraisal is against standards accepted as suitable for the manager concerned, and the process can be repeated time after time.

The whole MBO emphasis on the joint responsibility of a manager and his superior for the results the former attains means that 'playing God' becomes both less likely and quite inappropriate. It is also the case that because a manager invariably has a range of objectives, he is likely to succeed in some of them in any period, and so have a constructive basis for the appraisal interview as well as a feeling of accomplishment as a foundation for further personal growth. This applies to every manager simultaneously. It is not a competitive system in which some can succeed only at the cost of others.

When MBO in relation to appraisal was initially introduced, some writers spoke of it removing the subjective element from judgments, and of making achievements measurable. From what has been said above in the sections on 'Factors in Job Performance' and 'The Judgmental Process', such claims can only be regarded as grossly overstated. Nonetheless, assessment based on results, and wherever possible couched in quantitative terms, does mean that judgment is focused on performance against standards, even though both good and bad results have to be evaluated in the light of all the circumstances, including the real possibility that some poor target setting may have occurred. The degree of objectivity involved is increased by MBO and multiplies the chance of a subsequent constructive interview, as well as, hopefully, leading to effective future action by both parties.

Finally, how were the results achieved? For example, did the manager neglect the remainder of his job to concentrate on quantified targets? Or did he prejudice the future of his unit by neglecting maintenance of plant and development of people? Did he show good unit performance at the cost of others in the work flow, or by hazarding colleagues' objectives?

Koontz proposes 73 positive questions under the headings of planning, organising, staffing, directing and controlling, which are intended to reveal the quality of a man's managing.[27] They do not relate at all to any technical or functional elements in a manager's job. Certainly these questions would expose any discrepancy between the quality of results achieved and the methods used, so reducing the likelihood of the situation where, say, a sales manager has outstanding results because of favourable market conditions and rises rapidly in an organisation because of the reputation he has gained, moving through senior jobs before there is sufficient time for the consequences of his decisions to be demonstrated beyond reasonable doubt.

Other appraisal techniques

If appraisals based on performance objectives are the type most widely accepted at present, other techniques which are adequate and appropriate for some purposes are also available. These include appraisals based on the essay type of approach, in which the appraiser comments freely or under a very few headings on an individual's strengths, weaknesses and potential. Commonplace as a reference for someone's suitability for a job, they are usually very subjective and difficult to compare, and require some analytic skill and literary ability in the writer if the person appraised is not to be under-rated. They may highlight some factor not taken into account in prepared forms, but probably indicate nearly as much about the writer as the subject.

In some situations, simple rating scales, checked off by the appraiser and possibly having a space for any desired elucidatory comments, may be sufficient. Sometimes used for rating large numbers of foremen, these certainly involve a low cost in time and are useful within their limits. In the past, rating scales have often been used in combination with the traits approach, but performance items or attitudes can be included equally well; to concoct an example :

'This supervisor :

1   Shows little interest in accident prevention

2   Interested only during safety campaigns
3   Regularly checks that his men follow safety rules.'

Sometimes superiors are required to rank their staff, either from best to poorest, or in categories like 'above average', etc. or along a normal distribution. Techniques like alternative ranking or paired comparison ranking provide assistance in carrying this out. However, much depends on the criteria to be used and the degree of subjective judgment involved, as well as the weighting to be employed where several factors are to be taken into account. These techniques can be useful for selecting one person for some fairly straightforward purpose, but the study by Thompson and Dalton[28] points to some of the grave dangers which can arise in using them for comparing performances, especially if the approach used means that half of those assessed have eventually to be told that they are 'below average', an arbitrary and destructive measure leading to a downward performance-appraisal cycle.

It is not unknown for 'critical incidents' or other examples of actual behaviour to be recorded for eventual discussion with a subordinate. The disadvantages of storing up criticism, the 'little black book' atmosphere that may result, and the differences in standards of judgment and in biases which frequently appear during the discussion, all suggest reservations about this approach. It does provide a basis for realistic coaching soon after an event, however, including the exploration of the different standards and values.

'Work sampling', in the sense of watching a subordinate carry out a selection of his duties, in addition to studying what can be learnt from available and appropriate data, is rather similar to 'critical incidents'. It is particularly useful where the job structure is such that boss and subordinate do not interact much, or if the superior is unfamiliar with particular aspects of the subordinate's work. A sensible form, drawing attention to some salient points, is given by Kellog.[29]

The difficulty in judging a manager on 'his' results, when these are influenced or determined by events beyond his control has led to the suggestion that the item to be evaluated should be decisions made or not made. This would require assessment of the quality of the decision taken in the light of the information then available, rather than the outcome, which might be a matter of circumstance. Difficulties, such as making reasonable allowance for time or other pressures when the decision was taken, clearly remain, but for jobs in banking, say, where the quality of decisions might be the critical element, the approach deserves trial.[30]

The usefulness of these methods is mainly as a supplement to performance-based review, or where something simpler is required because of the numbers involved and likely value of the procedure, or to meet specific objectives. Oberg has recently examined these methods and some others from this point of view.[31]

Judging potential

Judging future managerial success is for many companies the second most important aim of appraisal schemes. Yet, partly because of the limited research undertaken in this area, we know little about the effectiveness of appraisals of potential. The poverty of investigation reflects the long time-span needed, and various theoretical difficulties. More work has been done on the effectiveness of managerial judgments and the values of psychological testing, areas where these problems are less pronounced.

Typically, organisations include in their appraisals some questions about the potential of the manager being assessed. The British Steel Corporation's appraisal form illustrated in Figure 13:2 distinguishes between a manager's potential at about the same general level, but in more demanding jobs; his or her suitability for the next level; and potential beyond that. Unilever divide their management structure into three strata, and ask whether a manager is thought likely to reach the stratum (which is not necessarily the job level) above his own. Standard Oil of New Jersey ask for the title of the highest position the individual can reasonably be expected to attain. Other firms enquire about a man's likely ceiling.

How should an appraiser decide his subordinate's potential? In some cases various criteria are suggested, such as the degree of decisiveness shown, self-confidence and care taken by the manager in developing his own subordinates. Past performance is some guide, and in particular the way the manager actually manages. It is possible to ask what things this individual has done particularly well, and less well, and whether any trends are apparent. It is probably especially valuable to consider the manager's career interests, and possibly his interests outside the job. In some instances the manager's wife's views are significant. Inevitably the concept of general potentiality is imprecise, and even if the level of job is taken into account, the function, or possibly even country of operation is often unstated. Among the obvious objections, perhaps four stand out.

First, in the absence of valid criteria, and especially for jobs several levels higher than that held by the appraiser, how is judgment to be made? Can it be more than guesswork? In this situation, moreover, the appraiser's judgments are going to be considered and assessed by his own superiors, so he is quite likely to be influenced by what he thinks they favour. He may very well tend to 'play it safe' and avoid recommending anyone who does not appear to be very good indeed, or who seems unusal or 'off-beat'. Second, if little or no guidance is given to managers on how they should identify potential, how can the results be compared satisfactorily?

The third difficulty comes back to the blanket nature of the recommendation being made. The quality of performance results from an interaction between the nature of an individual and the situation in which he finds himself. It is not solely a matter of an individual's ability, motivation, knowledge and skills, but also of the particular problems, boss, colleagues and culture in which he is operating. It is not safe to assume that excellence in one situation can readily be transferred, that is that present high performance can be extrapolated to another job. Each organisation—and often parts of it—has its own value system, and sometimes these differ so much that success in one part would be almost sufficient to disqualify a man from success in another.[32] It is not the case that the qualities required at different levels of an organisation are entirely the same, or ones which anyone can readily develop. To take one example, success in one culture, such as the USA, has frequently been shown not to guarantee success in a Western European country, or Africa.[33] Finally, what will be required of senior managers in ten or twenty years' time, and have appraisers the same view of what this is, as well as how it can be developed?

Most managers, while admitting the validity of these arguments, would regard them as 'academic' in the pejorative sense. Statements like, 'You can tell a young man of real potential when he walks through the door', although perhaps deliberately exaggerated, reflect many managers' view of the problem, and indeed few of us find it difficult to make overall judgments about the potential of younger members of our own occupation. In any particular career there do seem to be indicators of quality of performance which the experienced practitioner believes he can sense. However, little is known about the validity of judgments of this sort, although it is possible in the light of what has been said earlier to identify some of the considerable assumptions implicit in the extreme statement quoted.

We do know that the quality of judging others is not spread evenly : some are very much better at it than others. High intelligence and academic ability, specialisation in the physical sciences, aesthetic and dramatic interests, good emotional adjustment and integration, and social skill are among factors which correlate positively with ability to judge the personality characteristics of others.[34]

Whether it reveals anything about the perceived value of appraisals or not, two studies have shown that they are not always acted upon.

In the first one, Miner's data come from five divisions of a large US manufacturing company.[35] The managers had been appraised separately on their effectiveness in their present job, and their potential for advancement, using the pooled judgments of several superiors familiar with their individual work. In one division, with 76 managers, 25 per cent were promoted over four years. The 25 per cent comprised 11 per cent who had been rated high on effectiveness, 14 per cent rated low.

In another division, with 100 managers, 39 per cent had been promoted over three years. These comprised 27 per cent who had been rated high on effectiveness, 12 per cent rated low; 19 per cent of them had been rated high on potential, while 20 per cent were rated low.

In each of the other three divisions quite significant numbers of managers regarded as having high potential were not promoted, whereas men classified as of low potential were. Miner does not try to explain these discrepancies, unfortunately, neither does he suggest whether unmentioned factors, such as specific job knowledge, for example, justified the promotions made despite the appraisal results.

In the second study, Ferguson reported that 'in General Electric and other companies', apart from 'a few exceptional' ones, less than 30 per cent of the identified leading candidates for jobs actually achieve them. He reports that research shows also that less than one-half of those who achieved top-level managerial jobs had appeared on the lists of those with greatest potential early in their careers, or been paid in the top quartile of their age group. Finally, twice as many individuals from the lower nine salary deciles of an age group became 'company leaders' as are drawn solely from the top decile.[36] Unfortunately Ferguson does not enlarge upon his statements, or quote how the results were arrived at. It is not clear either whether the conclusions about potential which Ferguson quotes were judgments of superiors, the results of psychometric testing, or some combination of the two.

Testing is one of the areas where the non-psychologist must rely heavily on the expert. A thorough recent examination of the validity of predictive studies concludes, ' "Judgmental" prediction methods, as exemplified particularly by executive assessment procedures and peer ratings, are generally better predictors than psychometric procedures, although allowance must be made for the generally small samples involved'.[37] 'Psychometric procedures' refers mainly to the large number of general tests said to indicate potential, some of which appear effective at supervisory levels, but which have been found less useful for managers. A psychologist working within a firm would be able to adapt his approach to the values and reward system of the organisation, however, and analyse the individual in his interactions with the structure, so in all probability achieving better results.

Something of this sort was being done recently in the Talent Review Program of General Electric in America. The company was concerned at developing insufficient general managers, and the fact that it was taking fourteen years after a graduate joined the company before his capacity for a general managerial post was established. As a result a central management manpower planning and development consultant was attached to each group of the organisation to evolve lists of people ready for general responsibilities. After the candidates have been sorted and ranked by head office functional personnel, the consultant has a four- to seven-hour 'accomplishment-focused' depth interview with each candidate to assess his managerial potential, experience, skills and attitudes. This, after discussion with the manager's superior, forms the basis for a development plan for the manager concerned.[38]

A rather similar approach but on a much larger scale and at lower organisational levels is that of the assessment centre, which has recently become increasingly widely used in the USA by companies such as IBM, General Electric, A.T. & T., General Motors, Standard Oil (Ohio) and Sears, Roebuck. Based on wartime officer selection techniques, they test candidates in simulated situations such as management games, in-basket exercises, and leadership discussions. After a long period of being concerned with first-line supervisor selection, the centres are now increasingly concerned with selecting middle managers for promotion.

Their reports are said to be 'remarkably valid',[39] with, for example, twice as many A.T. & T. managers chosen after assessment centre evaluation doing 'better than satisfactory' as those not so evaluated.[40]

It may be noticed that, apart from the General Electric scheme just mentioned, almost every assessment of potential starts from the manager's immediate superior. That a 'school of experience' man of 60 is necessarily well equipped to assess young graduates, for example, is less than obvious, and sometimes there must be a case for, say, a management development specialist at least watching the progress of such expensive recruits, and ensuring that they are judged in more than one situation and by more than one person, lest they be filtered out of the system by junior managers of lesser ability who are jealous, or just out of sympathy with the younger men's attitudes.

Appraisal forms

The purpose—or purposes—that appraisal is intended to serve in any organisation are revealed most clearly in its appraisal form. Typically this is intended to be the record of the assessment, the indication of training or development needs, and a basis for the remote comparison of individuals being considered for promotion or other job changes.

One relatively recent form, that produced by the Management Appointments and Developments Section of the head office of the British Steel Corporation (BSC), is illustrated in Figure 13:2.[41] This is not shown as a model for other companies to copy; what is appropriate to meet one set of objectives is not ideal for others. Indeed, BSC are still making some changes to the form, and page 6, 'Agreed personal performance objectives (if appropriate)', has recently been added to highlight this area. It is also the case that some of the larger units of BSC, while following the general format, have made changes of their own. This approach has also been followed in the new (1972) Civil Service Department form, the major parts of which are standardised, although departments may add to it to meet any specialised requirements. There is a fairly detailed commentary on the use of the BSC form, entitled 'Management Assessments', issued in April 1971. This pamphlet is intended for all managers who have to make assessments or to be asssessed within the scheme. In addition the Corporation has arranged a series of local training seminars which extends to each level being included in the appraisal at

STRICTLY CONFIDENTIAL   Full name

British Steel Corporation
Annual Assessment 197

Function _____ Division
_____ Location

1 Personal details

Full title of position held

Date appointed to present position _____ Date of birth

Full title of immediate superior

Assessor's position (if different from above)

1

Agreed personal performance objectives (if appropriate)

8 Notes on the interview

(Note what has been agreed with the job holder regarding his performance. What indications have you given him about his career prospects and development/training plans? Remarks in this section on personal performance objectives may be expanded on page 6)

Signature _____ Date _____

9 Comments of assessor's superior

(Comment on the assessment as a whole and, in particular, on the development training recommendations)

Signature _____ Date _____

10 Recommendations of management development committee

(Note recommendations together with any general comments on the assessment)

Signature _____ Date _____

4

6

STRICTLY CONFIDENTIAL   Full name

STRICTLY CONFIDENTIAL   Full name

STRICTLY CONFIDENTIAL   Full name

2 Review of performance

(Summarise the individual's performance during the past year)

3 Job holder's section

(To be completed by the Assessee and may include ideas about his future development)

4 Development potential

(Consider the individual's potential for more demanding jobs or for different jobs at the same general level)

5 Summary of potential

(Tick one box and answer final question)

Is not, at present, capable of performing his job satisfactorily ☐☐

Promotion not foreseen within 3 years because

Potential for limited promotion (within the same managerial level) ☐
State for which jobs, regardless of availability, he is suitable

Has potential for promotion within 3 years to a higher managerial level, after further training or development ☐
State for which job, regardless of availability, he is suitable

Has potential for immediate promotion to a higher managerial level ☐
State for which job, regardless of availability, he is suitable

Do you consider that he may have potential, after   YES/NO
development, for further promotion beyond the   NOT YET KNOWN
next higher managerial level?

6 Development plan

(Make recommendations if appropriate, other than training courses, for the development of the individual)

7 Training requirements

(a) Specialist/Technical
(Give details of any courses you propose for the job holder)

(b) General management
(Make recommendations for development training courses)

2

3

5

Figure 13:2   Example of an assessment form   This is a six-page form which is folded where indicated by the dotted lines about the appropriate time. The Civil Service Department have also trained staff in assessment and in using their new form, partly through programmed learning techniques.[42]

'Management Assessments' gives the overall objective of the scheme as ensuring the maximum contribution of managerial manpower to the business objectives of the Corporation, and distinguishes five sub-objectives:

1 Conserving and improving resources by identifying individual abilities and potential
2 Improved performance in the current job
3 Identifying the individual's immediate training and development needs
4 Assessing potential, 'and, where appropriate, indicating to individual managers their career possibilities in next few years'
5 Encouraging self-development.

Perhaps the most interesting aspect of the form is the division between the performance and the potential aspects. Until the recent use of page 6 for (future) performance objectives, the measurable objectives previously agreed with the job holders, which the pamphlet recommended, were dealt with in the section 'Review of performance', in the 'Job holder's section' (if he desired) and in the 'Notes on the interview'. The pamphlet reinforces what is said under the latter heading by mentioning that it will include measures which can be taken by either of them to further improve future performance. Incidentally, it should be noted that the assessor's 'Review of performance' of his subordinate (section 2) has not necessarily been shown to the latter, who may have been asked to fill in section 3 beforehand. Although the form merely calls this the 'Job holder's section', the explanatory pamphlet lays down that the manager 'must have the opportunity to comment in writing on his performance'.

The section on 'Development potential' is supported by advice that an outline should be given of the individual's potential in terms of the qualities, knowledge, experience, aptitude and abilities 'displayed in doing his job, or for which there is other evidence'. Beyond this, such traits as 'the degree of decisiveness shown and especially whether it is firmly and accurately based', 'self-confidence in the face of unexpected or unfamiliar situations', 'ability to work constructively with colleagues, with subordinates and with superiors', and the care shown in developing subordinates, are some of the suggested points for comment. On section 6, 'The development plan', the pamphlet remarks that 'frequently' there will be no development plan to propose, and that plans unlikely to be realised should not be put forward. In addition there are three pages of notes for assessors on the conduct of assessment interviews.

In one variant on the head office BSC form and procedure, the 'Review of performance' is completed by the superior and the form given to the manager who 'then has the opportunity to comment in writing on his performance', as well as suggesting how he would like his career to develop. Also, the manager 'should be invited to read and initial' the 'Notes on the interview', and there is a marked space for that purpose immediately above the space for the comments by the assessor's superior. There has also been a supplementary sheet inserted into the head office form entitled 'Job description, part 2, targets' which will presumably now be replaced by the 'Agreed personal performance objectives' on page 6 of the head office form.

Conceptually there are few problems in the design of the appraisal forms, and not many problems prior to their completion, apart from the topic just touched upon, whether or not the subordinate should see his assessment, in whole or part. After completion, however, the same problem arises again, this time in the form of confidentiality versus usefulness. Broadly, the argument is that if the form is seen only by the assessor, the reviewing committee and those relatively senior management development personnel who have to handle it, it will be filled in more frankly and therefore be more valuable than if the form is, for example, available to appointing committees outside the unit or function that employs the manager. At present, assessment forms provide the basis for lists of managers classified according to their potential, who may be available for particular jobs. These lists are used in internal executive searches.

There is an argument for managers being able to see their superior's assessment of them on the grounds that this is conducive to trust between manager and superior, and to a sense of realism on the part of both. It can also be argued that providing assessments, or at least reviews, are made on a reasonably comparable basis, the benefits (to those assessed) from making, say, the last three forms available in cases of possible promotion, demotion or dismissal, are greater in terms of fairness than the consequences of reduced confidentiality. However, this is a matter of some emotion, at least in the early stages of a new appraisal scheme.

It is also one of the many areas in which a study of the practice of a sample of organisations and the underlying reasons would be helpful.

Appraisal interviews and counselling

If a prime purpose of management assessment is to improve a manager's performance in his present job, the appraisal interview must be critical to success. Improved performance is going to come primarily from changes the manager makes in his own behaviour, and such changes are only likely if and when he has been convinced that they are desirable. Unless the appraisal is felt to be fair, and the interviewing and counselling session conducted in a way that is acceptable to him, he is unlikely to be convinced. In fact there is evidence that the way the superior handles the interview is the best predictor of whether constructive action will follow from it.[43]

At first sight the very real desire of most managers to 'know how they are getting on', so often reflected in the *cri de cœur* that they can only assume they are doing satisfactorily because they continue to get salary increases, would suggest that managers would welcome the opportunity of discussing their progress, developmental needs and career prospects. Yet much of the evidence is that appraisal interviews are potentially hazardous, and frequently dysfunctional if not disastrous, particularly to the relationship between manager and superior.

The most fundamental critique of traditional performance appraisal stems from research carried out in the General Electric Company of America, and reported by Meyer, Kay and French.[44] They devoted particular attention to appraisal interviews, for the reason already given. In particular they interviewed managers and subordinates separately about their experiences of appraisal sessions, arranged a later experiment with assessors who deliberately used high and low participative styles, observed 92 interviews and checked the results on performance over the following 12 weeks against what the superiors had hoped for when they made their comments. Finally they conducted a one-year study to validate their conclusions and also a new system which the research had developed, called 'work planning and review'.

All this was done in a plant where the appraisal system was already judged to be good. Before the investigation, appraisals had been based on job responsibilities and not on personal characteristics, and appraisers had had intensive training which included conducting appraisal interviews. In addition the scheme was strongly supported by the plant manager and personnel staff, so that 90 per cent of the staff concerned were actually appraised and interviewed annually.

The major conclusion from the first part of the project was that traditional appraisals did not achieve their intended results. Criticism led to defensiveness, and had a negative effect on the achievement of goals, whereas praise had little effect. Furthermore, discussion of salary increases so dominated interviews that afterwards neither superior nor subordinate had been in the right frame of mind to plan performance improvements. On the other hand, the mutual setting of specific goals, rather than criticism, did lead to improved performance, and subordinates' participation in the setting of goals contributed to this.

In the first series of interviews, which lasted from 30 to 90 minutes, an average of 32 specific performance items were covered in each case, of which 13 were criticisms. The typical subordinate reacted defensively to 7 of these—for example, denying the point, blaming others or providing excuses. In addition, the more criticism a man received, the more defensive he became. In the opinion of the observers there were few constructive responses, and it was suggested that the defensiveness arose because the great majority of those appraised found themselves less highly rated than they had personally expected, so that the interview had been a deflating experience. This explanation applied to managers of high as well as of low ability. Other research has also shown that self-ratings tend to be considerably more favourable than ratings by superiors,[45] and this explanation is further supported by two investigators from the Harvard Business School, who commented, 'Performance appraisal touches on one of the most emotionally charged activities in business life—the assessment of a man's contributions and ability. The signals he receives about this assessment have a strong impact on his self-esteem *and* on his subsequent performance'. They found that reduced ratings, even of men who were still graded as above-average performers, led to discouragement, and this to reduced effort, so starting a vicious cycle.[46]

The General Electric follow-up study, made ten to twelve weeks later, is notable for two findings. In general, those who had received an above-average number of criticisms in the interviews showed *less* goal achievement in the period than their colleagues who had been less criticised, although they had scored only slightly lower on total ratings and so were presumably not significantly less able. Second, after the first series of interviews, each man appraised had been asked to name the most criticised aspect of his performance. At the end of the follow-up period, improvement in these particular areas was 'considerably less' than the achievements in other areas. The critical interviews had apparently reduced performance instead of improving it.

The General Electric Work Planning and Review Programme is a form of management by objectives, with a stronger emphasis on appraisal than is usual in MBO. Discussions take place, considerably more frequently than once a year, on progress towards past goals, on the solution of current problems and on future goals. 'The intent of the method is to create a situation in which manager and subordinate can discuss job performance and needed improvements in detail without the subordinate becoming defensive.'[47] Salary reviews are conducted separately, and 'no summary judgments or rating [are] made'.

As it happened, Meyer, Kay and French were able, after their first experiment, to compare the results obtained by half the managers in the works trying out the new Work Planning and Review Programme, while the remainder stayed with the traditional performance appraisal. The results of attitude survey questionnaires, before and after an experimental year, were very clear. In particular, members of the WP & R group had far more often taken specific actions to improve results than had their colleagues. They also commented on : getting more help from their superior to improve job performance, feeling that their abilities and experience were used more, feeling that they were trying to attain the right targets, finding their managers having greater receptivity to their new ideas, and getting better value from the performance discussions they had had. These had often taken the form of the subordinate reviewing developments and performance since the previous meeting, so that the manager 'was automatically cast in the role of a counsellor', not a judge.

An earlier experiment by Blake and Mouton supports these findings.[48] They contrasted the effects of the traditional authority-based appraisal of how well a subordinate has carried out his duties with a 'collaborative interview based on a goals system and oriented towards mutual goal setting for future performance'. The latter approach showed :

1   Significantly more even sharing of power between superior and subordinate

2 Greater sense of being part of a team
3 Much higher satisfaction for both parties.

Under the traditional approach the subordinate felt little responsibility to change his behaviour, despite being so counselled, because he had no belief that he was able to change the situation. Under a goals approach, both superior and subordinate felt 'a moderately high degree' of responsibility for changing behaviour.

Other psychologists have also commented on the problems involved in criticising subordinates. Maier suggested many years ago that satisfactory experiences for interviewer and interviewee go together, so that appraisal can be a constructive experience for both.[49] Difficulties arise when the superior judges and the subordinate questions the judgment made. Likert, speaking of the practices current in 1959, suggested that they 'compel the superior to behave in a threatening, rejecting and ego deflating way. . . . this . . . seriously impairs the capacity of the *superior* to function effectively.'[50] Indeed, there are reported cases of managers 'cooking' the appraisal system to justify salary changes, and of a rank-ordering scheme leading to managers inevitably regarding and treating those 'below average' as inadequate, and this leading to a spiral of low expectations and low performance.[51]

The increasing use of MBO approaches (where properly carried out) has gone a long way towards changing the appraisal interview from being an almost entirely 'manager-to-subordinate' situation, to being a two-way relationship, with the interdependence that customarily exists in real life demonstrated in the joint setting of objectives. Advice from the superior is concerned with what actions the subordinate should take, and not with how the latter should change himself, that is, his personality. In addition, the superior puts his cachet on the suitability of the targets, accepts responsibility for providing organisation and resources appropriate to them, and in these ways, and through coaching and monitoring, shares responsibility for performance. The situation shown in Figure 13:1 has become a constructive one, and is no longer potentially threatening.

A recent analysis by Burke and Wilcox[52] of the nature of effective appraisal interviews essentially confirms the validity of the General Electric studies. These authors distinguish four essential characteristics:

1 A high level of subordinate participation, indicated by, for example, the superior doing more listening than talking.

2 A helpful and constructive attitude by the superior. The greater the threat to the manager's self-esteem, the more his defensiveness, the less favourable his attitudes towards the appaisal system, and the less the subsequent improvements in job performance.[53]

3 A mutual approach to solving job problems, with a common interest in developing the subordinate.

4 Mutual setting of specific short-term goals for the subordinate, which led to more than twice as much improvement in performance as the making of criticisms without goal setting.[54]

Is this American evidence relevant to Britain? Most practitioners would accept that it is, and agree that improved managerial performance is only likely where the climate encourages managerial growth. Just what this means and how it can be achieved has been explored at length in the literature of organisational psychology and organisational development,[55] but in McGregor's convenient shorthand, it requires a philosophy much nearer Theory Y than Theory X. Within this the superior may more readily move from being a judge who issues both rewards and remonitions to being a coach who encourages individuals to develop themselves.

At present many British managers do not fully appreciate the case for focusing on future objectives, and for being helpful, or 'supportive' towards subordinates. Indeed the very word 'supportive' commonly seems to suggest to managers that it is another of their responsibilities to help carry 'lame duck' subordinates, and this arouses resentment. However, the move in recent years towards Theory Y by many of the companies best known for their awareness of the significance of the process of managing, such as Shell, ICI, Unilever and BAT, shows that this type of change is possible, and that, over time, given positive leadership by example as well as exhortation, and suitable training, much can be achieved.

Two practical questions require mention. What should be done about discussing salary changes or promotion prospects, which has often been done in the appraisal interview, and to what extent, if any, may criticism usefully be made of a subordinate? On the first point, attempting to deal with appraisal, salaries and prospects at one time is an instance of multiple objectives leading to poor results on each. It is now generally agreed that the discussion of either salaries or promotion prospects is incompatible with the atmosphere required for successful counselling, and should be dealt with in separate interviews. Quite possibly, as Rowe suggests, discussions on prospects should take place between the manager and his boss's superior, every two or three years.

What has been said about criticising subordinates is often misunderstood : in particular it is not suggested that all criticising is bad, or always to be avoided, but that criticisms in a counselling interview tend to lead to defensive attitudes, and to resentment, and that this gets in the way of constructive action. Comments on specific incidents, or inadequacies in results or methods used, often require to be made, and should be made at the time, or in the next informal review session, and thus got out of the way as soon as possible. Criticism can often be quite effective in getting someone not to repeat something. Probably because of the attitudes engendered, it is less effective in encouraging positive action. Perhaps managers should always ask how far criticisms of a subordinate are likely to lead to improved future performance before they indulge in the luxury of giving vent to judgments from their position of superiority. However, joint goal-setting and the mutual consideration of difficulties and of the resources needed tend to lead to constructive action. On both of these practical points, there is the same underlying difficulty : the roles of judge and of counsellor cannot easily be combined in one interview.

Finally, interviewing is not something that comes naturally to managers, so training is essential. The Civil Service Department, having recently changed the basis of its appraisal interviews onto job performance, past and future, from personal qualities, has engaged in such a training effort. It has made a 45-minute film called *The Man on the Job*, accompanied by a training manual, as one part of its campaign. It is also running three-day courses at the Civil Service College to train departmental instructors in the aims of the system and in how to interview, by means of practice sessions which are intended both to remove faults and establish confidence. The film emphasises the need for preparation by both parties before the interview, shows how a trained interviewer can, as a result of the training, prevent a counselling session from going wrong, as well as the need for follow-up action on the information obtained in the interview.

How often should appraisal take place?

One of the benefits of appraisals being based on results and managerial practice is that the appraisal is part of the process of managing, and not something extraneous. There will be various informal reviews of progress anyway, of a frequency appropriate to the task being done or, broadly, the managerial level. In addition there will be more formal appraisals for particular purposes.

Under management by objectives, each target is likely to have its own appropriate review dates, both during progress towards the objective (when methods used will be one important focus) and on completion of the task, or at the end of an agreed time period. These are likely to be relatively informal reviews, and should be sufficiently frequent to avoid either favourable or adverse comments becoming unduly disconnected in time from the events to which they relate. Reviews may also be desirable when targets have to be changed.

In a junior managerial post, it may be that the tasks are relatively routine and unchanging. If so some of the objectives may be discussed on a convenient calendar basis such as monthly. For other objectives a time span of quarterly reviews or possibly even longer may be more appropriate where the manager is experienced. A full appraisal of progress and the setting of further objectives might well be held every six months. The appraisal of training needs might take place at alternate six-month reviews, and salary adjustments at the same frequency (though not at the same meeting).

The head of a function where change is frequent might have fortnightly or even weekly review and goal-setting sessions on some matters critical for the firm—say its cash flow, or sales progress on a new product. Other goals might be informally reviewed monthly or quarterly, and formal appraisals of overall progress take place quarterly or half-yearly. Objectives for the next year, or even five years, might be reviewed and updated on a rolling basis at each quarterly meeting.

There is a general feeling at the present time that annual formal reviews are too frequent, though no comparative studies of different time spans appear to have been made as yet. Annual discussion of development programmes is normally sufficient. It is useful to discuss career prospects more frequently with, say, relatively recent entrants at lower levels, than with senior managers. In the former case various forms of career progress besides promotion are not only relevant, but more of a burning issue, and are also likely to occur more frequently than the major moves of the executive, who is presumably much more settled in the organisation.

Review and comparison

It has been remarked that appraisals are usually made by a manager's immediate superior, and that this evaluation is later reviewed by the latter's own boss or the management development committee for a unit of the organisation, such as a works, division or function. Typically the secretary of such a reviewing committee is a professional management development man, and he sends the committee's findings, in abstract, or possibly in detail for managers above a certain level, to a higher unit—or functional—management development committee. Sometimes the committee secretary is on the staff of the central personnel department, so that he is 'above' any local pressures, and more importantly, brings organisation-wide standards to bear on the unit's high flyers, for example, so that there is a broad similarity of treatment for men believed to be of approximately similar ability.

Usually the review of appraisals of the top two or three levels in an organisation is made by the chief executive and some board members with responsibility for appointments at these levels. In Standard Oil of New Jersey the Compensation and Executive Development Committee, consisting of the Chairman, President and three Executive Vice-Presidents, meets for half a day each week to consider the development of the top 250 executives and their planned replacements. This suggests that in most organisations the management development emphasis moves increasingly from improved performance in the present job to concern with potential for higher posts as the seniority of those appraised rises.

There are four major reasons for reviewing appraisals at a high level. The first two—the problem of making judgments of a man as objective as possible and the need for someone to compare men assessed by different superiors—are obvious. In addition, managers of lower units can normally only assess, recommend and plan development on the basis of needs in their jurisdiction. Ultimately management development has to be based on company requirements. Frequently talent is unevenly spread in the units and functions of a large organisation, so superior reviewing bodies are concerned to try to use the total resources that the company possesses to the best advantage. For this reason, there is typically a network of lower-level reviewing bodies meshing in to that chaired by the chief executive.

At a more mundane level, there is a good deal of evidence that unless superiors do review and comment upon the appraisals made by their staff, the attention given by the latter to appraising is reduced, forms are filled in casually, and the consequences are likely to be harmful to managerial morale.

In my experience, where reviews are taken seriously by senior managers or the management development committee of the works or function, penetrating comments by the superiors are quite frequent. In particular, the additional height in the hierarchy improves the overall view which can be taken, so that comments on possible development plans, cross-posting and other recommendations are noticeably wider and done from a company-wide point of view. In one company, in instances where the original raters were known to have particularly high or low standards, reviewers seemed to have gone to considerable trouble to form their own impressions of those being assessed, and to correct (in their judgment) their immediate subordinate's veiws.

At some point, choices have to be made between different managers, and this is always a ticklish business in terms of the possible reactions from the managers concerned, and management morale generally if it is felt that the wrong decision has been taken, quite apart from the direct disadvantage to the organisation. With the traits approach, and five-point ratings from very good to very bad, for example, it was easy and attractive to turn these into numerical ratings, and add up total scores for managers, which in effect compounded the weaknesses in the traits approach.

With performance-based appraisal, scoring is virtually unknown and it is a matter of assessing the suitability of each individual for promotion or transfer. Assuming that the work done by different managers is not directly comparable, questions like the following have to be asked:

1 Were the evaluated achievements in results and in performance as a manager outstanding, average or poor, in absolute terms, and in comparison with others?
2 Can any distinguishing characteristics of the manager under review be identified, and if so, what relevance have they to the purpose of the comparison?

Two practical comments may be added. The more precisely identified the job for which a man is being considered, the more likely senior managers are to make a good judgment in the light of assessments and their own experience. Second, the closer the man's previous jobs (or special assignments, for example) have been to the proposed new job, the more helpful the past assessments are likely to be. A grading of an individual as 'potential for director level' could be quite misleading for some jobs, however accurate it is in itself.

Individual appraisal the right approach?

Over the past decade, individual appraisal as such has come under increasing attack from several directions. Katz and Kahn, the social psychologists, were quoted early in this chapter as regarding individual appraisal as 'partaking of surveillance' and out of accord with democratic values. Likewise, it has been said to encourage dependency and paternalism.[56]

Dissatisfaction with existing approaches led one region of the US Internal Revenue Service to develop two-way 'exchanges of expectations', with superior and subordinate considering how to improve the *relationship* between them. However, it was found that few pairs of managers welcomed this approach. Although there were some gains in mutual understanding, most subordinates had difficulty in stating their expectations of their bosses. Further examination of the organisation led to the identification of multiple sources of power, such as line authority and functional authority, and the emphasis changed to seeking better ways of using these power networks. This in turn has led to 'a concern for how individuals and groups are going about [their] accomplishments' rather than what is being accomplished. It is argued that the process (which has only been outlined here) produces greater commitment and individual responsibility than performance appraisal at either individual or unit level, partly because, it is said, the relationship in which the superior is controller of his subordinate is now a myth.[57]

Other writers have also developed the last point, saying that management will be increasingly participative in the future, or is anyway carried out by teams of managers.[58] Still others argue that the difficulties and subjectivity involved make appraisal invalid, or that appraisal changes a collaborative, trusting relationship into something less constructive which is bad for both assessor and assessed, so that the disadvantages outweigh any benefits.

So far, no one has tried to assess the numerical significance of those situations in which lateral relationships prevail, or where individuals work in teams to such an extent that their contributions cannot meaningfully be isolated, in comparison with the large number of more traditional situations where the quality of different managers significantly influences results. Are there really very many of the former, or is it less a reflection of real managerial situations than a pretext for an aversion to having to make hard judgments?

On the second point, the subjectivity of appraisal is an undoubted fact, but to confuse this with error is another matter. In this respect assessments are no different to many other managerial decisions, including selection, salary increases, redundancy and many disciplinary matters. Given the apparent inevitability of judging, it seems best to concentrate our efforts on doing so as effectively, fairly and openly as possible.

On the third point, the nature of managing is such that friendly, collaborative team relationships are not possible all the time even in small units. Where they exist in large ones, there has been a good deal of experience in Britain and elsewhere of organisational purpose deteriorating into cosier personal objectives. Tough-mindedness, in William James's sense, is one of the requirements for the successful manager.

The arguments against individual appraisals—whether grounded on its supposed incompatibility with democratic values, its alleged irrelevance to modern management situations or its imperfections—may apply in some instances or cultures. However, until we reach an age of perfect trust and highly motivated performance, some form of appraisal and counselling is likely to continue in most large organisations, anyway, and to be preferable to some as yet inadequately specified alternative. *Better* appraisal should be our immediate concern.

Appraisal in practice

When one contemplates how appraisal and counselling are done in very many firms, and how they are typically not done in most non-profit organisations, considerable opportunity for improvement is obvious, both in Britain and most other countries.

Appraising for the improvement of performance in the near future leads only to relatively straightforward problems. Presenting the results to managers so that they take action to effect improvement is more complex, for two reasons. First, the organisational climate and prevailing management styles must be conducive to individual experimentation and development. Broadly, this is only likely where the climate can be characterised as much nearer McGregor's Theory Y than his Theory X.

Second, the psychological evidence on how individuals react to being appraised is very clear. Assessment against agreed standards, with the emphasis put on how to do better in the future, with the help and encouragement of the superior, is likely to lead to individual commitment. On the other hand, critical, verbally punitive appraisal almost always leads to reduced performance and possibly to psychological withdrawal. Virtually the same thought can be put another way : when managers ask to be told how well they are doing, they are really wishing to be assured that they are doing well. And this is part of the human condition, not some conscious piece of bloody-mindedness.

Some comments on aspects of practice may also be offered. Assessment should be against agreed standards, because this reduces appreciably the difficulties both of appraising and of counselling. If some halo effect is inherent in any assessment, or in the evaluation of results, it is likely to be reduced when the superior has assessed a manager several times and gained experience both of judging this subordinate within the latter's system of relationships, and judging the significance of other variables such as the environmental. This argues for appraisal more often than annually and a normal job-holding period of not less than three or four appraisal cycles. Many firms would also benefit from examining more specifically than they do now, the methods used in achieving the results, as Koontz advocates. Little attention has been paid in Britain to appraisal by people other than the immediate superior. Assessment centres, and appraisals by peers, subordinates and groups of superiors, all offer possible advantages.

The appraisal of potential does not seem to have been studied to any significant extent; the value of the evidence available is not clear, but it does raise questions about the validity, or usefulness, of much of the assessment of potential currently being done. Moral judgments about 'crown prince' systems may be one reason for it, but at present a good deal of managerial effort may be wasted. This is an area where some good research studies are urgently needed.

Like many other management systems, effective appraisal and counselling schemes require regular nourishment from top management, so done as to ensure that there is something—preferably positive—in it to make the task of appraising worth while for the appraisers. A scheme has to be acceptable to the managers involved, or it is likely to cause harm. And schemes need to be supported by training, since neither appraising nor counselling come naturally to us.

A good appraisal and counselling scheme is costly in terms of managerial time and effort. However, done in the way suggested, it is part of the task of managing, and not something extraneous to it. In this way, it has a great deal to contribute to improved organisational performance immediately, and also in the long run by ensuring that the most able candidates are promoted. The potential returns are very high.

Notes and references

I should like to thank my colleague, Mr A. G. Lees, for the helpful comments he made on an early draft of this chapter and Mrs J. M. Newman for her excellent typing of the various versions.

1   Thompson, P. H. and Dalton, G. W., 'Performance Appraisal: Managers Beware', *Harvard Business Review* (January/February 1970).
2   Whisler, T. L. and Harper, S. F., *Performance Appraisal: Research and Practice* (Holt, Rinehart and Winston, N.Y., 1962), discuss most research up to that time, and reprint many of the major articles.
3   Katz, D. and Kahn, R. L., *The Social Psychology of Organizations* (Wiley, 1966), p. 240.
4   BIM, *Management Appraisal Practices*, Information Summary 133, 1967.
5   BIM, *Performance Appraisals: What Managers Think*, Information Summary 136, 1969, p. 5.
6   Campbell, A. D., Dunnette, M., Lawler, E. E. and Weick, K., *Managerial Behaviour, Performance and Effectiveness* (McGraw-Hill, 1970).
7   Kappell, F. R., Chairman, American Telephone and Telegraph, quoted in Labovitz, G. H., 'In Defence of Subjective Executive Appraisal', *Academy of Management Journal* (September 1969).
8   See, for example, part 1 of Costello, T. W. and Zalkind, S. S., *Psychology in Administration* (Prentice-Hall, 1963).
9   These statements are drawn from Labovitz (see note 7) and Costello and Zalkind where the evidence for them is given. Many other statements to similar effect could be cited.

10 Quoted in Lopez, F. M., *Evaluating Employee Performance* (Public Personnel Association, Chicago, 1968), p. 163.

11 Rowe, K. M., 'An Appraisal of Appraisals', *Journal of Management Studies*, Vol. 1, No. 1 (March 1964), p. 5. If this is because the supervisors wished to avoid having to tell anyone that he or she is 'below average', their instincts were sound, as will be seen later.

12 Koontz, H. and O'Donnell, C., *Principles of Management*, 5th Edition (McGraw-Hill, 1972), p. 458.

13 Elliott, A. G. D., 'Revising a Merit Rating Scheme', *Institute of Personnel Management*, 1955; quoted on pages 12–13 of the BIM book referred to in note 4.

14 Miner, J. B., 'Bridging the Gulf in Organizational Performance', *Harvard Business Review* (July/August 1968), p. 104.

15 Taft, R., 'The Ability to Judge People', *Psychological Bulletin*, Vol. 52, No. 1 (January 1955), and reprinted in Whisler and Harper (see note 2).

16 BIM Information Summary cited in note 5 and, for the last point, Greiner, L. E., *et al.*, 'Putting Judgement Back into Decisions', *Harvard Business Review*, 48:2 (March/April 1970).

17 Beach, D. S., *Personnel* (Macmillan, N.Y., 1970), p. 325.

18 Hollander, E. P., 'Buddy Ratings: Military Research and Industrial Implications', *Personnel Psychology*, Vol. 7, No. 3 (Autumn 1954), pp. 385–93, reprinted by Whisler and Harper (see note 2), with other material on this topic.

19 Korman, A. K., 'The Prediction of Managerial Performance: A Review', *Personnel Psychology*, Vol. 21 (1968), pp. 313–14.

20 Levinson, H., 'Management by Whose Objectives?', *Harvard Business Review* (July/August 1970), p. 132.

21 Lawler, E. E., 'The Multitrait-Multirater Approach to Measuring Managerial Job Performance', *Journal of Applied Psychology*, Vol. 51 (1967), pp. 369–81.

22 Their approach has recently been at least partly defended by Kavanagh, M. J., in 'The Content Issue in Performance Appraisal: A Review', *Personnel Psychology*, Vol. 24 (1971), pp. 653–68.

23 McGregor, D., 'An Uneasy Look at Performance Appraisals', *Harvard Business Review* (May/June 1957).

24 Rowe, K. M., 'An Appraisal of Appraisals', *Journal of Management Studies*, Vol. 1, No. 1 (March 1964), pp. 6–9. Koontz, H., *Appraising Managers as Managers* (McGraw-Hill 1971), pp. 22–4.

25 Andrews, K. R., 'Is Management Training Effective? II Measurement, Objectives and Policy', *Harvard Business Review* (March/April 1957), p. 68.

26 See Koontz, *Appraising Managers as Managers*, cited in note 24; the point is discussed further below.

27 Each question is related to the relevant passages in Koontz and O'Donnell, *Principles of Management*, 4th Edition (McGraw-Hill, 1968).

28 Thompson, P. H. and Dalton, G. W., 'Performance Appraisal: Managers Beware', *Harvard Business Review* (January/February 1970).

29 Kellog, M. S., *Closing the Performance Gap*, AMA (1967), pp. 84–5.

30 Lopez, F. M., *The Making of a Manager*, AMA (1970), p. 276.

31 Oberg, W., 'Make Performance Appraisal Relevant', *Harvard Business Review* (January/February 1972).

32 Miner, J. B., 'Bridging the Gulf in Organizational Performance', *Harvard Business Review* (July/August 1968), pp. 108–9.

33 Miller, E. L., 'Identifying High Potential Managerial Personnel', *Michigan Business Review*, November 1968. 'High Potential for What' (unpublished) goes further into these and other aspects of the topic.

34 Taft, R., in 'The Ability to Judge People', *Psychological Bulletin*, Vol. 52, No. 1 (January 1955), and reprinted by Whisler and Harper (see note 2).

35 Miner, J. B., 'Bridging the Gulf in Organizational Performance', *Harvard Business Review* (July/August 1968), pp. 108–9.

36 Ferguson, L. L., 'Better Management of Managers' Careers', *Harvard Business Review* (March/April 1966), pp. 141–2.

37 Korman, A. K., 'The Prediction of Managerial Performance: A Review', *Personnel Psychology*, Vol. 21 (1968), pp. 295–322. Quotation from p. 319.

38 I am grateful to Mr D. B. Moody for this information.

39 Byham, W. C., 'Assessment Centres for Spotting Future Managers', *Harvard Business Review* (July/August 1970).

40 Ferguson, L. L., 'Better Management of Managers' Careers', *Harvard Business Review* (March/April 1966), p. 147.

41 I am indebted to Mr J. E. A. King, Head of Management Appointments and Development, for permission to reproduce this form.

42 Civil Service Department : *Second Report, 1970–71*, HMSO, p. 25.
43 Meyer, H. H. and Walker, W.B., 'A study of factors relating to the effectiveness of a performance appraisal programme', *Personnel Psychology*, 14 (1961), pp. 291–8, quoted by Burke and Wilcox (see note 52).
44 Meyer, H. H., *et al.*, 'Split Roles in Performance Appraisal', *Harvard Business Review* (January/February 1965), contains most of their findings. It has been reprinted in several books of readings.
45 Miner, J. B., *Personnel Psychology* (Macmillan, 1969), p. 93.
46 Thompson, P. H. and Dalton, G. W., 'Performance Appraisal : Managers Beware', *Harvard Business Review* (January/February 1970).
47 Meyer, H. H., *et al.* (see note 44), p. 128.
48 Blake, R. R. and Mouton, J. S., 'Power, People and Performance Reviews', *Advanced Management* (July/August 1961); and in several books of readings.
49 Maier, N. R. F., *The Appraisal Interview: Objectives, Methods and Skills* (Wiley, 1958).
50 Likert, R., 'Motivational Approach to Management Development', *Harvard Business Review* (July/August 1959).
51 Reference 1.
52 Burke, R. J. and Wilcox, D. S., 'Characteristics of Effective Employee Performance Review and Development Interviews', *Personnel Psychology*, 22 (1969), pp. 291–305.
53 Anderson, J., 'Giving and Receiving Feedback', in Dalton, Lawrence and Greiner, *Organizational Change and Development* (Irwin, 1970), goes further into these matters.
54 French, J. R. P., Kay, E. and Meyer, H. H., 'Participation and the Appraisal System', *Human Relations*, Vol. 19 (1966), p. 11.
55 See, for example, Katz, D. and Kahn, R. L., *The Social Psychology of Organization* (Wiley, 1966); or Schein, E. H., *Organizational Psychology* (Prentice-Hall, 1970); the six pamphlets in the Addison-Wesley series on OD, or Fordyce, J. K. and Weil, R., *Managing with People* (Addison-Wesley, 1971); Paul Hill's *Towards a New Philosophy of Management* (Gower Press, 1971) records the company development programme at Shell UK Limited.
56 Fitzgerald, T. H., 'Appraisals : Personality, Performance, and Persons', *California Management Review* (Winter 1965), p. 84.

57 White, F. B. and Barnes, L. B., 'Power Networks in the Appraisal Process', *Harvard Business Review* (May/June 1971).
58 Levinson, H., 'Management by Whose Objectives?', *Harvard Business Review* (July/August 1970).

14

The Management by Objectives Approach

Angus Reid, Corporate Planner, Tennent Caledonian Breweries Ltd

Management by objectives (MBO) is an approach which many companies now claim to have introduced, yet on closer examination these applications often turn out to be comparatively limited in scope. Frequently they affect only middle or junior management, with the result that they concentrate on improving performance of those managers within an existing framework of company aims—either specified or assumed.

MBO should be applied as a total approach to managing, so as to question the existing situation at every level, clarify corporate objectives and then provide the framework of organisation, plans and controls to achieve them.

Principles of management by objectives

Management by objectives is based upon the simple and obvious concepts that unless you know where you want to go you are unlikely to get there, and unless you know what results you want to achieve you are unlikely to achieve them.

An objective in MBO language is a definition of where a business—its board, its departments and its individual managers—wants to go. It has three essential elements; it must:

1 Define the starting point or present position
2 Specify the finishing point
3 State the time by which the goal is to be reached.

Whenever possible the end result should be quantitative or at least positively identifiable, for example:

Objective for a company: To increase profitability on assets employed from $x\%$ on $£A$ assets employed to $y\%$ on $£B$.
Objective for a production manager: To reduce losses from $a\%$ to $b\%$ by September 1973.

These objectives imply that a large amount of preliminary research and planning has been undertaken to establish their validity. If they are to be achieved, there must be a great deal of subsequent planning and coordination at all levels in the company. Company objectives should be directly related to the corporate aims of the enterprise. They should also be the fountain from which all lower-level objectives are developed.

Once the overall purpose of a company has been defined, it is possible to identify areas of performance that would be vital to the achievement of that purpose. These are known as 'key result areas'. This identification of key result areas aids further analysis by separating the essential from the nonessential and acting as a reminder of the really important headings under which objectives should be set.

Each key area is then subjected to a critical review of present performance. This leads to a consideration of constraints, problems and opportunities and on to courses of action that might be taken to improve results.

However, the setting of objectives by themselves rarely achieves the goal. Every objective must be broken down into defined action to be taken by subordinate units and managers, by specified times, before it comes to life. This action itself must be carefully planned and controlled to produce those predicted measurable results which will directly contribute to the attainment of the objective concerned.

Installation of MBO in a company

Management advisers should be appointed, preferably from within the company, and trained. Their function is vital until the process is well enough established to be accepted as the way of managing within the business. They assist top management in clarifying objectives and ensure that these are understood by other managers.

They assist each job holder and his senior to achieve mutual understanding of key results, levels of performance and the associated controls.

They help to draw, from the managers, problems and suggestions and opportunities for improving results. They encourage managers to plan for improvements. They help seniors to identify ways in which they can help subordinates to improve. In short, the adviser is a catalyst who increases the rate at which all the desired reactions take place.

Each manager in the company from foreman, supervisor or area sales manager up to and including the managing director has his job analysed. In practice he does this himself with the active help of the management adviser and a management guide (MG) is produced.

The MG is not a job description of the usual sort. It specifies not only the main areas of responsibility of the job holder, but also the actual results to be achieved if he is performing each task well, and the means by which the progress can be measured and monitored. The finalised MG is agreed with the job holder's senior.

The job holder and his senior agree short-term objectives for certain of the areas enumerated on the MG, or as a contribution to company objectives. These objectives are to be achieved within a defined period, and a job improvement plan (JIP) is produced.

At defined periods the job holder and his senior hold a meeting to formally review the job, including actual achievement against short-term objectives.

This job review is not a performance inquest to apportion blame. It is only concerned with why things did not happen in so far as this helps to identify the action which can be taken in the future to achieve better results. At the end of the review further short-term objectives are agreed.

THE MANAGEMENT BY OBJECTIVES APPROACH

Management guides

Purpose

When a manager's duties are analysed it can usually be shown that 20 per cent of the activities account for 80 per cent of the results achieved. The management guide focuses attention on these critical areas and it thus differs from a traditional list of duties and responsibilities. The management guide serves the following purposes:

1   It provides a list of those results which a job holder has to achieve to ensure the attainment of good overall results by the company. These are referred to as 'key result areas'.
2   It records the currently feasible levels of results which the job holder has committed himself to attain or maintain in respect of his key result area. These are referred to as 'standards of performance'.
3   It lists the sources of information which will be used to measure the actual results relating to key result areas.
4   It thus provides a realistic basis against which to review management performance.

The management guide consists of two parts and when completed helps to provide a basis of understanding between every job holder and his senior.

Instructions to a manager on compiling a management guide

Part one

Main purpose of job
Give a concise answer to the questions: What am I doing to earn my salary? What is my contribution towards the company's success or profit pattern?

Position in organisation
Directly responsible to whom? (Give the title of your immediate superior.) —To whom do you go for a rise?

—To whom do you go for a day off?
(If you think you have two 'bosses'—write them both down.)
Subordinates directly supervised : (job titles only).
—To whom do you give direct instructions?
—Who comes to you for a rise or day off?

Size of job
This should indicate the size of your job in quantitative terms of financial, human and physical resources, i.e. numbers of men or machines, geographical size of sales territory, sterling value of sales of capital equipment, numbers of articles produced or sold or maintained, for example :
(a) Personnel : 2 section managers, 10 foremen, 200 workmen (annual wage bill £——)
(b) Stores : Spares and consumables valued at approximately £——
(c) Equipment and facilities : Machinery and buildings valued at approximately £——
(d) Revenue and expenditure : Approximate annual value of purchases.
(e) Projects (for technical staff) : Estimated annual value of all projects dealt with
(f) Volume : Estimated annual value of sales of production
(g) Or other indicators which demonstrate the financial importance of the job—such as the value of the annual expenditure budget.

Limits of authority
What can you not do in connection with your job?
What can you do to a limited degree?

Part two of the management guide

This part is divided into three areas :
—Key result areas (KRA)
—Standards of performance
—Means of measuring results.

Key result areas
First, you should refer to the total list of key result areas for the company or for the department within which you work, and identify those in which you are involved to a significant extent.

It is important to state at this stage that you are not trying to make a list of all your jobs and responsibilities—it is not a job specification—only the parts of the job which make the major contribution to the success of your position in the company.

Having listed the areas in which you consider you have a major responsibility, write a short sentence defining your contribution in that key area.

If you find that your sentence contains more than one active verb, you are probably combining tasks. For instance, an area sales manager could write under 'Sales' :

> To work out sales targets for each territory and review actual sales against targets each week and to take action such as is necessary to achieve the forecasted total sales turnover.

This is really three tasks, namely :
1   To achieve forecasted total sales turnover
2   To set targets for each salesman
3   To ensure achievement of sales targets.

Standards of performance

The performance standards should answer to the following description :
1   *Impersonal.* They should relate to the job and not the job holder. In view of this it may be necessary to indicate other departments or sections which can influence the level of results.
2   *Realistic.* Each standard should help to define the results that will be achieved if the task is being performed to the full satisfaction of your superior. It should not be a statement of ideal conditions or minimum acceptable conditions. It should, however, nominate a level of results at least as good as current performance, and preferably better.
3   *Relevant.* Standards should define results which, if they were not being achieved, would influence you and your senior to plan a course of remedial action. Each standard should be an indicator towards achieving the main purpose of the job.
4   *Precise.* It is important to avoid expressions like 'adequate', 'appropriate', 'approximately'. This is most easily satisfied when results can be directly measured in terms of quantity, quality, time, cost, etc., as in the case of production or sales turnover. In more difficult instances,

such as jobs of an advisory nature, it may be more convenient to refer to the consesuences of not doing the job well. Thus some of the standards for a designer's job may refer to the frequency with which production problems arise in manufacturing the parts to the specified drawings or the incidence of queries about ambiguities in the drawings.

In order to define the conditions for satisfactory performance of a key task precisely, it may also be necessary to use several complementary standards. In this case they should be lettered, *a, b, c,* etc.

5 *Acceptable.* The standard should not be based on guesswork. If it is not possible to determine reasonably accurately the level of results which are currently feasible, then further controls are necessary.

6 *Appropriate.* It is important to be clear whether the difference between the task being well done and not well done is related to time, how well, at what cost, how, etc.

Means of measuring results

The means of measuring results indicates how the job holder's superior is to become informed of whether or not he, the job holder, has performed his key task well. This may be by :

1 Visual inspection by the superior.
2 Weekly meetings with the superior to discuss results.
3 Weekly/monthly/three-monthly reports to the superior.
4 Submission of details at monthly intervals.
5 Possibly immediate notification to the superior whenever performance comes outside standard limits.
6 For quantitative standards the controls should be an identified document, such as an operating statement.

If no control is available, say so, and follow with suggestions (in the control column). If the cost of establishing the control is not consistent with the value gained by being able to assess performance against standard, then the chances are that the standard should be eliminated.

Performance record

Every manager's MG involves information collected by him, examined against current targets, acted upon and later passed to his senior.

THE MANAGEMENT BY OBJECTIVES APPROACH

Also the MG of all his subordinates will require that he examine their performance by either:

1 Receiving reports; or
2 Making periodic checks on their activities.

This does not mean that MBO introduces a separate system of controls, in addition to what exists already. What should happen is that the analytical approach of MBO should be used to overhaul the existing pattern of controls to ensure that it tells the right people what they need to know at the minimum cost.

As a handy running record of actual results against KRAs, a sheet entitled 'performance record' can be introduced to assist managers in checking their own performance against targets. It will list, for example:

1 Receiving figures and reports from subordinates at the required intervals
2 Making the daily/weekly/monthly checks on subordinates' activities as laid down in the appropriate MG.

On this sheet should be listed all the performance standards relating to all the KRAs on a manager's MG and the current targets reported in the 'planned performance' column. The frequency of checking and the actual results can then be entered to show the trends.

Job improvement plan

Once each job holder's involvement in company KRAs has been clarified, he can begin to determine the short-term objectives he should endeavour to achieve during the next 12 weeks or thereabouts.

Compiling the JIP

To arrive at these short-term objectives the job holder and his senior examine the current situation relating to each KRA, to see if any of the results need to be improved and, if so, by how much.

At this stage the senior will be taking into consideration :

1 The company objectives required by the board or objectives agreed with his own superior
2 Previous discussions he may have had with the job holder, perhaps when he was preparing or assisting to prepare company plans
3 Problems or opportunities arising within the job holder's own unit or section.

The outcome of these discussions will be a set of interlocking job improvement plans, each of which will show :

1 The company objective number
2 The contribution stated in 'objective' terms of the manager concerned
3 The subdivision of the objective with supporting contributions from each of the job holder's subordinates, his own personal contributions and any supporting action required from his senior or from managers in other functions
4 The present and target results, quantified where possible
5 Space for noting results progressively, during the period covered by the plan.

Approach

Considerations to be borne in mind in selecting items for inclusion in a job improvement plan include the following :

1 Subjects which are directly related to cost reduction should be given priority.
2 A quicker return is likely to come from those items where the job holder can make significant progress on his own authority without waiting for supporting action by colleagues or higher management.
3 The most fruitful areas are those where present results are known, required results can be specified and progress towards these specified results can be measured.

Further action

Approval
The senior will discuss the draft JIP with his senior to ensure that it is consistent with overall company objectives.

Circulation
Within one week of the meeting at which it is drafted, the final version of the JIP should be in the hands of the job holder concerned. The only other full copy will be retained by his senior and both copies may be hand-written.

Amendment
Like all plans, the JIP may have to be modified in the light of subsequent events such as hold-ups, changes in procedure, etc. Whenever circumstances make it impossible to complete action, they must be reported to and agreed with the senior when they arise. Reasons given at the performance review for not achieving the action are likely to cause embarrassment if they relate to factors which had been known for some time but not reported.

Conclusion

The JIP, mutually agreed between manager and senior and prepared in the manner described, is an essential part of management by objectives, since it :

1 Compels clear thinking about the objectives that are of critical importance at any given time.
2 Provides a practical form for expressing priority results expected and the means of attaining them.
3 Together with the management guide it is an equitable and acceptable basis for reviewing a manager's performance.
4 Provides an opportunity for a manager to indicate where he requires support from higher management.

The quarterly review

At the end of the agreed short-term period—say 12 weeks—the job holder and his senior will meet to review the job formally—the job, it should be noted, and not the manager who is doing it.

It is important to strike the right note for a job review meeting. Essentially, it is a private discussion between a manager and his senior, where the MG is used as a basis for assessing how the job is going. The nature of the discussion should be friendly and helpful, but also constructive and jointly critical of the results that are being achieved.

It is not *primarily* a review of the job holder, rather a review of how well the job is fulfilling its defined purpose. Although the review illuminates the job holder's performance, it also spotlights the strengths and shortcomings of the senior. Therefore, it is wrong to create the impression that the purpose of the review is to diagnose the inadequacies of the job holder.

The job review is not a performance inquest. It is not primarily aimed at finding out who is to blame for past shortcomings. It is mainly concerned with the action that can be taken in the future to ensure that what is not happening now will happen thereafter.

The first review will certainly be attended by the management adviser and subsequent reviews by the adviser or senior's senior on a few occasions.

All concerned should have studied the quantifiable information specified in the MG and will therefore have compared actual achievements with the target objectives, before the meeting takes place.

Procedures before the review meeting

Quarterly performance review
Before the review meeting the senior should arrange for the quarterly review form to be updated. The document shows the job holder's actual performance against agreed standards of performance over a number of review periods, and should be available at the meeting, containing, in the case of quantifiable standards, actual results for the period to be discussed.

Job improvement plan
Before the review meeting the senior and job holder will individually have completed the 'actual results achieved' section against the short-term objectives (STO) set out.

First stage of the review meeting

The first stage of the review meeting is to examine the job holder's performance against agreed short-term objectives. The job holder is asked in respect of each STO : 'Has it or has it not been achieved?'

If the target has been achieved, the job holder should be congratulated, then the following question should be asked : 'Should the same target remains for the next period or can an improved target be set?' If a new target is to be set, this becomes one of the next period's short-term objectives.

If the target has not been achieved, there should be neither recrimination nor blame, the following questions will simply be asked :

1 Was the shortfall within your control?
2 Was supporting action and help given?
3 What action can *we* take to see that it is achieved during the next period?

From these questions will emerge the action needed to achieve the objectives in the following period—they will normally fall into one of the following categories :

1 Problems to overcome or suggestions to be considered
2 Steps to be taken by the job holder
3 Supporting action that the senior manager will take to assist his subordinates in achieving the target during the next period.

Second stage of the review meeting

The second stage of the review meeting is to examine the job holder's performance against the agreed standards of reach KRA listed in his MG.

The job holder is asked in respect of each KRA, 'How well do you feel you performed this task?'

In the case of quantitative standards of performance, any statement the job holder makes in answer to the initial question posed above will need to be supported by his actual achievements against the agreed targets, as shown on the quarterly review form.

For qualitative standards, the job holder's performance will have to be measured by the quality of reports or plans submitted or the results of plans or programmes.

For example, one KRA for a manager could be : 'To ensure that human resources are available to meet present and future objectives of the company'. Standards of performance for the KRA may be :

1 Training needs are identified and met;
2 Succession plans are prepared.

The job holder will then be reviewed on the success of the training programme he has introduced and the quality of the succession plans he has prepared.

In advance of the meeting the senior will enter his comments on the job holder's performance in relations to qualitative standards. Remarks such as 'satisfactory' are inadequate. Full comments should be written about how well the job holder achieved his key result.

Supplementary questions

Where a job holder thinks he has carried out a job well and the results indicate otherwise, the senior should ask questions about specific points, for example: 'Do you feel that your training programme contains sufficient internal training which could be carried out by yourself and other managers?'

This use of questioning avoids direct criticism and encourages the job holder to re-examine his own performance.

Further action

As in the first part of the review, the job holder should be congratulated if he achieves the required standards of performance and as they work through all the KRAs the senior should make notes of those standards in relation to which further action is required in terms of :

1 Major improvement
2 Slight improvement
3 Present level.

The joint decisions of the manager and senior are entered on the quarterly review form, by placing the corresponding letter in the appropriate column and writing comments on what is required in the next period. It is quite possible that the target figure for some quantitative standards of performance is either increased or decreased.

KRAs which the job holder and senior agreed 'need more attention' or 'require a major improvement' will provide areas for STOs during the next period.

At this point, the manager and senior should also agree and record any changes necessary in the management guide itself.

Resetting short-term objectives

The job holder and senior agree the areas for STOs for the forthcoming period from :

1   The KRAs that 'need more attention' or 'require a major improvement'.
2   STOs that have been redefined or were not achieved from the previous period.

The dates of the next review period are also agreed. The review stage is then completed and the job holder and senior, either at the same meeting or during the course of the next week, agree the particular targets they think should be achieved during the next period and how these targets can be achieved.

They will then be in a position to discuss and agree the new JIP. The agreed STOs are recorded on a new form complete with details about how the job holder will endeavour to achieve them. A copy of this form is issued to the job holder and senior.

The annual review

Each senior should be asked to complete an annual review for each of his immediate subordinates.

Aims

1   To assess overall performance
2   To assess suitability of individual managers for promotion or alternative types of work
3   To identify the type of development needed to enable each manager :

(*a*)   To perform his existing job better
(*b*)   To cope with changes in the character of his job
(*c*)   To be ready for promotion

4   Salary review.

Points to be considered

1   Factors which cause the manager to perform well against management guide and job improvement plan standards

2 Factors which if modified would enable him to perform better
3 Technological and other changes likely to affect the character of his job within the next few years
4 Additional skills and knowledge which will make the man more suitable for promotion or cross-posting
5 The manager's career ambition
6 His suitability for promotion or transfer in the near, medium and long-term future.

Identification of training needs

Current performance
The senior should assess the job holder's performance in each KRA of his job as detailed in his MG. This can be done by examining results of the reviews held during the previous 12 months and STOs set during this period. The results should be summarised to indicate the job holder's major strengths and features requiring development.

Examples for a factory manager might be :

Over the last twelve months he has achieved all the performance standards for his KRAs and 90 per cent of his short-term objectives. In particular he :

— plans his approach to task well
— present information in a precise and clear manner
— analyses problems in a clear and thorough way.

At present he gets too involved in detail which should be delegated to subordinates. This means he is having to work late most nights to keep up to date and his subordinates are failing to accept their full responsibilities.

Future requirements
The senior should think of the changes in company policy which will or might take place over the next three to seven years and consider new management skills or technical knowledge which the job holder will require to continue to carry out his present job efficiently, such as :

— the need to build up high-level contacts within supermarket chains

- a knowledge of consumer market research techniques and their application within the company
- the development of area sales managers into area marketing managers.

The senior should then think of the broadening required to increase the opportunity of being able to use the man in other capacities at at a higher or on the same level.

Summary of performance and potential

Potential

The senior should ask the job holder about his career wishes over the next three to seven years and enter his comments on the form. The senior should then enter what he considers is the job holder's potential in one, three and seven years.

An example of entries for a packaging manager might be :

1 Hopes to become a plant manager within the next five years
2 1 year — Present position, as he requires more experience of production planning
   3 years — Suitable for plant management if given training in costing and works industrial relations
   7 years — Unable to assess beyond plant management.

Grading of performance for year under review

The senior should consider the job holder's achievement against performance standards and short-term objectives over the previous twelve months, together with his management of subordinates. The result of this analysis will enable the senior to determine the job holder's grading for the previous twelve months.

Annual personal development programme

The identified training needs will normally be met in one of the following ways :

1 By projects and experience
2 By reading and guidance
3 By off-the-job training.

When discussing the training to be given, the senior should remember that it is more effective to build on a man's strengths rather than attempt to cure all his weaknesses.

Projects and experiences
A project may be selected which the subordinate can carry out in his spare time or in addition to his normal day-to-day duties by either replanning his activities or having some of his responsibilities removed for the period of the project.

An example of a project for a production manager to be carried out in addition to his normal day-to-day duties might be :

Prepare a detailed six-month training programme for operators, including subjects for talks, exercises and suggested speakers.

Examples of projects for area sales managers which might be carried out by reducing some of their workload for a limited period are :

Review the company's promotional plan over the previous three months and evaluate its results on sales.
Prepare an analysis of trade margins and methods of discovering and determining them.

Experience may be arranged for a subordinate so that he gains knowledge of how other departments, managers or companies operate, and the problems and difficulties that have to be overcome by such means as the following :

— carrying out a recruitment exercise
— acting as a holiday relief in a different department from his own
— being seconded to another department for a set period of time
— visiting an outside factory in the same or a different industry.

In every case the subordinate should be asked to submit written reports on some particular aspects of the project or experience, including recommendations where applicable.

Reading and guidance
The management adviser and training department may have a recommended reading list for the majority of management functions and techniques, and a subordinate can be requested to read one of these

books and give a two-page review of the book or give a report stating if any of the theories or techniques in the book are adaptable for company use.

A senior or specialist may be appointed to guide a job holder in a particular aspect of his job. For example, a district manager may be weak on personnel selection and the personnel manager may be appointed to assist in making a study of the problems affecting this aspect of the job.

The guidance manager should submit a report on the aspects covered under his guidance.

Off-the-job training

Off-the-job training can be one or more of the following :

1 Special project
2 One-day seminar
3 Three-month course.

The courses and seminars can be internal and organised by the company or external away from company premises.

Subordinates attending either internal or external seminars or courses should be asked to submit a report :

1 Outlining any aspects which could be utilised profitably by the company.
2 Stating whether the course is suitable for other members of the company.

Conclusion

Looking at all the problems, perhaps the major pitfall to be avoided is a natural tendency to concentrate at the outset on the system itself and the associated documentation rather than on the purpose and the basic concepts involved. As understanding is developed and the basic soundness of the approach is accepted so will the need for a more disciplined and systematic approach become apparent.

Management by objectives is effective only when it becomes the accepted way of managing in an organisation. This means that every manager must understand and accept the concepts and be seen by his subordinates to be applying them in the practical management situation.

Part 3

MANAGEMENT DEVELOPMENT IN ACTION

'What do they do at . . .?' Many managers find the most convincing testimonial for any new development to lie in its successful implementation by someone else first. The dangers of this approach are that problems and capacities of organisations vary, and the ideal solution to a problem in one situation may be inadequate in another; but we remain curious.

Here we have the case histories of what has been done in a number of industrial situations and other areas of occupational life, such as education and the hospitals.

15

Management Development in Manufacturing

David Casey, Director of Training and Development, Wall Paper Manufacturers Limited

Introduction

The case study described in the article originally published in the IPM journal *Personnel Management* is reproduced on pages 284–293 as one example of the kind of development activity taking place in Wall Paper Manufacturers Limited, a major division of Reed International. It is by no means the only kind of activity taking place since major programes exist at the centre of Reed and at unit level throughout the company. It is quoted because it aroused considerable interest when first published and because it is, I believe, an indication of a trend in this and other large organisations away from formal management training courses. In this introductory note I will give some of the original beliefs on which this particular cadre exercise was based and indicate what some of the underlying trends seem to be.

We believe that the identification of talent does not take place of its own accord and the process has to be developed by which young men of ability are given company-wide visibility and early exposure to the gaze of senior men who will make decisions about manning the top levels of the organisation. This is not to say that an identification programme obviates the need to recruit competently. On the contrary, an effective recruitment process is the *sine qua non* of any development activity and must be first class. But even when it is first class, changes take place; young men develop late, mediocre performers suddenly find fresh vitality in a changed role or the changes in the work itself, because of major shifts in our social and economic environment, create a new situation to which some managers respond better.

For these reasons we devised a system for exposing to general view those middle managers in the business who are thought by their senior colleagues to have potential.

This does not imply any diminution in the responsibility which each division and unit carries. We believe the responsibility for developing managers is a shared one. Each unit carries the major share but the centre is not free of responsibility, since there are some perspectives which can only be seen at the centre. For example, the comparison of standards between one division and another. Similarly the training function bears a part of the responsibility and cannot hide behind the excuse that 'The managers in this or that unit are not interested in developing their subordinates'. Consideration of this shared responsibility leads us to see cadre exercises as an additional tactic to overall strategy for the development of the business and the managers within it and we recognise that the main strategy must rest with the divisions themselves.

This means in practice that many points of view must be reconciled in developing the overall design. Divisions must take part in running the programme and in the end the participant who is returned to his division must look to that division for his short-term career development, even if his exposure at a higher level has influenced his longer-term career prospects. The follow-through relies very much on the thoroughness of personnel practices in each division. Unless manpower planning is practised and appraisal and reward systems are effective, the cadre experience will be largely wasted.

Looked at from the point of view of corporate strategy, adopted to maximise the total contributions of peope who work for us, this exercise is one example of a trend away from educating individual managers and towards improving the effectiveness of the business as an organism by development activities. The trend is a national one and has not necessarily been articulated by organisations as a shift in policy.

In cadre exercises the role of the training staff has shifted from the former authority position as the source of knowledge on training courses to that of designer of a learning situation. The 'teachers' are now the senior executives, other management colleagues and the business situations themselves. Another shift is in the training material used, the case studies are real, the problems live and vital to the business. However, the men who attend are still attending as individuals and are working on business problems which are not their own; there is some way to go before cadre can be seen as an OD activity in which management teams are helped through their own current problems. Perhaps it is a halfway house in which both individual managers develop and company problems are solved. There are many examples in Reed International of full OD efforts in which training resources have been deployed in helping parts of the organisation through particular phases of their work. This is not the place to report on them.

Brief mention of one other example of a halfway house, which seems to be developing from a standard training course, may serve to illustrate the trend towards concern for the organisation as a startpoint for development activities, rather than concern for the individual manager.

Recent changes to a well-established residential fortnight devoted to 'leadership of working groups' have helped to bridge the gap between the newly trained manager and his effective re-entry and improved contribution to his business. Previously, individual managers were nominated for the course, briefed (often all too briefly) by their bosses, attended the course and returned home. Successful application of the learning was infrequent in spite of a high reputation which the course enjoyed.

Changes were introduced in an experimental version of the course in early 1972 as follows. First, two trainers visited the man's unit and in a far-ranging discussion with the candidate and his boss, explored reasons for the nomination, the business situation in which the candidate was placed and explained their own attitudes to the course, and how they intended to run it. This achieved the commitment of the boss, the orientation of the candidate and brought the trainers up to date with each work situation before the course began.

Second, the students returned home after a week's learning about leadership for a two-day project in which they analysed their own leadership in terms of what they had learned and began to plan improvements. Then they returned to the course for further discussions and practice and firmed up a definite plan of action for themselves.

Both of these changes were planned as a result of research findings from an on-going research of the effectiveness of our courses. After the experimental course we were delighted to find a considerable improvement in research results related to 'relevance of the learning to your job'. But we were unprepared for the flood of opportunities which arose as a direct result of the two-day analysis of the backhome situations! Not only did the new design bring learning on a training course into the real work situation in a meaningful way, the reverse also happened : managers saw the need to bring advisers and consultants into their own factories to help with what they now saw as problems in their own business.

This example, taken together with the article which follows, illustrates, I think, the growing need to detach management training from its own self-importance and use the trainers' real skill which is not preaching from a platform, but designing learning opportunities within the business. Our experience has been that if this can be done managers learn more, and can apply what they learn more quickly. And, incidentally, the trainers develop faster too and become more credible to their colleagues in the process.

Individual growth in a company context

There are two streams of activity which often become separated. One is business activity concerned with turnover, manufacturing, new products, profits, cash flow; the other is management development, training needs analysis, assessment of potential and even MbO when this is an activity centred on the personnel department. Even when corporate planning is an established routine, the manpower planning part can be trivial and concentrated on the numbers game. Why is it that the two streams become separated?

No trainer would disagree with the thesis that these two streams should integrate if the company is going to move forward long term. The problem is how to do it. I have a personal concern that it may be getting more difficult as the economic situation puts more pressure on business, so that managers' priorities are constantly being re-established in the business areas. On the other hand, the jargon in behavioural activity is growing from day to day and some people become so specialised that it is difficult to understand what they are saying.

One way to bring the two streams together may be to couch management development in such a way that it gets under the skin. This implies management development as an irritant producing some discomfort. It is common knowledge that one way to achieve results is to work through the top man who is committed to management development. This can certainly guarantee getting under the skin of some of the junior managers. But it is not the only way.

Consider also the direct effect of business projects undertaken within the company when it is known that changes in management, organisation, company policy and so on, will be the direct result of such projects. Another possibility is to expose individual managers to direct measurement by overt assessment in situations where they can be seen throughout the company. Any of these tactics produces a level of discomfort and therefore a possible setting for a realistic development activity.

These notes provide the background to an experimental activity which we have tried to design so that certain factors get under the skin of managers and directors. For example, in our management development exercise we have involved top management as tutors in spite of their initial hesitation. We have claimed a good number of days from senior managers, when they were reluctant to give their time. We have encouraged top managers to assess their subordinates; many of them felt very uncomfortable about this at first. We have turned the students (on this exercise they are senior men themselves) loose in crucial sectors of the business to recommend action that should be taken to improve the business to those people running that sector. This activity is disturbing for everybody concerned. And the students understand that they are being assessed with regard to their future potential. There is of course a wide spectrum of reaction among the students to this knowledge, from those who find it positively invigorating to others who find it worrying, but nobody accepts it with complacency.

The spin-off value of management development activity of this kind is potentially very great, the level of spontaneous activity on the part of the students, for example, has surprised and delighted us, and the chain reaction effect is impressive.

History of the project

There is some history in my group of project-based training, the main element of which has been visits by groups of managers to units within the organisation. During these programmes assessment and training have taken place at the same time. The debate about the viability of assessing a man while he is learning is as old as the activity itself. The protagonists for mixing the two claim that we are all being assessed by each other all the time so why not be open about it? Others claim that assessment pressures ruffle the calm needed to learn. They also make great play of the difficulty of simulating activity which is near enough to the real thing to make assessment of managerial characteristics valid.

In an attempt to disentangle learning from assessment we have this year established a fortnight's business project for twelve students released in three teams of fours into different parts of the company. The students are senior men with potential. We have steadfastly refused to call these projects 'business problems' preferring 'business situations'. We have reasoned that when men become managers nobody brings problems to them already defined; one of their major tasks is going to be diagnosing specific problems from a heterogeneous business situation. In Professor Revans's terms, we want our men faced with real problems and not puzzles to which there is known to be a finite answer hidden away somewhere.

During this fortnight they are assessed by senior directors against agreed characteristics which we believe are possessed by successful general managers within our own company. We hope we are picking our future general managers in this way. It goes without saying that in the fortnight there is a lot of learning—but this is almost incidental, the main thing is the assessment.

However, the men need training for the task and this training started four months ahead. We assumed that twelve men who are mostly strangers to each other—our group has 20 000 employees—would have needs of two kinds: a common group of needs such as how to structure the approach to a business problem, how to work together as a team, etc., and personal needs, which might well be unique to the individual, such as a deeper understanding of marketing for a production manager, increased interviewing skill for a man who had missed out on this training in the past, and so on.

Common needs were catered for by a residential week in July. Individual needs were handled in the three summer months. Each man has a personal programme designed for him, flexible to his own personal arrangements including holidays and monitored by at least one trainer. No assessment was carried out in either of these training activities.

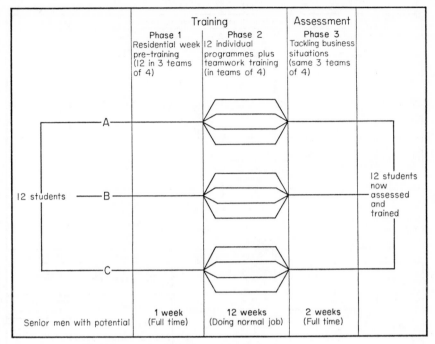

Figure 15:1   Structure of the WPM programme

Again this can never be wholly true since it is impossible to avoid assessing people, but the training was carried out by trainers who were deliberately excluded from the assessment team. Where the assessment team members were introduced as teachers and counsellors we were at great pains to emphasise to them and the students that they were now discharging a different role. On the whole they found it easy to adjust from one role to the other, although certainly there was some tension which was directly due to the knowledge that in the end this exercise would be one of assessment. The tension, however, was considerably less than in the past when we have mixed assessment with training.

Figure 15:1 is a diagrammatic representation of the whole programme. Already we have found some big faults in the design. A major one is the gap of three months between the pre-training week in which the men learned how to structure business problems and the actual task of doing this in phase 3 in October. Interestingly enough, this has been self-

	Set objectives and design programme						
	Business situations		Training		Assessment		
	Divisions	Centre	Divisions	Centre	Divisions	Centre	
Feb						Crude criterion "General manager"	
Mar	Situations suggested		Design training strategy		First assessment (selection)		
April		Situations chosen				Teams formed	
	Man briefed in general terms		Man briefed		Man briefed		
May–June			Prepare training programme		Assessing team formed · Criteria refined (characteristics)		
July			Pre-training week		No assessment		Pre-training
July–Sept			Personal training programmes		No assessment		Personal training
	Business situations tackled		Business situations tackled		Assessment		Business situations
Oct–Nov	Report to board and local management		Further training as required		All assessments collated		
						Feedback MD + DCE	
Dec					Feedback DCE + BOSS + trainer		
Jan					Career plans		
	Evaluate and plan for next programme						

Figure 15:2   Planning timetable for the WPM programme

correcting, since all three teams spontaneously added mini-project work to the individual programmes planned in phase 2. Next time we will build this kind of activity into the design. Another elementary mistake was in not consulting the bosses of students in diagnosing their training needs.

The whole operation was run by a steering group of six people under the chairmanship of the managing director. The three separated strands —assessment, training and impact on the chosen business situations— now had to be woven into an integrated programme. It will be easier to understand if I describe these three processes separately but Figure 15:2 puts the whole picture together and shows how they are related.

Assessment

This was clearly the main objective of the exercise, and everybody knows this. The original nominations for the programme came from the divisions and each divisional chief executive (DCE) put forward up to six nominations from his division. He was encouraged to use the judgment of his own managers and his personnel executives in making his selection. The criterion against which he was selecting was fairly crude: 'men who in a few years' time will head up a fairly major unit'.

None of these nominations were rejected by the centre although there were five times as many as could be accommodated on the first programme; they were put on ice for future projects. Three teams of four were formed using the following criteria to establish the mix of four men: functional expertise, mix of divisions, ability to handle the business situations already chosen and overall personality balance of the team of four.

Forming the team of assessors was the most difficult part. We were determined to get senior line managers and in the event we have six assessors, four of whom are divisional chief executives. We felt the whole exercise would be more acceptable if everybody knew that the assessment was being carried out by senior line men who were responsible for divisions. After all, it is their job to assess middle managers and their skill in doing this would be improved in the process.

The assessors refined the criteria to be used by them during phase 3. The logistics of the exercise prohibited each assessor getting to know all of the students in depth. We therefore established criteria at two levels: ten to be used where the assessor had a depth contact with the student when the assessor was sitting down in 'shirt sleeve' conditions with the team as they worked through the business tasks; and three to be used for students who had been observed from time to time but never really studied in depth. Each assessor will make 4 assessments in depth and up to 8 at a shallower level.

Afterwards we plan to collate the assessments and feedback to the individual. First he will have a private session with the managing director and his own DCE, followed by a session with his own DCE, his immediate boss and his own training officer. It is at the second discussion that the plans for the man's future will be made so that the division will feel responsible for his future development.

There are two parts to the training. First a residential week with three objectives of structuring the approach to business situations, improving teamwork and individual training needs analysis. The main part of the week was concerned wtih business cases and the activity was graded to become gradually less academic and more practical. We started with four business cases taught by London Business School and then moved forward into current company cases and finally into current cases run by the divisional chief executive responsible. It was at this stage that the DCE's had a teaching role. All this training took place in the same teams of four which would be together in October. There were several training officers from division present and they took sessions devoted to teamwork and worked through the business cases from the teamwork point of view.

Secondly, on the last day of the course we analysed individual training needs. Students were encouraged to analyse their own needs with the help of the divisional training man and a training information room which had been laid on for the occasion, staffed by three information officers from BIM, Industrial Training Service and our own company. Each individual programme is unique and a lot of ideas have come forward from the men themselves. In all cases the divisional training man is fully involved in working through the programme for the three months with the student.

Business situations

We decided that the situations should not be confined to single units but should be areas of business activity, e.g. a sector of the market place or a product which spans more than one unit or division.

The students do not know what these business situations are and this remains a secret until the first day of the phase 3 fortnight. They do, however, already know that the brief will be short (no more than a quarto page) and they are familiar with the way in which the brief will be expressed since on the pre-training week business situations were expressed in similar terms. Briefing will be carried out by key executives who know this part of our business very well. Then the teams will be allowed access with complete freedom to collect any information they need and talk to anybody. They will decide how best to use all resources available to them.

At the end of the fortnight they will report back to the managers of the business in company with the board of directors. The managers to whom they report will have freedom to decide what action to take if any, as a result of the visiting team's recommendations.

Involvement

If commitment is going to be widespread, at least five distinct groups of people must play their part and they must feel their part is important. The participants themselves, the bosses, the senior directors, trainers associated with the participants and any outside teaching resources used. Further, to be comprehensive the programme will include training needs analysis, training, assessment, briefing, debriefing, career follow-through, validation and evaluation. Hence the people involved and operations carried out build up to a comprehensive model with many variables.

Organisation issues are important too, adding a further dimension of complexity. The main organisation issues with us is that we are de-centralised, so roles and decision points need to be clearly thought through and understood by all. At the WPM centre we tread warily but at the same time benefit by our relative autonomy from the centre of Reed International. This gives us freedom to act.

Involvement takes time. It is not until you write it down in some form that you realise the time needed to plan and execute such an operation. The chart in Figure 15:2 shows that to operate a fortnight's programme takes a year!

We have tried to be comprehensive but the alarming thing is that our omissions are very significant. For example, we have done no evaluation of this whole programme at all. Next time if we can cope with further complexity we will build in a research programme to evaluate the benefit of the whole operation.

We are already thinking of more than one programme each year. We know major omissions and faults need rectifying. The picture forming is of a few central development activities every year, each at the centre of a web of interrelated activities and tying up the resources of a variety of trainers and managers in various roles.

Spin-offs

The indirect benefits of this kind of work are becoming clear and are greater than anticipated. Among the most important to the organisation as a whole are :

Directors' skills as teachers have been developed. They have learned that their contribution can be of unique value and that they can really enjoy it! They have understood more about assessing potential and training needs analysis and in these areas they have developed their skills further.

Manpower planning. Our method of planning for succession and expansion at the top involves continuously combing through the organisation for talent and measuring this against the opportunities likely to arise. Our first attempts at this were either too mechanisic or, at the other extreme, so casual and haphazard that they lacked credibility.

We now find that several different activities are throwing up lists of names established from different criteria, each of which contributes to the total picture of talent available. If we methodically search all these lists, which are themselves in constant flux, we don't miss people. The list of nominations for the programme under discussion has provided further raw material for this work.

Business situations. It is surprising what a help to the business the ideas generated can be. Most managers are surprised at the depth of understanding reached by the visiting teams and they often get new insight to their own problems.

The relationship of the company to business schools. This is an area of personal interest because I took part in the recent BIM/CBI survey for the Council of Industry for Management Education and I believe that the relationship between a company and a business school depends on the close personal respect and understanding which exists between key members of each organisation. In bringing in Dr Denis Thomas from London to help us with the formal teaching part of this programme and with some aspects of its design, we feel we have consolidated one of these practical links.

Individuals taking part have also benefited in significant ways :

Managing their own learning. One illustration of this is the spontaneous way in which the teams decided that they needed some training in the three months of phase 2 not just as individuals but also in teams. They used the resources of those trainers available to them very well and have planned a series of exercises to improve their teamwork. Individual training programmes are also being managed very much by the man himself, using trainers as helpful resources.

Career development of senior divisional executives is lodged squarely within each division. At the same time the training specialists allocated to each division, responsible to the divisional chief executive, are fully involved. There has been a stirring of consciences within some divisions. At the same time we hope, although this has yet to be proven, that transfer from one division to another will be facilitated.

Early conclusions

It seems important to pick on something for focusing management development activity. What is chosen may not be critical provided it gets under the skin of managers in their day-to-day work and seems vital to them.

If this activity is then made comprehensive and everybody rightly concerned is fully involved, the spin-offs are perhaps more beneficial to the organisation than all the 'systematic management development programmes' put together.

A first look at quantification for this exercise in the perspective of our total number of managers is depressing. It is easy to cry 'all this for twelve men out of 750?' This clearly poses a problem but I believe the numbers are misleading. Involvement produces understanding and many of our managers and directors now have a firmer grasp of some basic principles of learning. These principles can now be applied by as many as 50 managers and directors involved in some aspect of this programme. There is a good chance that some of the principles will be used to further the day-to-day on-job development of managers and in the end this is what matters since managers can only really be developed by themselves and by their bosses in their normal jobs.

16

Management Development in the Construction Industry

Roy L. Spiers, Group Personnel Services Manager, Taylor Woodrow Group

The Taylor Woodrow Group, a first generation organisation, consists of over 100 subsidiary and associated companies with a turnover in excess of £100 million. It operates in all continents of the world with a staff and labour force in excess of 12 000 people. Much of its work is in the construction industry.

Unlike a manufacturing company, which sells goods in competition, a construction company sells a service and, in most cases, by competitive tendering. Production units can only begin to operate when the client has decided to make use of the company's services. Projects vary in size and time available for completion. They may involve from two to two hundred staff and vary in duration from four months to four years.

In such a changing situation, how is it possible to organise management development and make it relevant to the needs of the organisation? This chapter explains some of the work which has been undertaken in more recent years. At times eyebrows may be raised at what appears to be an informal approach. However, as any personnel manager knows, professional idealism on its own is useless, in the end it is results which matter and that means growing managers to meet the changing needs of the organisation. To succeed, the personnel manager must gain the cooperation of every manager. He will do so only if the managers are able to understand what is being attempted and believe it to be appropriate. We still have a long way to go and even if we have the right formula for today the need will almost certainly be different in a few years' time. Even then we will be developing the individual manager and, more important, the management team.

Organisation of personnel services in the group

The board of the parent company, Taylor Woodrow Limited, consists of executive and non-executive directors. Each of the executive directors holds an executive appointment in one of the subsidiary companies, and is a member of the board of that company. Group policy is established by the parent board and is disseminated to the subsidiary boards which are responsible for implementation in a way appropriate to the particular business of the company. The same applies to personnel and training policy. The parent company lays down the philosophy and framework, leaving each company to develop detail.

The personnel function

There are three ways in which companies provide a personnel service to the managers:

1 In the smaller companies the managing director takes full responsibility, with his private secretary providing the personnel administration service.
2 In the medium-size companies the personnel service is provided by the company secretary with, in some cases, specialist assistance.
3 The larger companies have a specialist personnel department.

There is one further vital link in that it is necessary to coordinate the personnel activities and avoid duplication of effort. This service is provided by the Group Personnel Services Department. In more recent years the largest part of their contribution has been in the area of manager and management development.

MANAGEMENT DEVELOPMENT IN THE CONSTRUCTION INDUSTRY

Developing the manager

Identifying whom to develop

In an idealist way it can be said that every manager is enriching his career while he is a manager and, therefore, a development programme should cover all managers. Nevertheless one has to accept that on a long-term basis, and considering development programmes on a cost-benefit basis, it is usually appropriate to invest most effort in a comparatively limited number of people at any one time. The problem arises in deciding in whom this investment should be made. Taylor Woodrow Group policy is that this decision must be made by the senior management of each company.

The managing directors are asked to prepare a list of managers they wish to include in the development programme. In preparing the list they must take into account three factors:

1　The individual's past performance
2　The likely future needs of the company
3　The career aspirations of the individual manager.

These lists are updated each year.

Assessing the individual's need

Originally this was left entirely to the senior management of the company. They tended to convert the need into a plan of action usually entailing attendance on a managerial course. It became very apparent that with the rapid development in the scope of management training this was not making the best use of resources. The managers themselves were also beginning to question whether they were competent to make such a decision without professional advice. However, in making any changes in the assessment procedure we had to make sure that the senior managers were still involved. They had to be able to understand the process and make the decision of what action should be taken.

It was, therefore, agreed that the assessment process should be divided into three stages as follows:

1   An initial assessment, against a predetermined checklist to be under-
    taken by a senior manager
2   A 'career development' interview conducted by an independent
    manager and a representative of the Group Personnel Services
    Department
3   A review in which the result of the initial assessment and the career
    development interview would be compared.

This process has proved to be workable and one which is seen to be fair
by the majority of managers included in the development programme.

Generally the reports prepared during the assessment follow a similar
pattern. The senior manager's initial assessment concentrates on performance in a particular line job and a possible future appointment in
the same management line. The career development interview tends to
bring out more about the managerial skills and career aspirations of the
individual.

Because the career development interview is conducted by people
outside the manager's immediate subordinate/superior relationship it
tends to be very open and revealing. Care has to be taken when reporting
to the senior manager as this confidence must not be destroyed. The
report on the career development interview is therefore written to show :

1   Main strengths of the manager
2   The type of appointment in which he is likely to be most successful
3   Any particular weakness
4   Suggestions for future training and development.

In this assessment process the most difficult task has been to develop a
standard for the senior managers to use in their initial report. They were
therefore asked to submit their own ideas on what factors should be
considered and on what basis these factors could be judged. Because of
the different activities of the various companies it has not been possible
to use the same list of factors throughout the group. Nevertheless the
basic system is the same and many of the factors are common to the
various company assessment forms. The items covered by the senior
managers' assessment are shown in Figure 16:1.

In trying to find a method for judging the factors it became apparent
that managers tended to compare themselves with others on the extent
of their expertise. Phrases such as 'he is an expert at ——;' 'He has a

MANAGEMENT DEVELOPMENT IN THE CONSTRUCTION INDUSTRY

CONTENT OF SENIOR MANAGER'S ASSESSMENT

1. Present position/appointment
2. Potential position/appointment
3. Priority in development programme
4. Summary of past experience
5. Brief description of current duties
6. What he/she has done well
7. What are his/her weaknesses
8. What is needed to develop him/her for the potential appointment
9. Skills, knowledge, techniques to be graded:

Administration and procedures
(a) Office organisation and procedure
(b) Buying and storage
(c) Timekeeping and wage payment
(d) Accounting and financial
(e) Measurement and valuation
(f) Bonus and incentive schemes
(g) Computer applications and systems

Legal
(h) Contract Law
(j) Regulations for construction work
(k) Regulations relating to employees

Production
(l) Progress and planning
(m) Costing
(n) Work study
(p) Site services
(q) Plant maintenance and use

Human
(r) Communication
(s) Interviewing
(t) Negotiating
(u) Trade union and labour relations
(v) Welfare and safety

Technology
The items under this heading vary considerably with the particular occupation of the manager

Figure 16:1   Content of senior manager's assessment

working knowledge of ——;' 'He is sometimes able to ——;' 'I would go to him for advice on ——' were commonly used in describing skill, experience, knowledge, technical ability, etc. As a prerequisite was to develop a system which would be understood and used by the managers, a series of grades were devised which used similar phrases as those quoted above. The various grades are shown in Figure 16:2. By comparing these three parts of the assessment it is possible to gain an indication

299

GRADINGS

A. Expert knowledge, ability, skill etc. Consultant grade, top expert to whom anybody would refer for the informed opinion.

B. Very good knowledge, ability, skill etc. Professional, able to deal with all problems in his own sphere without guidance.

C. Working knowledge, ability, skill etc. Able to deal with many problems in his own sphere but needs time to cope with completely new situations.

D. Some knowledge, ability skill etc. Not able to deal with problems on his own without initial guidance, but can identify problems.

E. Slight or no knowledge, ability, skill etc. Would always need advice.

The above gradings are used in three parts of the senior managers assessment.

CURRENT APPOINTMENT To indicate the degree of ability expected of the manager in his current appointment.

POTENTIAL APPOINTMENT To indicate the degree of ability expected of holders of the potential appointment.

CURRENT PERFORMANCE To indicate the degree of ability achieved by the manager in his current appointment.

Figure 16:2 Gradings

of what is required to improve performance in the present appointment; what help is needed to achieve the potential appointment; whether talent is being wasted or likely to be wasted in a future appointment.

Planning the action

The final stage after reviewing the assessment is to decide what action should be taken. Obviously at this time account must be taken of the current production needs of the company and any individual development programme must slot in with these needs. There are three main headings under which the plan is prepared.

First there is action which can be taken by the individual without any help from outside other than that which sets him on a line of action. We have found that in many cases the individual can develop himself by :

1   Developing and broadening his reading habits
2   Broadening his contacts with people in similar positions but in other parts of the group

3   Joining institutes, societies or associations and attending their meetings and conferences.

The decision to do these things must be made by the individual but he is not always aware of the benefits, therefore he often needs some help and encouragement in the initial stages.

The second form of action relates to the individual's job experience. Four possibilities can be considered.

1   Leave him where he is to grow in his current appointment.
2   Transfer him to some other appointment within his company.
3   Temporarily attach him to another department.
4   Transfer him to an appointment in some other company in the group able to provide the appropriate experience.

Possibilities 1, 2 and 3 can be done entirely by the individual's company but 4 requires cooperation by another senior manager. The Group Personnel Services Department provides guidance on what is available but it is then the responsibility of senior management to arrange for the most appropriate transfer.

The third line of action results in the individual attending a formal course. Use is made of a number of development courses and programmes run by external organisations but in the last few years a programme of internal courses has been introduced.

The structure of these courses is constantly under review as the experience gained from running each course is used to develop later courses. However, the broad pattern of courses is firmly established and can best be reviewed under two headings:

1   The career development 'O' level courses
2   The career development modular courses.

Detailed information about the content and structure of the courses is given later in this chapter, but at this stage it is worth considering these two headings and what they mean.

The reader will have noticed the use of the words 'career development' rather than 'management development'. This reflects part of the group's philosophy. We feel that everybody should be given the opportunity to develop his career in a way suited to both his needs and the company's needs. Equally the group's needs and the individual's personal circumstances change from time to time. Career development programmes only give the individual the opportunity to develop his career. Whether or not he is to become a successful manager and whether or not he takes advantage of the opportunity given to him depends upon how well the company sells the opportunity as well as the individual's personal motivation. The dangers arise from people thinking that because they are attending a 'management development' course they are guaranteed stardom as a top manager. All we are really doing is to point the way to the stars.

Within the Personnel Services Department there was a great debate about how we should identify the various levels of career development courses. Dangers arise in using words such as 'junior management', 'middle management' and 'senior management'. The usual problems arise from first defining who is junior or senior and second the participant's feelings when he is attending a junior course while one of his peers is attending a middle level course. In the end we decided to take a leaf out of the educationalist's book by having 'O' level, 'A' level and 'S' level courses. In this way it is very quickly understood that before taking the 'A' level course, for instance, the individual must have taken the 'O' level course or have proved his competence at that level.

The modular courses were started initially as a quick means of filling an immediate need. However, since then their popularity with managers and apparent success has meant that they have had to be retained in the career development programme. Each module relates to one of the subheadings under item 9 in Figure 16:1. Any number of these modules can be assembled to form a course to meet the needs of any number of managers.

Career development ordinary level course

The participants attend the course for three separate weeks with a period of approximately three months between each week of the course. Each week has a distinctive flavour and part to play in the overall objective. For this reason it is considered desirable to give time between each week to digest the various concepts and put some into practice before starting on the next stage.

MANAGEMENT DEVELOPMENT IN THE CONSTRUCTION INDUSTRY

The purpose of week 1 is to :

1   Develop skills in communications
2   Develop interpersonal skills and effectiveness when working in groups
3   Develop an understanding of leadership
4   Develop an understanding of the Taylor Woodrow Group.

The week starts with a session in which the participants, in syndicates, begin to identify problems of their working situation. Our aim is twofold in that we want them as soon as possible to get used to the idea of working in a group and also to relate the course programme to their own job situation. In the next session we set them a project to be worked on during the week. Briefly it requires the course members, together, to prepare a presentation, which they make at the end of the week, aimed at helping all participants to develop their understanding of the Taylor Woodrow Group. A comprehensive library of information is made available to the course and they are able to consult the tutors or make contact by telephone with managers in various parts of the group. The effectiveness of the presentation depends entirely upon how much they have benefited from the work done during the other part of the week. One day is devoted to communications with particular emphasis on effective writing, effective speaking and case presentation. Two days are devoted to group effectiveness and leadership. So far as is practicable, the participants learn by observing other course members who are undertaking various exercises. These are analysed and discussed with the tutors bringing out salient points. Closed circuit television proves useful in helping the process of analysis. This method of learning was considered to be most appropriate after experience gained in using the Industrial Society's Action-centred Leadership course developed by John Adair. Formal lecturing is kept to a minimum but some of the work of behavioural scientists like Herzberg and Maslow has to be presented in a formal way although even this is introduced through exercises undertaken by the individual participants.

In week 2 of the course the aim is to develop the participants' knowledge of, and skill in applying, the various techniques used in controlling construction projects. The subjects covered include :

1   Planning and programming
2   Method improvement techniques

3 Plant selection and maintenance

4 Estimating, tendering, costing, measurement and valuation.

All this is brought together through a planning and programming project undertaken at the end of the week.

The final week is devoted to the consideration of a construction project as a whole with emphasis on external factors influencing the managing of the project. Subjects covered include :

1 Contract law

2 Employment of subcontractors

3 Working conditions and safety

4 Industrial relations

5 Statutory regulations.

An exercise at the end of the week requires the participants to manage a project in which various incidents are introduced to reinforce the lessons of the entire course. The complete structure of this course is shown in Figure 16:3. More advanced courses are now being developed.

Career development modular courses

As stated previously, these courses were introduced to fill an immediate need. During the assessment stage it was found that many people, in some cases already holding management appointments, were unable to be as effective as was desired because their past experience had not brought them in contact with particular aspects of managing projects. A further study showed that in most cases these were activities which were usually the responsibility of specialists employed either on the construction project or in a head office. Evidently, because the manager had virtually no knowledge of the specialist's job or function, he was unable to communicate with him and did not know when to seek his advice. The problem became more acute when the manager was responsible for controlling a specialist whose job he did not understand. A specialist in this context includes such people as buyers, timekeepers, wages clerks as well as professionals like accountants, quantity surveyors, systems analysts, etc.

MANAGEMENT DEVELOPMENT IN THE CONSTRUCTION INDUSTRY

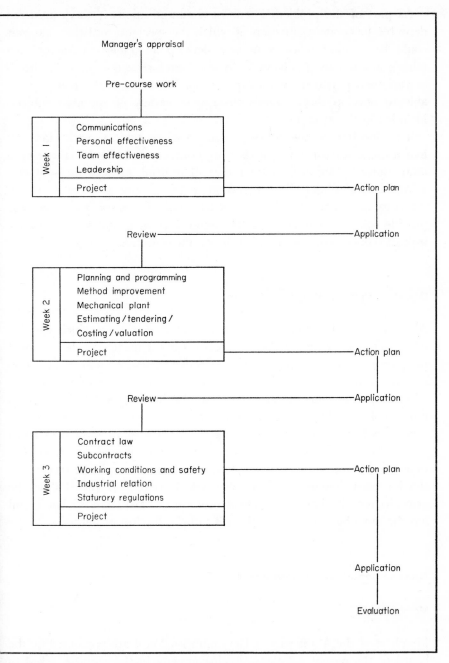

Figure 16:3 Structure of the career development ordinary level course

As part of the problem is one of communications it was considered desirable to create a situation in which the specialist and the managers could be brought together to help develop an understanding of each other's job and its problems. Help was therefore sought from the heads of various departments within the group. With their assistance we were able to develop short courses covering a variety of specialist subjects included in the assessment list.

The duration of the courses for the various subjects varies between half a day and two days but they are normally assembled to make up a total course lasting at least three days. The heads of departments themselves usually undertake the formal lecturing and give assistance in exercises. A course tutor is also resident with the course participants to provide continuity, to act as a catalyst in discussions and to keep control over the course to ensure that it achieves the objectives.

Developing the management team

Already mention has been made of a number of ways in which the idea of managers working together as a team is brought into the development programme; for example, the team effectiveness exercises in the 'O' level course and the involvement of specialist managers in the modular courses. The senior managers of each company also have a special role in team building by holding conferences and discussion groups. There is, however, one further part of the development programme which makes a significant contribution. In 1944 a scheme was started which at that time was known as the Junior Board of Management. More recently its title has been changed to the Management Development Board. Over the years its constitution and working procedures have changed but it still has the same basic objective which is to help develop managers.

Management development board

Membership

Members of the Management Development Board are appointed by the board of the parent company. Each company in the group is asked to make nominations of suitable managers. At any one time there are twelve members of the board. It is essential that there is a constant supply of new blood yet board members must be able to achieve continuity in their working. To this end members serve for eighteen months with four members retiring and four members joining every six months. The board has no permanent chairman, as it is essential that all members play an equal part. Meetings are held at intervals of four weeks and members take the chair in rotation. Each has one vote although it is seldom necessary to resort to formal voting. Five members need to be present to form a quorum but members are expected to arrange their business to ensure almost 100 per cent attendance.

For the purpose of preparing agendas, covering meetings, producing minutes and keeping records, the board is allotted the services of a male secretary and female minute writer. Members are paid an honorarium.

Constitution and aims

No executive powers are vested in the board as a body but the members do, of course, retain powers as individuals to act within their normal duties as a manager in one of the group's companies. The aims of the board are defined in its constitution under sixteen subclauses but these can be brought down to four main areas :

1   Aims related to finance and profit
2   Aims related to the human aspects of management in the group
3   Aims related to the overall efficiency of the organisation
4   Aims related to future business and policy.

From these aims it will be seen that the board is given a very wide brief within which to work. The overall emphasis is on encouragement to think about problems which affect the group and work out ways and means of implementing solutions.

Procedure

As has already been mentioned, the board meets at regular intervals with one of the members acting as chairman. A formal agenda is prepared for each meeting and the business of the meeting is minuted. Within two days of the meeting the minutes are circulated to the board members and to the group chairman. He carefully considers the minutes and any recommendations, giving a formal reply in writing. It may not be possible for every recommendation to be accepted as in many cases these will have to be considered in relation to overall group policy and current business commitments. In these cases a full explanation is given to the board about why a recommendation is rejected. This may be done in writing or through personal discussions.

Besides the system of formal meetings the board undertakes a number of special projects. For these it sets up working parties or subcommittees and creates links with managers from both within and outside the group. The projects concern a current issue which in some way or other relates to the group's business activities. A few examples of the projects undertaken are :

1 Recruitment and employment conditions
2 Out-of-town shopping
3 Cost index systems
4 Export
5 Productivity agreements.

Success or failure

There is no doubt in the minds of both senior managers and the people who have served on the board that it makes a valuable contribution towards the development of managers. The reasons for this are many but can be summarised as follows :

1 There are clear aims and objectives with virtually no limitations.
2 The board is left to conduct its own business. If it is failing then it is told so.
3 It is provided with all the information it needs to do its job properly and trusted to use confidential information with discretion.
4 It gives top management a second viewpoint on many important matters and in so doing creates a direct link with people on the ground.
5 Managers develop a broad general-management outlook rather than a specialised or departmental outlook.
6 Individuals become involved with other parts of the organisation and gain knowledge and experience which would not normally be available until they were in a senior management position.

Concluding comments

In a case study such as this it is not possible to give a complete picture of all aspects of career development in a group of companies so large as Taylor Woodrow. There has been no mention of job descriptions, management by objectives, manpower planning or any other phrase normally associated with management development. This has been intentional because although these techniques are used by some companies in the group they are by no means universally accepted. There is, however, one area which is common to all our career development programmes, that is problem solving. What we are trying to do is develop managers who will be able to cope with problems as and when they arise and at the same time be looking to the future so as to be able to make effective use of our most valuable asset, people.

17

Management Development in the Hospital Service

*Jack Howarth, Regional Training Officer and
John H. Dafforne, Deputy Regional Training Officer, Manchester
Regional Hospital Board*

The organisation of hospital services in this country in their present form
dates from July 1948 which saw the birth of the National Health
Service. Before then, hospitals had existed in three noticeably different
forms—the voluntary hospital service, local authority hospitals and
mental institutions. The voluntary hospital service included a range of
types of hospital which differed in their form and administration because
they were controlled by the people who had been responsible for raising
the finance for them and who had then from their own number elected
a hospital committee. This hospital committee would normally put the
running of the hospital into the hands of a matron who would be responsible for almost the entire range of activities in so far as they were
even remotely connected with nursing—including, for example, catering,
linen supplies, rations and provisions of medicine and equipment. The
general administration would be in the hands of a secretary whose main
task was to raise money for the running of the hospital. There was

little attempt at medical administration; this activity was usually in the hands of the honorary medical staff through the medium of a medical board.

Local authority hospitals were founded under the provisions of the Local Government Act of 1929. They were rate aided and their size depended on the size of the local authority that controlled them. Their administration was very strictly controlled so that, although they were backed by the full resources of the local community through the rates, they could often only provide a service that was inferior to that provided by the voluntary hospitals. Salaries, wages, planning and purchases were usually based on central council departments. The matron was responsible for the nursing activity and the hospital secretary controlled clerical and administrative activity.

Because of fears of abuse, mental hospitals were governed by various Lunacy Acts, the Criminal Justice Act and the Mental Treatment Act of 1930 and regular visitations by commissioners of the Board of Control were required. These very strict regulations required specific and detailed books of records which meant that the mental hospitals were in the main very closely supervised and, as was the nature with any form of government-financed institution, were run very much on a shoe-string with little authority or autonomy in the hands of the hospital secretary.

Growth of hospital management

In the voluntary hospitals which provided the bulk of the services before the 1946 Act and which most certainly provided the outstanding hospital treatment, the system of management was one which had grown from the system of founding the hospital. That is to say, a court of governors was usually drawn from the body of subscribers or donors and the boards or committees which controlled the hospitals were self-perpetuating by virtue of the fact that, as subscribers or donors, they were responsible to themselves for appointment.

The boards of governors had little or no knowledge of medicine or nursing and so they were obliged to place all the control of nursing services in the hands of a specialist nurse (usually given the title of matron) and, following the practice adopted by Florence Nightingale in the hospitals at Scutari, the matron usually had responsibility for the housekeeping. The secretary was responsible merely for collecting income and for carrying out routine office duties. In the early part of the nine-teenth century, the post of hospital secretary became recognised as a career in its own right, nevertheless the control of the hospital resided mainly in a number of committees operating under the umbrella of the board of management. These would form main committeees, sub-committees, committees developed for the purpose of considering one particular item, *ad hoc* committees and committees relating to each of the hospital departments. Despite the lack of management expertise and the existence of a complex and uncoordinated structure the voluntary hospitals continued to develop and it says much for the enthusiasm of the subscribers and the determined efforts of the matrons and secretaries that the hospital service in the United Kingdom reached a level of efficiency comparable with that anywhere else in the world.

When it was decided that the nation's health should become the nation's responsibility a unifying Act was passed in 1946 which brought together the three parts of the service—the voluntary, the municipal and the mental hospitals—together with the executive councils and the local health authorities. As was inevitable with a unifying Act, it was some time before the mistrust which each partner felt for the others was finally vitiated and the growth of confidence was further delayed by the concept of centralised administration whereby functional activities were carried out at the unit hospital but day-to-day management and control was exercised by a central committee and its group officers. In turn, the management committees were coordinated, advised and in some cases supervised and controlled by regional hospital boards. Continually increasing costs resulted in a series of reports all of which pointed to the need for improved administrative and management procedures inside the hospital service. The Bradbeer Report of 1954 and the Guillebaud Report of 1955 both commented upon administrative activities and were followed by a report on the grading structure of the administrative and clerical staff of the hospital service (the Hall Report) in 1957. From 1960 the emphasis began to be laid upon management and three major reports appeared in the latter part of the 1960s which have influenced the hospital service in evolving a pattern of management development. These were the Farquharson–Lang Report of 1966 on administrative practice of hospital boards in Scotland, the Salmon Report of 1966 on senior nursing staff structure and the Godber (or Cogwheel) Report of 1967 on the organisation of medical work in hospitals.

Growth of management development

Training as such has always formed a major part of hospital activities and the training of both nurses and doctors in their technical fields can be a model for teachers in many other fields of activity. However, training on a regional basis was only developed in the mid-1960s and was considered to supplement rather than replace training at the local level which had traditionally been the practice in the hospital service.

The first training to be organised at regional level was introduced for administrative and clerical staff following the receipt in 1956 of Ministry Circular HM(56) 32 'Recruitment and training of hospital administrative staff'. By 1961 the Manchester Regional Hospital Board had mounted a very modest programme of training for administrative and clerical staff, catering officers, domestic superintendents and ward sisters. Following publication of Ministry Circular HM(61)80, 'Recruitment training and promotion arrangements for administrative and clerical staff of the hospital service', in 1961 a Regional Training Office was appointed in the Manchester area and from this date training facilities have increased progressively. Assistance has been sought and given in the early stages by the University of Manchester principally through the facilities made available in the Extra-Mural Department.

By 1964 in was apparent that the region was carrying out sufficient training to merit its own training establishment and the staff college at Rossendale came into existence. This accommodation, in the grounds of Rossendale General Hospital, had been used as residential accommodation for nursing staff and has since been converted to provide lecturing, tutorial and residential accommodation for up to 30 students. In 1965 the formation of the National Staff Committee and of Regional Staff Committees complemented the work being carried out under the aegis of the Regional Training Officer and provided a means whereby national and regional trainees could be drawn into the service with a view to dispelling some of the parochial image formally associated with the hospital service.

The impetus given to training throughout the country by the Industrial Training Act of 1964 was supplemented so far as the hospital service was concerned by the publication of the Salmon Report and the report by a subcommittee of the Standing Nursing Advisory Committee entitled *The Post-certificate Training and Education of Nurses* (London : HMSO,

1966). These reports followed by the Godber Report of 1967 led to a further expansion of work and the procurement of more residential training accommodation at Brindle Lodge, near Preston, where a further 24 students can be accommodated. It can thus be seen that from comparatively small beginnings, over the period of a decade, management training in the hospital service in the Manchester region has now reached considerable proportions.

In April 1974 the three parts of the health service (the hospitals, local health authorities and executive councils) are to be integrated to form one service and this will lead to a further extension of the work being undertaken. In preparation for this increased work the Manchester Regional Hospital Board has opened a third residential centre in the grounds of Monsall Hospital and intends to increase the use which it makes of the University and other further-education establishments in the area.

Developing managers for hospitals

Training objectives

The principles underlying the management training practised in the Manchester region are based upon:

1 The need to teach techniques, routines and procedures both in theory and by on-the-job practice.
2 An acceptance of the need for staff at all levels to achieve job satisfaction, calling for an emphasis in training on interpersonal relationships and associated skills.
3 The need to take account of staff attitudes towards their work and towards other staff in the hospital, in the group, in the region and throughout the National Health Service.
4 The advantages to be gained from an interchange of experience and information which can be built into training programmes by drawing trainees from different backgrounds in terms of geographical areas, the type of hospital, the discipline within which the student works and the type of job on which the student is engaged in his or her day-to-day activity.
5 A continuing need for expansion in the service to be provided for

while bearing in mind the fact that activities must be coordinated within the group, within the board and within the service.

Problems of management training in the hospital service

The major problem associated with training hospital managers, whether they be doctors, nurses or administrators, is that in the past the majority of practitioners have been primarily concerned with their own technical expertise and have therefore not seen themselves as managers at all. Historically the training of doctors, nurses and hospital administrators has led them to concentrate on medical excellence, high standards of patient care and the operation of effective systems of control.

Over the years the responsibility for hospital administration, which was originally largely vested in the matron and subsequently in the matron and the secretary, has come to be exercised by a triumvirate consisting of doctor, nurse and administrator, responsible finally to a committee of predominantly lay people, with little specialist knowledge in the areas within which the functional managers are expert.

Each of the three main functional areas is strongly disciplined and the result has been a rather regimented approach to the management and control of hospitals. Because of the size of the organisation and the complexity of procedures which need to be subjected to strict controls, the administrator has had to develop highly standardised systems in order to exercise a strict measure of control over both costs and quality. The paramilitary nature of the nurse's calling has resulted in a formal discipline somewhat akin to that associated with the armed forces, as exemplified by the wearing of uniforms, badges of rank and decorations which indicate the extent of the nurse's experience and/or technical efficiency.

Medicine has, understandably, adopted a very high degree of professionalism and so doctors have developed very strict and stringent rules and procedures. There has consequently been a conservative and restrictive approach to the administration of the practice of medicine within the institutions; a conservatism which has seemed almost reactionary in the face of the enormous scientific and technical changes which have taken place in the world of medicine. Technological changes in medicine, nursing and administration have been such that the members of the management team have found themselves being forced farther apart rather than closer together because they are not sufficiently familiar with the intricacies of each other's disciplines to be able to converse freely. In two respects only have the three sides of the management structure seen the problems of management development from a common standpoint. They are all agreed that hospitals are 'different' and that it therefore seems unlikely that management theories developed for manufacturing or service industries can have an application in the hospital field. They also tend to associate management practice with the entrepreneurial activities of the profit-making industries and, because the concept of practising medicine in the hospital situation for profit is an anathema to the British hospital service, there has been a rejection of any move to introduce management training into the service.

In addition to these outright hostilities the potential trainer of management in the hospital service has been faced with other opposition which may not have been so inevitable in other spheres of activity. Change, which tends to be resented in all institutions, also brings with it in the hospital service a very real and sometimes justified fear that change in methods, change in technology, change in structure—all of which result in changes in patient care and techniques—may have detrimental effects in the short term if not indeed in the long term. Consequently, change is resisted more strongly in the hospital service than it would be in an industry such as advertising, where technological change, change in methods, change in marketing procedures, etc., is seen as being not merely inevitable but also desirable.

Another major problem has been in breaking down barriers between the three branches of the service, barriers between different levels in the hierarchy, barriers between different hospitals now in the same group but previously in different areas and financed under different schemes, barriers based upon the natural resentment felt by those working at the interface of the community against the central administrative structure, barriers existing between newly appointed and longstanding holders of posts which are particularly noticeable in an organisation such as the hospital service where the majority of managers will have joined the service at a very early age and then remained for a life-long career. The complex nature of the organisation of the hospital service has posed further barrier problems in considering the development of managers who have to relate their own job and the role which they undertake in the overall organisation.

Some of the older mental hospitals are virtually townships with many of the staff actually living on the hospital site and the site being provided with all the services necessary for its existence, even in some cases power and water supplies. This extremely complicated administrative structure exists to support an equally complicated technical structure within which skills are being exercised in a wide range of recognisably different professions. Each of the many skills and disciplines represented in the organisation of a structure of this size and complexity must be given its correct representation and this representation given its correct weighting in the decision-making processes which are needed to operate a complicated system of consultation, coordination and control.

Management training methods

Following the publication of the Salmon Report in 1966 most of the management teaching in the hospital service has been concentrated in the nursing disciplines. Earlier attempts to introduce some form of training for management at the more junior levels of the administrative grades have been combined with this increased training for nurses to introduce integrated courses for nursing and administrative staffs at senior and middle management levels. Only occasionally have courses been run which have included medical staff and most of these have been at the most senior level. It is possible that medical staff do not see any management content in their own roles, particularly at the more junior levels, and it is difficult to convince people of the need to study management merely to appreciate the management roles of the people alongside whom they work.

The majority of training has followed the traditional form of choosing courses to introduce the concepts of management and to lead the student into a consideration of the behavioural sciences, the legal implications, the economic implications and the accounting problems which are encountered. This traditional approach has been supplemented by developing group and individual practical work and adopting the project as a major training medium and also by financing fundamental research into the nature of management in the hospital service. Some of the most interesting work has been carried out at the University of Wales and the University of Aston by Derek Williams. In the Manchester area Professor Chester at the University, and John Pantall at the Manchester Business School have carried out further work. A more recent innovation has been the joint sponsorship of a research assistant at the Manchester Polytechnic by the Polytechnic Department of Management and the Training Department of the Regional Hospital Board. The result of this research has been to underline the ways in which management in the hospital service has facets in common with management elsewhere and is at the same time peculiar in the demands which it makes upon its managers and thereby demands training directed specifically towards the management of a hospital or a group of hospitals.

One result of these attempts to determine the actual content of the hospital management job has been the revelation that the analysis of management activity in the hospital starts from differentiated ground and then draws the roles together into an administrative superstructure; whereas it is more normal for consideration of management in the industrial or commercial world to start from areas of common ground and then to separate into areas of specific activity .

Nurses as managers

If there can be said to be a key role in the hospital service it must be that of the nursing sister concerned with running what is recognisably the prime hospital unit—the ward. At the level of the sister (grade 5, 6 or 7 in the Salmon rating) the ward is a tightly knit and well-controlled unit which can be seen to have its own specific task and in which the sister can be seen as the manager of an easily identified resource area. At this level the medical staff and the administrative staff contribute towards the ward activity without in any way seeking to control other than by such general mechanisms as the daily return of bed state or the advisory activities of the medical staff who supplement nursing care by specifying patient treatment. Both above and below ward level it becomes more apparent that a distinct managerial role is played by the administrative staff in particular and, at the more senior level, by the medical staff.

As managers, nursing staff have considerable advantages derived from the profession within which they have been trained and the environment within which they have worked for much of their lives. Their profession requires them to develop a 'bedside manner' involving perception, sympathy and the ability to deal with people under stress situations. Training in these particular areas is the most difficult form of training for managers and yet the nurse has developed these skills almost as a by-product of her technical training.

Most nurses are rightly proud of possessing these skills and yet they do not see them as being in any way appropriate to their management job. In fact, possibly in keeping with the paramilitary style which has been adopted in the past, some nurse/managers seem to take a pride in being harsh, abrupt and authoritative when dealing with staff to such a degree that they alienate sympathy rather than develop confidence and claim mutually rewarding relationships. If the skills used in dealing sympathetically and firmly with the patients could be translated into the management sphere of the nurse's work and correctly aligned to the setting of objectives, the nurse/manager would greatly enhance the management performance within hospitals without in any way jeopardising the standards of technical competence and professionalism within the nursing service.

The environment within which nurses have worked since the time of Florence Nightingale has also developed two most praiseworthy managerial habits which are often sought after in the industrial and commercial world as a Holy Grail to be recognised and longed for but rarely achieved. One of these concepts—that of sapiential authority—is so far recognised as to be incorporated in official documents and textbooks including the Salmon Report. Sapiential authority is authority based upon knowledge and experience, not upon a position of the hierarchy. A senior nurse who has had little contact with geriatric patients will always be willing to listen to and be guided by a more junior member of her staff who has the experience her superior lacks. What is equally important is that the more junior member of the staff takes no advantage of this power residing in her knowledge and the task of management within the organisational structure is in no way hampered by the fact that the superior has had to admit to comparative ignorance in the face of a person of lower grade.

Nurses have also long accepted the principle of 'acting up' and 'acting down'. If an assistant matron is absent from duty, matron could take over some of her job thereby 'acting down' into the assistant matron's position and the administrative sister or indeed any one of the ward or theatre sisters will 'act up' and undertake certain other aspects of the assistant matron's job. In this manner all the important elements of the job are covered during absence. This procedure is an admirable way of training junior staff by instituting a form of automatic and easily acceptable delegation, keeps senior staff in touch with what is going on and provides a point of contact which results from people working on the same job and which helps to get over one of the main barriers to communication—that arising from different levels in the hierarchy.

Nurses are also, as part of their tradition, committed to full participation in training as trainers and trainees. Nurses are traditionally trained by nurses and, when the management activity is recognised as forming part of the job of the senior nurse, nurses will automatically assume the responsibility for incorporating this part of the work into the training of their subordinates. In this way acceptance of management as part of the nursing role will result in a commitment to a programme of management development on the part of the line manager in the nursing section of the hospital service.

Course design

Because of the extremely detailed training required for both nursing and medical work and the high degree of technical efficiency required in the implementation of the day-to-day job, it has been difficult to gain acceptance of the managerial task by either doctors or nurses, because they feel that they are acting outside their own skills, and outside the prime purpose of the hospital activity. They are, in effect, wasting their talents by undertaking a management role. To consider what management is in the hospital service, it must be seen against a background of the service itself. Essentially, the hospital activity is oriented towards people and, what is probably more important, people in a situation of considerable stress throughout the time when they are in contact with the hospital managers. For this reason the tendency is for the managers in the hospital situation to concentrate to a very large extent upon the patient in much the same way that the manager in the school (head, deputy head or head of department) concentrates upon the needs and wants of pupils. The need, as in the school situation, is for the manager, by delegation, by coordination, by training and by controlling, to enable his staff to attend to the 'direct' needs of the pupil or patient—a role for which they are fitted by their own training and by their proximity to the workplace. Management training in the hospital service must therefore be aimed more at changing attitudes and thereby affecting behaviour than at passing on knowledge. It has been well established that attitude change is best affected by behavioural change in a practical situation which is seen to call for deviation from the normal behaviour pattern of the person under training. Unfortunately most hospital programmes have been traditional in nature and have depended on inputs of the material common to commercially based management courses. In the more successful hospital courses the emphasis has been upon change and has been achieved by practical work in which the managers under training have acted in a manner which deviated from normal hospital procedures. If this has been seen to be successful and desirable and has been considered acceptable it has led to some subsequent behavioural change in the work situation.

The intention is not to produce a change in behaviour which will enlarge the skills previously employed by the nurses and medical staff; it is rather to add to the existing managerial skills so as to make for a higher level of overall efficiency and provide a framework within which their subordinates can operate more effectively. Additionally, there is a belief that the managerial skills exercised by medical, nursing and administrative managers will serve to complement each other, thereby improving the efficiency of the hospital, the group or the service as a whole.

Inevitably a great deal of the lecturing on hospital board courses has to be carried out by persons inside the hospital service because of the specific nature of the content. One of the problems involved in course design has been that of coordinating the efforts of the hospital-based lecturers with those of the lecturers from academic institutions. In the Manchester area this has been attempted by using a course tutor, usually a member of the hospital board staff, whose work situation is similar to that of the course student but at a higher level—for example, a secretary will act as the tutor for an integrated course of middle managers or a principal nursing officer as the course tutor for a group of first-line nursing officers. Course tutors have been successfully trained by workshop weekends during which they can be introduced to the basis of their work and can gain some knowledge of and informal acquaintance with the lecturers from the colleges with whom they are to be associated.

There has been very little attempt at 'vertical slice' training in the hospital service in the Manchester region. Courses have been designed to deal with horizontal slices of the management structure. The courses most commonly in operation are for (1) senior managers, (2) middle managers, (3) management appreciation, (4) first-line managers and (5) supervisors. Of these, the first-line management course is specifically for nursing staff but all of the others are interdisciplinary—the supervisors' course being for administrative, paramedical staff and supervisory ancillary staff. The first-line management course and the management appreciation course deal with nursing grades in the Salmon range of 5, 6 and 7. The differentiation is that the management appreciation course is not only interdisciplinary (including administrative and para-medical staff of equivalent grades), but is also intended for staff who have been in post for some little time, whereas the first-line course is intended for nursing staff newly appointed to, or about to be appointed to grade 6. It is felt that the exposure which would be experienced by the newly appointed manager training in a multidisciplinary group is not desirable, but that managers with a fair degree of experience should benefit. It appears that this is the case.

One unfortunate feature of the courses is that, through no fault of the training staff, medical staff are rarely involved in these courses. Para-medical staff (radiologists, physiotherapists, etc.) are regularly involved and on some of the senior management courses medical staff in these particular areas are also present. It is, however, extremely unusual for surgeons or other medical staff to take part in management training courses at levels other than senior management, although it goes without saying that their presence would be extremely beneficial at middle management level. It may be that their particular skills are such that they are employed primarily for their professional ability. However, people of this order are vitally involved in the management of the hospital because (1) they put demands on the system in order to practise their professional skills and (2) they hold authority in the various technical and administrative committees upon which they represent medical opinion. It is impossible to develop meaningful case study and practical exercise work without students taking the part of the medical staff who are essential to the running of the hospital and yet it is rare to find medical staff on the courses who could give an accurate interpretation of the findings of groups when considering medical matters.

Conclusion

One factor which is not lacking in management development in the hospital service is support—even initiative and pressure—from the top. The Department of Health has realised that most of the complaints about the service and the inefficiencies and abuses from which the (comparatively few) justified complaints arise are the result of ineffective management rather than lack of commitment or technical competence. Given the right management structure and given managers who ally managerial competence with the technical skills which they already exercise, the majority of the minor spots and blemishes on the winsome face of the National Health Service will be removed.

Resources are certainly being poured into the area and as soon as an acceptance and appreciation of the managerial task is general throughout the nursing and medical professions we can anticipate immeasurable increases in the standards of efficiency which must reflect in the improvement in patient care that is the aim of all members of the Service.

18

Management Development in the Insurance Industry

*Vernon Walker Jones, Manager (Personnel), Legal & General
Assurance Society Limited*

Legal & General is a composite office dealing with all branches of insurance. Founded in 1836, its UK staff now number over 6000.

The Chief Administration comprises about 2500 staff and is divided between offices in London and Kingswood in Surrey. The sales force is divided into seven regions each controlled by a regional manager and then subdivided into area and district sales offices. Management development is the responsibility of the Personnel Department which also controls the training function and manpower planning.

Structure of Legal & General

The Chief Executive Officer, who is also a Main Board director, has five divisional heads reporting to him (see Figure 18:1).

Below the first reporting level are officials with the titles of assistant general manager and/or manager according to the ranking of their respective positions. Managers in the actuarial division have titles appropriate to their profession.

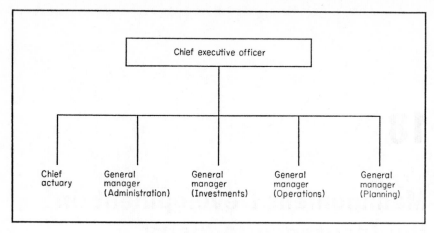

Figure 18:1   Structure of top management in Legal & General

The remaining officials and staff are graded from 8 down to 1 and each grade has a salary band with upper and lower overlapping limits.

Official titles are given to staff in grades 8 to 6 and job titles to other staff according to their function (see Figure 18:2).

Corresponding grades are arranged for specialist departments such as Management Services, Estates and Accounts.

Introduction of a formal management development scheme

Before the launching of our formal scheme, management development relied largely on the intuitive skills of existing managers in finding and developing new managers.

Grade	Title
8	Controller
7	Assistant Controller
6	Superintendent
5	Chief Clerk
4	Section Leader
3	Deputy Section Leader
2	Clerk (trained)
1	Clerk

Figure 18:2   Examples of titles of officers and jobs

Salaries were reviewed annually on the birthday month and reports submitted to the Personnel Department. A question in the review form asked whether the staff concerned had potential for promotion and the reviewing official was required to give gradings (1–10) to each of 10 qualities—some of which were rather subjective.

The decision to have a formal scheme of management development was taken at board level and the Chief Executive Officer and his senior advisers were involved at each stage of the preparation.

It was decided that the scheme would initially include all officials and staff down to and including grade 3 even though some in the lower grades had relatively minor supervisory duties. The purpose was to develop management in depth.

Objectives of the scheme

The objectives of the scheme are to ensure that :

1   Each member of the staff is employed effectively in the job in which he can make the greatest contribution.
2   The progress of each member of the staff is assessed fairly and objectively, and that he is given the opportunity to develop his ability to enable him to reach the level of responsibility for which he is best fitted.
3   The future requirements of staff at all levels can be satisfied.

Management by objectives

From the outset the principles of MBO were the foundation on which the scheme was built.

A pilot MBO scheme was launched in one department at about the same time as management development and the managers concerned soon recognised that the two subjects were compatible and, indeed, interdependent.

It was foreseen at the outset that, where MBO-style job descriptions were not already in existence, assessing officials would have considerable difficulty in assessing performance objectively over a previous period of 12 months.

This problem was acknowledged and the importance of properly written job descriptions was emphasised. Assessing officials were recommended to use the first cycle interview to formulate and agree MBO-style job descriptions which would set out standards of performance and controls in key tasks for the forthcoming review period.

The following basic rules were made :

1 That each member of staff concerned should be assessed by the official immediately in charge of him
2 That no official should have to carry out more than 15 assessments (This resulted in some cases in assessments being carried out by grade 5 staff.)
3 That all assessments would be confirmed by 'grandfather' and seen by 'great grandfather'.

Launching procedure

A manual was prepared which described the scheme in detail, giving examples of how the various forms should be completed. The Chief Executive Officer sent a preliminary notice to each member of the staff explaining the principles and objectives of the scheme. A presentation of the scheme was made by the General Manager (Administration) to all officials (down to grade 6) at the Annual Conference in May 1970. Each received a copy of the manual.

The Manager (Personnel) (responsible for the administration and control of the scheme) met divisional and departmental heads to explain the working of the scheme in detail and to deal with any queries.

Guidance notes were issued to all who would be carrying out assessments. Assessment interviews were carried out throughout the Society during October 1970. Before the assessments each of the staff to be assessed received a form entitled 'Preparation for the annual interview'.

The completed reports were returned to the Personnel Department where a central card index was established, designed to record performance and potential ratings.

The reports were analysed and training programmes prepared for the forthcoming year.

Results of the first year's cycle

At the completion of the first year's cycle in which 2109 assessments were made, a voluntary feedback occurred from managers at all levels.

Generally speaking, they reported that the scheme had been well received. There had been some apprehension at first but from most of the staff the ultimate reaction had ranged from 'favourable' to 'enthusiastic'. The first cycle of the scheme was judged to have :

1 Improved relationships between most managers and their staff
2 Highlighted the need for adequate job descriptions
3 Provided information leading to an assessment of the real training needs.

The problems encountered in the first year were :

1 Managers found difficulty in establishing 'norms' for grading in-dividual performance. Our conclusion was that their problem was one of interpretation of this particular part of the manual.
2 The reports contained too many 'essays' which were sometimes difficult to translate into positive action or provide data for manpower planning.
3 A number of managers had not fully accepted that management development is a line function and consequently tended to abdicate their full responsibilities, particularly in so far as training was concerned.
4 The sheer weight of numbers presented a record-keeping problem.

Changes made for the second cycle

Based on the experience of the first year, the following were the main features considered in planning the second cycle :

1 Post-experience 'workshops' should be held to enable assessing officials collectively (in groups of 15 to 20) to discuss the problems they had encountered in the first cycle with the Manager (Personnel) and his assistants. The aim was to achieve a consistent approach throughout the Society.
2 Managers required more time to complete their interviews.
3 Personnel Department should collate some of the information pro-duced, analyse it, and feed it back to divisional and departmental heads in such form as could be used by them for future planning.
4 Maximum possible use should be made of the computer to minimise

time-consuming manual operations, and to form the basis for the manpower planning exercise.

5   A retrieval system should be designed for the computer to assist the Personnel Department in providing an advisory service for promotions or staff movement.

The second-year cycle

The revised scheme was submitted to a number of officials at varying levels, all of whom contributed useful suggestions for further improvement based on their personal experiences. The basic features of the present scheme are as follows.

Each assessing official arranges an interview date for each of the staff concerned and gives him the form 'Preparation for annual interview' (Figure 18:3). The object of this form is to ensure that staff understand the purpose and key points of the interview and, therefore, are ready to make their own contribution. Question 4 is particularly important as it emphasises that action is required by both participants as a result of the meeting.

The assessing official makes his assessments prior to each interview, consulting, where necessary, with any colleagues who may be able to make a useful contribution regarding specific performance over the period under review.

The interview is carried out (see pages 338–339).

The assessment form is shown to the next two senior officials for approval and endorsement.

The assessment form, together with others from the same department or division, is returned to the Management Development Unit of the Personnel Department.

All assessment forms are checked to ensure that they have been completed correctly. Copies of the form MD1A (computer input form—Figure 18:4) are sent in batches to the computer section dealing with this exercise.

Punch cards are prepared by the computer section from the copy MD1A forms and a number of analyses prepared for the Management Development Unit.

The MD1 forms are filed by the Management Development Unit under strict security measures.

MANAGEMENT DEVELOPMENT IN THE INSURANCE INDUSTRY

MANAGEMENT DEVELOPMENT

(CAREER AND PROMOTION PLANNING)

PREPARATION FOR ANNUAL INTERVIEW

Management Development is a continuous process of which the annual interview is a vital part.
In order that the maximum benefit shall be obtained, it is essential that you should prepare for this meeting because the more you are able to participate the more you will benefit from it. You will, of course, have had regular day to day contact with your immediate senior but the importance of meeting formally is that you can discuss together your work over the previous year, agree what can be done to improve your performance in your job and make plans for the development of your career.

Before the interview, consider how you would answer the following questions:

1 Have you a clear understanding of the purpose of your job and what is expected of you?

2 Have you agreed with your immediate superior what are your key tasks?

3 How well do you think you have done the job during the last year?

4 What do you think can be done to help you to improve your performance and prepare you for future advancement:
   (a) by yourself?
   (b) by your manager?
   (c) by the Training Section of Personnel Department?
   (d) by any other department?

5 What do you think are your particular strengths and weaknesses?
   Are your strengths being utilised to the full in your present job?
   Do your weaknesses affect your performance? If they do, what can be done to rectify them?

6 What are your ambitions?
   Do you want to develop in your present work or are you interested in work elsewhere in the Society?

7 If the opportunity arose would you be prepared to move to:
   (a) anywhere in this country?
   (b) a limited area?

Remember that the objective is to reach **AGREEMENT** on:

1 The purpose of your job.

2 The key tasks which must be fulfilled satisfactorily if the purpose of the job is to be achieved.

3 The standards of performance, including methods of checking whether these standards are being achieved.

4 What can be done to improve your performance and to prepare you for future promotion.

Figure 18:3   Instructions for preparation for annual interview

STRICTLY PRIVATE AND CONFIDENTIAL   MD1A

NOTE: All boxes must be completed. Blanks must not be left. Please write legibly in red ink

Staff number

Copy from front page of form MD I
the number appearing below
the name

I   4

Date of birth

Copy from front page of form MD I
the last line of the label

5   10

Factor 2

11

Factor 3

I	2	3	4	5	6	7	8	9	10

12   21

Factor 4

22

Factor 5

M – Management
S – Specialist
B – Both
O – Rated D or E in factor 4

23

Factor 6

Now	End of year				
	I	2	3	4	5

If retiring, enter
're' for those years
following retirement

24   35

Factor 7

Enter appropriate departmental code
If no change envisaged enter 'O's

36   39

Factor 10

I	2	3	4	5	6	7	8	9	10	11	12	13	14

R – Required
N – Not required

40   53

NOTE: Ensure that all boxes have been completed

Figure 18:4   Computer input form

A	Exceptionally high level of performance
B	Quality of performance higher than would normally be required
C	Completely satisfactory and meets demands made on him
D	Performance does not always reach the required standards
E	Performance consistently below required standard
X	Has not yet had opportunity to show his abilities to the extent that judgement would be valid

Key tasks	A	B	C	D	E	X	Comments
1							
2							
3							
4							
5							
6							

Figure 18:5 Assessment of performance

The central card index is updated and the copy MD1A forms are destroyed.

Assessment form

The assessment form (MD1) has 13 sections requiring attention by the assessing official and, for 7 of these, factors are entered in the form MD1A (attached to MD1), Figure 18:4, which is used as the input to the computer record. The sections are as follows:

1 The key tasks of the job for the period under review are listed and an assessment made according to ratings A, B, C, D, E or X as shown in Figure 18:5. Comments are required where performance is graded other than C.

2 An assessment is made of the *overall* job performance using the grading table in Figure 18:5 and this is entered in factor 2 in form MD1A.

3 Ten specific qualities are listed (Figure 18:6) and ratings recorded in factor 3 of MD1A. Any particular weakness (indicated by D or E rating) which inhibits satisfactory performance is discussed with the individual. These ratings are a particularly important part of each individual record as they are used as a guide when considering suitability for other work or promotion.

4 An assessment of potential is made in accordance with the table shown in Figure 18:7 and recorded in factor 4 of MD1A.

5 The assessing official is required to indicate, in those cases where potential is rated A, B or C, whether the individual is suitable for future promotion in a line management and/or a specialist role. This is indicated in factor 5 of MD1A.

6 In the boxes in factor 6 of MD1A are entered the grades which are potentially possible for each of the next five years. If there is immediate potential then the next grade is entered under NOW. This factor provides the basis for listing staff considered ready for promotion and also serves to provide basic data for manpower planning.

7 If interest is expressed in another area of work this is indicated by a departmental code in factor 7 of MD1A.

8 Each of the staff is invited to comment on his present mobility and his answer is recorded in the MD1 form itself.

MANAGEMENT DEVELOPMENT IN THE INSURANCE INDUSTRY

Quality	A	B	C	D	E
1 Understanding of all aspects of job	Exceptional knowledge	Good knowledge	Satisfactory knowledge	Fair degree of knowledge but requires some help	Needs a lot of help
2 Quality in relation to basic standard	Very accurate and reliable	Accurate — rarely makes mistakes	Normally accurate and proficient	Tendency to make mistakes. Work must be checked	Unreliable — inclined to repeat mistakes
3 Use of initiative within the limits of job	Exceptionally enterprising	Self-reliant and competent	Normally able to deal with matters within his own competence	Follows the rules, but has little idea what questions to refer to his supervisor	Refers all queries to his supervisor
4 Quantity of work achieved in job	Exceptionally high output	Output above standard	Meets required standard	Tends to be rather slow	Output inadequate
5 Extent of supervision required	Capable of a high level of independent work	Requires a minimum of supervision	Is able to get on with his work with normal supervision	Needs encouragement to get on with his work	Requires constant supervision
6 Ability to adapt to changing conditions and requirements	Exeptionally adaptable	Adapts easily	Adapts to change satisfactorily	Slow to adjust	Does not adjust — suitable for repetitive work only
7 Attitude to job	Maximum possible degree of commitment	Very interested	Interested	Apathetic	Complete lack of interest
8 Extent of organising ability within limitations of job	Exceptional degree of organising ability	Organises himself and others efficiently	Competent organiser of own work	While recognising need, requires assistance to organise work	No ability
9 Degree of analytical ability shown	Highly perceptive Quick to grasp situations and present relevant and practical solutions	Normally considers all implications and possibilities	Analyses problems—sees obvious answers	Needs help to analyse problems	No ability
10 Ability to control others within the limits of job	Exceptional ability to motivate and control	Can lead in competence and confidence	Capable of communicating objectives and obtaining effective results	Ineffectual and lacking personal confidence	No ability

Figure 18:6   Personal factors

A	Potential for promotion 3 grades above present position
B	Potential for promotion 2 grades above present position
C	Potential for promotion 1 grade above present position
D	At this stage not possible to assess potential for promotion
E	No potential for promotion; has reached his limit

Figure 18:7   Assessment of potential

9   This is directly related to question 4 of the form 'Preparation for the annual interview' and reads as follows:

Training

Consider the assessment you have made in section 1 (performance in the 'key tasks') and what action has been agreed to improve his present performance and to prepare him for future promotion. Decide:

1   What action he will take *himself*, for example by studying for appropriate examinations, by selected reading, by undertaking specific projects, etc.
2   What action will be taken by *you*, for example by personal tuition, by departmental training, including courses, by job rotation, etc.
3   What assistance can be given by the Training Section of Personnel Department, for example by internal course, by external course or seminar, etc.
4   What help can be given by any other department.

The object of this section is to identify the training needs by direct reference to the performance in the key tasks listed in section 1. It is also intended to establish the responsibility for training. A form MD2 (Figure 18:8) is provided for use by the assessing official to record action which is agreed during the interview.

Training programme for   (Name)   (Title)

Assessing official

Department

NOTE:- This is a working form. When filling it in, please leave space for future amendments

Key task	Training to be carried out	Date to be started	Date to be finished	Training objective and review date	Notes on method

Figure 18:8 Individual training programme

1	Leadership	8	Appraisal interviewing
2	Delegation	9	Technique of training
3	Work planning and control	10	Report writing
4	Decision-making	11	Public speaking
5	Budgetary control	12	Statistical analysis
6	Computer appreciation	13	Job description writing
7	Recruitment and selection procedures	14	Target setting

Figure 18:9   Management training needs

10   Fourteen management skills are listed (Figure 18:9) and training required indicated in factor 10 of MD1A. The objective here is to identify the demand for particular training so that the management training courses can be planned. There was a tendency in the first year for the need to be identified merely as 'management training'.

11   This section allows for the assessing official to describe any other training need which is required to be met by the Personnel Department.

12   The assessing official writes a brief report, commenting on any particular matters arising from the interview, including the reaction of the staff concerned.

13   The assessing official signs the report which is then endorsed by the next two senior officials. Space is provided for any further comments.

Interview

The main objectives of the interview are to:

1   Discuss with the individual how he has performed during the period under review.

2   Agree with him what can be done to improve performance in the present job and for future promotion (if appropriate).

Guidelines are given as follows :

1 Start the interview by explaining what are its objectives.
2 Deal first with the strengths in performance of the job.
3 Discuss inadequacies in a helpful, constructive way.
4 Listen at least as much as you talk.
5 Stick to job performance and avoid consideration of personality unless this affects satisfactory performance.
6 Establish positive plans for training with particular reference to the subject of responsibility.

Job description

This is based on the principles of MBO and incorporates the following main points :

1 Statement of main purpose of job
2 Details of reporting levels
3 List of key tasks (the tasks where successful results are essential if the main purpose of the job is to be achieved)
4 The agreed standard of performance in each of the key tasks
5 The controls whereby the job holder can check progress
6 The personal activities of the job holder.

These job descriptions are kept by individual managers (with copies held by the job holders) and are intended to be working documents which should be constantly under review to ensure that they are kept up to date.

Use of a computer

This can produce an emotional reaction from staff if not handled properly. They may imagine that they have been 'dehumanised' and that their individual identities have been replaced by a series of symbols and electronic impulses. It must be made clear that the computer is merely being used to do more efficiently operations which otherwise would have to be done very laboriously by hand.

Particular care must be taken when arranging the program that there is absolute security as far as the input is concerned and also that the output analyses and listings are issued only to the departmental managers who control the staff concerned.

Output from the computer

Schedules are prepared from the computer as follows:

1 Lists of staff with immediate potential
2 Lists of staff with potential for promotion after one year
3 An analysis of the management training needs listed in factor 10 of the MD1A form
4 A projection of the potential assessments over the next five years. This is then compared with the staff requirements, in grades, shown in the corporate plan.
5 Lists of staff who have expressed interest in working in other departments, should the opportunity arise.

Schedules 1, 2 and 4 are provided for each departmental manager. They provide the information necessary for forward planning in his own department.

The analysis of management training needs is used by the Training Unit to plan courses and other training during the forthcoming year.

Training

The Personnel Department is responsible for training and runs a training centre controlled by the official who is responsible for the management development scheme. In this way our plans for training are based on 'needs' rather than 'wants'. Needs for training are basically established from actual performance in the key tasks but increasing emphasis is being placed on the training of staff at all levels in the skills of management so that the maximum benefit may be obtained from our most expensive resource—people.

Technical training is regarded mainly as a departmental responsibility but the central training unit in Personnel Department undertakes the training of departmental instructors. A most important aspect of this training is in the use of modern media such as audio-visual aids.

Manpower planning

The data produced from the management development scheme combined with the existing computer payroll file provide the basic source of information for manpower planning. Programs have been prepared for the computer to support a staff wastage study so that the forecasting of staff needs can be more accurately made. Data will be collected to form historical records of job experience to assist in the selection of staff for promotion and movement.

The potential assessments are collated and matched against manpower requirements over the five-year planning period so that an assessment can be made as to whether the present stock of staff is sufficient to support future expected needs or whether recruitment is necessary at any particular grades to 'fill in' the weak areas.

Management development and the line manager

From the outset it has been stressed that management development is a line function; staff will develop themselves given the right circumstances and proper encouragement. The responsibility of the Personnel Department is to maintain overall coordination with a strong element of control in so far as the maintenance and use of a central record system is concerned. The purpose of this central control is to provide a service to line management by conducting 'searches' which will eventually be assisted by a computer retrieval system.

Service by the personnel department

The success of management development must be judged by what it actually achieves, and line managers must see positive benefits accruing to themselves following the assessments and interviews carried out.

To this end there must be a 'follow up' by the Management Development Unit to discuss with the managers concerned:

1 Staff with high potential to ensure that adequate thought has been given to forward planning of individual careers.

2 Staff whose performance is judged to be below the standards required to decide whether training of any kind could raise performance to adequate levels or whether they could be better employed elsewhere.

The basic function of our own Management Development Unit is to create the circumstances which encourage self-development, offer an internal consultancy service, provide training to improve current performance and to ensure that each member of the staff achieves the highest position consistent with his or her competence.

19

Management Development in Agriculture

George Hayward, Principal Lecturer in Management Studies,
Anglian Regional Management Centre—Danbury Park

Agriculture is a land-using industry and is consequently geographically widely dispersed. Until the last two decades, an absence of significant returns to scale has resulted in a structure comprising small business units. The individual units can support only a small number of personnel in executive positions and the existence of a formal management hierarchy within a farm business is rare. There is thus little opportunity for specialisation of function by executive personnel. This situation has several important implications for management education.

First, the geographical dispersion of the industry and the low density of population of agricultural managers means that any management course aiming to train at a high level could only attract students of the necessary calibre from a large catchment area. Part-time study at a high level would be extremely difficult, if not impossible, because of the problems of distance.

Second, with the small number of executive staff per business and the small size of businesses, sponsorship by employers is most unlikely since key staff could not be released for any length of time without being replaced. The work carried out by the Agricultural, Horticultural and Forestry Industry Training Board in the provision of short courses and modular training will be dealt with later in the chapter.

Third, because the manager in agriculture must necessarily be versatile and competent over a wide range of management activities, any long course of study must be broadly based.

Full-time courses

A course meeting these criteria has now been running as a joint venture between Danbury Park Management Centre and the Essex Institute of Agriculture for two years. It is a full-time residential course designed to attract the already technically qualified agriculturist at a point in his career when the acquisition of managerial skills is critical to his further progress. The course is three terms in length, and the successful members on the joint management course will gain the postgraduate Diploma in Management Studies (Agriculture) which is approved by the Department of Education and Science.

If a potential manager is to undertake a full-time course, he will need to do so before he is heavily committed with a career, family and financial burdens. The course members are somewhat younger than those taking the current Diploma in Management Studies courses from industry but they have nevertheless already obtained a good sound background in agriculture on which to base their learning.

All the course members have been committed to a career in agriculture since leaving school at the age of seventeen or eighteen. All have completed extensive periods of practical experience as well as full-time vocational courses. In addition many course members are recruited from farming families where they will have been exposed to the technical and business problems of the industry from an early age.

The Diploma in Management Studies (Agriculture) course has the following objectives. It aims at developing within the course member:

1 The ability to determine and understand various management techniques and their application to agriculture
2 A broad understanding of the environment in which the agriculture industry operates

3   The ability to work effectively and responsibly with other people
4   The ability to arrive at, and convey to others, considered opinions on a wide variety of agricultural and industrial problems
5   The ability to integrate knowledge and experience in making appropriate decisions.

In order to gain maximum interplay between members and to ensure the widest participation, each course has been confined to a group of ten to twelve course members who are subjected to a wide variety of teaching methods, such as 'live' case studies based on both farms and industrial organisations, the use of closed-circuit television, seminars, and a dual environment of the Essex Institute of Agriculture which possesses modern teaching facilities and an estate of 500 acres devoted to the operation of commercial-scale agricultural and horticultural enterprises, and that of Danbury Park Management Centre which is an old country house in fine surroundings and one of the designated Regional Management Centres offering a wide range of courses to industry.

Within the broad framework of the course, an opportunity exists for individual members to develop special areas of study under staff supervision.

Course members also join the Diploma in Management Studies (DMS) students from industry on a range of 'live' case studies. The method of carrying out this aspect of teaching may be of special interest. Case studies based on activities at the Essex Institute of Agriculture have been written up by Arthur Longbottom, the Head of the Management Studies Department at Writtle, and a brief given to course members from the DMS (Agriculture) and DMS members from industry. Syndicates are then formed with the DMS (Agriculture) course members acting as consultants to those from industry. Cases are prepared and delivered to the combined group. The discussion and 'post mortem' on these live case studies are very wide and the learning situation greatly appreciated by both groups of course members. This is being extended to include 'live' industrial case studies which will involve the DMS (Agriculture) course members in reverse roles.

The Diploma in Management Studies (Agriculture) course is aimed at the technically qualified agriculturist who is on the threshold of a management career in the large-scale farm business, in advisory work, in private consultancy or in ancillary trades. The course is open to holders of a University degree, National Diploma in Agriculture, National

Diploma in Horticulture, National Diploma in Dairying, National Diploma in Poultry Husbandry, Higher National Diploma in Agriculture or Horticulture and allied fields. It is also suitable for those holding professional qualifications of the Royal Institute of Chartered Surveyors, The Chartered Auctioneers and Estate Agents Institute, The Chartered Land Agents Society and the Incorporated Society of Auctioneers and Landed Property Agents. In exceptional circumstances, candidates with proven ability and experience in an appropriate area may be admitted without the above qualifications.

Diploma in Management Studies (Agriculture) syllabus

Stage I

The course is divided into two stages spread over three terms but these are neither rigid nor inflexible and readily merge with one another. Stage I comprises the following subject areas:

1 Studies in management I
2 Human behaviour in the enterprise
3 Economics
4 Introduction to basic techniques of quantitative analysis
5 Introduction to the design of management accounting systems
6 Financing the business I
7 Work study and labour planning techniques.

In addition course members spend some time during this stage on case studies, individually supervised projects, tutorial sessions and on specific written assignments based on set readings.

Studies in management I. This part of the course provides an opportunity for the student to make a detailed study of the nature of management and the activities within the individual manager's own command. The course is highly participative and requires a great deal of self development from course members. Lecture-discussions, case studies, projects and researches into management literature are used as teaching methods and aim to develop the management skills in full. This aspect of the course also takes the course members into a wide variety of industrial firms so that he may make an assessment of managerial problems under many varied circumstances. The visits are prefaced by a briefing and then summarised after each visit. The course member with a background in agriculture gains an opportunity to see how industry works and to discover for himself how various management principles and techniques are applied under differing conditions.

Human behaviour in the enterprise. This aspect of the course is closely linked with 'studies in management' and seeks to assess the factors affecting the behaviour of individuals and of groups in the work situation. Origins of behaviour, perception and communication, development of attitudes, morale, leadership, fatigue and patterns of work, motivation to work and sources of dissatisfaction are dealt with together with the measurement of intelligence, personality and group attitudes, and the application of these measurements to selection and the maintenance of a satisfactory human relations climate in the working environment. A great deal of this work is carried out in syndicates.

Economics. This section of the course aims at giving the course member a brief introduction to the nature of economics. The intention is not to train students as economists but to give them sufficient background to comprehend economics and to interpret economic findings.

Introduction to the basic techniques of quantitative analysis. Again, this is an introduction to statistics which enables students to interpret quantitative data and shows them how to set out data in the most productive and understandable manner. Students are made familiar with measures of central tendencies, measures of dispersion, elementary sampling concepts, significance testing and elementary analysis of time series. Research papers on a wide range of topics directly related to agriculture are used to demonstrate the value of statistics and how to use the techniques in the interpretation of scientific findings.

Introduction to the design of management accounting systems. An examination is made of money in the business, assets, liabilities and net worth, balance sheet analysis and its use to management and the measurement and interpretation of trends. The profit area is studied with a view to showing the meaning of profit, the accounts necessary to calculate profit and profit as a measure of business efficiency.

Students are guided through assessment of the business, measurement or resources used, analysis of sales and expenditure, calculation of efficiency factors, interpretation of accounts and the presentation of information acceptable to management for control of the business. The various forms of budgets are discussed and principles of cost accountancy are examined in relation to their advantages and limitations in the agriculture businesses.

Financing the business I. The needs and sources of finance are studied for the farm business. The capital requirements of agriculture and the financing both of the national farm and individual farm business are explored and the need for capital investment to develop the business and yet remain competitive is studied.

Sources of credit are considered together with the credit worthiness of the individual business and the determination of security for loan capital. Sources of credit in the long, medium and short term are discussed and the relative advantages and disadvantages of borrowing money from different sources are considered.

Work study and labour planning techniques. Work study, method study, transport and materials handling, work measurement, activity sampling and other techniques are all assessed in relation to their use in agriculture. Labour on the farm is studied, the 'drift from the land', the seasonal nature of labour use and the substitution of capital equipment for labour. Attention is paid to labour recording and planning and the analysis of labour and its use and management. Remuneration of the workers, motives and reward of farm workers, minimum wages, piece work, working conditions and incentive schemes all form part of this subject area.

Stage II

Stage II comprises the following groups of subjects :

8   Studies in management II
9   Application of techniques of quantitative analysis
10 Business documentation and office organisation
11 Legal aspects of business decisions in agriculture
12 Financing the business II

13 Marketing I
14 Studies in management III and business policy
15 Staff management, personnel administration and industrial relations
16 The implications of taxation and estate duty in business
17 Marketing II—commodity seminars
18 Role of agriculture in the national economy.

This final stage is fully supplemented by a major case study, varying farm visits to supplement the learning situation, one complete individual case study, tutorials and supervised projects and reading assignments.

Studies in management II. This section of the course provides an opportunity for detailed study of the basic processes relevant to managing and case studies are used to integrate this area. The major processes of management, planning, organising, controlling, directing, allocation of resources and innovating are all examined in some detail and related to the needs of the manager in agriculture. These processes are also examined in the various industrial situations by means of visits and discussions following the visits.

Application of techniques of quantitative analysis. Once the student has grasped the basic essentials of quantitative analysis he then progresses to a study of the techniques and examines significance tests, correlation and regression, sample designs for quality control, optimisation using linear programming methods, Monte Carlo analysis, critical path method, inventory management, value analysis and ergonomics. All these techniques are related to the work situation and practical examples given.

Business documentation and office organisation. This important feature of the farm is not neglected and the office as a management support activity is considered and also the general office services, and an examination is made of clerical functions and procedures such as procurement and purchase accounts, stock control, sales ordering and invoicing, sales accounting, cash control, wages systems and management information. The physical layout of the office, use of machines, office forms and planning office methods are all given attention.

Legal aspects of business decisions in agriculture. The objective of this subject is not to supplant the use of professional legal advice but rather

349

to give an appreciation of principles of the law of contract, outline of the law of tort—especially negligence, trespass and nuisance. Various statutes affecting farmers are considered such as the Contracts of Employment Act, Redundancy Payments Act and the Industrial Training Act. A brief summary is made of trade union law and collective bargaining. Special attention is paid in particular to 'standard forms' of contract recommended by the National Farmers' Union.

Financing the business II. This area studies the development of farm business structure in relation to the money market, capital planning and investment appraisal. Financing of industry from savings, by issue of shares, from undistributed profits; loans, types of shares, the working of the Stock Exchange and speculation all have their place. The planned use of capital in agriculture, theories of investment, depreciation, earning power, returns on total capital and returns to marginal investment; capital appraisal, discounted cash flow, annuity payments, amortisation and pay-back methods are considered. During this course a visit is made to study some of the working of the City.

Marketing I. Marketing is assuming greater importance in agriculture and an introduction to the subject is made at this stage of the course in order to familiarise course members with basic marketing techniques, sales research, product promotion, market intelligence, advertising and export procedures. The current marketing of agricultural produce, the determination of guarantees, the calculation of deficiency payments for review products and the role of statutory bodies in the marketing of agricultural products are explored.

Studies in management III and business policy. In this final part of the course emphasis is laid on the problems and policies of top-level management and on analysis and problem solving using complex integrative types of case studies. Major aspects covered are a study of management by objectives related to the agricultural environment and of corporate planning for the enterprise.

The study of business policy serves to integrate all other subject areas so that subjects such as marketing and finance fit into a balanced view of the enterprise. Management 'tool' areas such as economics and human behaviour are given a correct perspective and course members are assisted to make a transition from academic studies to the practical application of concepts in the business situation.

Staff management, personnel administration and industrial relations. The course members examine manpower planning and the demographic, social and economic influences. Studies are made of communications, changing attitudes and communicating the managers' point of view. Job analysis is explored and the recruitment and selection of staff together with job evaluation methods and staff appraisal. Students give attention to the contract of employment and to industrial training with its implications on the agricultural industry.

An examination is made of the legal framework for industrial relations. Industrial conflict, collective bargaining, the role of shop stewards and trade union structure with special reference to the agricultural industry are made a part of this section of students' work.

Implications of taxation and estate duty in business. An introduction to tax administration in the United Kingdom is given and distinction made between business and private expenditure. Allowable deductions and prohibited expenses are considered with regard to calculating taxable profits. Capital allowances on plant, buildings, patents and scientific research are discussed. Limited company formation and estate duty are major components of this area of study.

Marketing II—commodity seminars. Groups of individual commodities are described and appraised by student groups who present their findings to the class as a whole. Various aspects of each commodity such as current supply/demand position, trends in production and factors influencing demand, current marketing arrangements, current problems and possible solutions and likely future developments in the marketing systems are reviewed. The following commodity groups are covered in seminars; root crops, cereals, milk and dairy products, fat stock, vegetables, fruit and processing crops, and eggs and poultry meat.

Role of agriculture in the national economy. Mention is made of the efficiency of resource use in agriculture, the development of current policy, the need for selective expansion and agriculture as an import saver. Consideration is given to the strategic and social importance of agriculture. For the future, attention is paid to the possibility of price and income stability, the prospects of food surpluses, the European Economic Community and the common agricultural policy of its members; also the cost of United Kingdom entry and the implications for British agriculture.

Assessment

All the potential managers on this course are continuously assessed on course work, written assignments and examinations. Special attention is given to their work on a live case study and on their solution to the problems posed. Assessment is made by a panel of academics, practising farm managers and industrialists. It is felt that the blend of academic work combined with industrial expertise in an agricultural setting is a milestone in managerial education.

Other courses

Although the information given above is based on the joint Danbury Park Management Centre and Essex Institute of Agriculture scheme, a very similar course is also being operated by Seale Hayne Agricultural College at Newton Abbot and Plymouth Polytechnic. This course is similar to the one detailed above and also qualifies for the Department of Education and Science award of the postgraduate Diploma in Management Studies. This joint venture approach between Agricultural Colleges and Management Centres is one of great interest and has aroused considerable comment outside the area of agriculture.

A further noteworthy venture is a post-diploma course in agricultural marketing and business administration which is run by the Harper Adams Agricultural College, Newport, Shropshire, in conjunction with the Management and Business Studies Department of the North Staffordshire College of Technology. This again is a full-time course lasting one year and is aimed at training personnel for business posts at managerial level in various commercial organisations, cooperatives and marketing boards, and the larger scale farming organisations.

This course is of three-term duration with emphasis on tutorials and seminars. Students are involved in a number of projects which involve considerable research and outside visiting. Emphasis is also laid on the assessment of data with a view to reaching reasoned decisions in managerial situations. The course is in two sections :

1   Agricultural marketing
2   Business administration.

Agricultural marketing covers economic theory and statistics; the marketing functions; market intelligence, research and advertising; marketing legislation, organisation, structures and institutions; merchanting, distribution and sales organisation; and international trade.

Business administration comprises business law and organisation; capital, credit and investment appraisal; insurance; taxation requirements and effects on business; management; labour management and organisation; data processing; office organisation and communications.

Other full-time courses are available in management for agriculture but the ones mentioned above are of particular interest because of their cooperative nature and because of the benefits ensuing from contact with other educational institutions and with students from different areas. Details of the various courses may be obtained from *Agricultural Education*, a booklet prepared by the Department of Education and Science and the Central Office of Information, 1971, obtainable from HMSO.

Short courses

The Agricultural, Horticultural and Forestry Industry Training Board is very much aware of the need for management training in the industry, and has plans for future developments. A representative working party meets regularly to provide advice on the implementation of the Training Board's policy in management training. As a result of the survey of training needs it is considered that the actual training should be carried out in modules not exceeding four days in length and held at times most convenient to the industry. This training will be carried out in conjunction mainly with the education services. The needs of individual managers may be catered for by their attending the module or modules which will be of the most value. These modules may be taken in any order, but introductory modules will be held in order to familiarise trainees who have had no previous training with the total concept of management within the business and later with the content of more specific modules.

Considerable care will be taken to determine the objectives of these modules and to ensure that they fill a genuine need and one which is not already being adequately provided by other organisations. The Board feels that such needs will be most acute where the manager cannot easily and at a reasonable cost rely on outside experts, where the requirement is a continuous and frequently occurring one and where 'attitudes of mind' or 'thought processes' rather than simple mechanical techniques or knowledge are required.

Effective use of managerial time

A factor of great interest in agriculture, as in all other areas of management, is the effective use of managerial time. Quite a number of books and articles have appeared in management literature on the use of time in various functions but a recent article by Ansell and Giles makes a very detailed study of how the farmer spends his time. This paper is of great interest to those teaching management and especially management in agriculture as one of the questions arousing especial interest is how managers, either self-employed farmers or salaried managers, spend their time. The report sets out to provide the answer. It is based on time sheets kept by sixteen farmers and farm managers, all members of the Berkshire Branch of the Farm Management Association. It appropriately commences with a quotation from Drucker, 'Everybody has the problem of time : for of all resources it is the scarcest, the most perishable and the most elusive'.

The manager has the job of being concerned with the organisation as a whole and it is the task of combining the various resources, men, money and materials into a profitable enterprise that makes the allocation of time so important. Time to the manager is the scarcest of commodities and one which he often finds the most difficult to manage, for not only has he to carry out various functional tasks but he is also concerned with managing other people with all the attendant problems. On top of this he has to think and plan ahead for the future and not just work from one crisis to another. To be able to think and plan ahead effectively, he must therefore have 'chunks' of discretionary time in which he can sit down and think.

In order to avail himself of this discretionary time it is essential that the manager keeps some form of record of how he spends his working time and then proceeds to analyse this with a view to improving his work pattern and ascertaining the most effective way of organising time. In the study mentioned, the farmer or farm manager was asked to complete a time sheet like the one in Figure 19:1 for the first week in each month for a whole year. It was appreciated by the authors that by choosing the first week in each month, some distortion could arise due to not taking account of various duties that only take place at the month end, but it was felt that this was not greatly significant in view of the limited time probably spent on these duties.

From the example shown it will be seen that the day is divided into fifteen-minute intervals and as guidance the following headings were suggested :

1   Manual
2   Trading—buying and selling
3   Issuing instructions
4   Clerical
5   Inspection
6   Supervision
7   Gathering information
8   Planning
9   Other work (not connected with the farm).

The fifteen farms ranged in size from 134 to 4092 acres and the average length of the managers' working week was calculated to be 59.5 hours in respect of farm work on all of the sixteen farms. The range of hours worked was from 42 to 84.25 hours. Not surprisingly, the authors found that the type of work undertaken by the managers varied greatly and this is shown in Figure 19:2.

The work goes on to draw up management profiles for the six small and medium-sized farms (134 to 337 acres) and the nine large farms (963 to 2387 acres) for the manual work and non-managerial work. Manual work tends to dominate on the small farm and managerial work dominates on the large farm as would be expected. However, a most interesting conclusion drawn is that the time spent on managerial work is remarkably constant within each of the profiles from month to month. A point noted was that of fragmentation of the day, in other words the manager takes up a job, drops it for something else and then takes it up again. This is very similar to the pattern of the manager working in industry who shows this fragmented and very episodic profile to his work pattern.

Week commencing			Day	
7 am	Issuing instructions	3 pm	With owner	
	to workers and			
	organising days			
	work			
8 am	Checking livestock and	4 pm	Meet rep - buying	
	treating sick pigs		Checking temperatures of sick pigs. Examine	
	Dealing with		sows due to farrow	
	correspondence		Inspect jobs done during day	
9 am	Meal	5 pm		
			Meal	
	Telephone calls			
10 am	Transporting pigs	6 pm		
	to slaughterhouse		Not working	
11 am	Buying-spares	7 pm		
	etc. and travelling		Travelling	
12 noon		8 pm		
			NAAS talk on	
			grassland management	
	Meal			
1 am		9 pm		
	Issuing instructions			
	to workers		Travelling	
2 pm		10 pm		
	Discussion of			
	valuation and		Not working	
	trading account			

Figure 19:1   Specimen time sheet for a farm manager

Source: Ansell & Giles, *The Farmer and his Time*

Code number	N	F	D	R	S	O	C	I	G	J	K	A	M	H	B	E
Acres	134	157	207	303	325	337	963	1090	1400	1440	1876	1949	2003	2082	2387	4092
Type of Work	%	%	%	%	%	%	%	%	%	%	%	%	%	%	%	%
Manual Work	71	73	82	79	61	83	5	32	5	15	12	5	27	16	20	—
Trading	2	3	1	3	2	1	10	6	5	6	4	13	10	7	7	6
Issuing Instructions	1	4	1	1	3	4	7	4	14	9	4	10	5	7	6	6
Clerical	12	8	6	5	19	2	29	16	22	8	17	15	15	13	13	23
Inspection	2	5	2	2	3	4	17	13	14	29	33	24	21	18	20	15
Supervision	1	—	1	6	5	2	7	2	17	26	10	14	8	24	12	6
Gathering Information	7	2	5	3	1	3	11	11	13	3	10	15	9	2	12	24
Planning	4	5	2	1	6	1	14	16	10	4	10	4	5	13	10	20
Total	100	100	100	100	100	100	100	100	100	100	100	100	100	100	100	100
Average hours per week per farm (to nearest hour)	74	58	54	72	84	53	66	57	62	56	62	43	59	48	57	42

Figure 19:2 Pattern of total farm work

On each farm in order of size and by type of work

Source: Ansell & Giles, *The Farmer and his Time*

MANAGEMENT DEVELOPMENT IN AGRICULTURE

The report is well worth reading and illustrates a very valuable technique in the training of managers in agriculture. If more managers would carry out a self-recording technique for how they spend their time and then carry out analyses on their various tasks they would gain a much clearer picture of the role of a manager. Facts become much sharper when set down in written form and the analysis of data can be carried out as and when the manager can find the time! Careful analysis of the raw data can be valuable in examining the nature, duration and method of solution of the various problems which find their way to the manager. If these problems are recorded over a period of time in some precise form the manager will have a ready record of his own problem solving behaviour and can then decide what he personally can do about it. The manager will be enabled to record the percentage of time spent on various jobs and can then discuss its proportions with other farm managers to determine whether there is any common pattern running through their day.

The work done in this area by Ansell and Giles was followed up by a further study commissioned by the Farm Management Association in which 450 questionnaires were distributed with a total response of 311 (69 per cent). The whole of the United Kingdom was covered and a total of 276 questionnaires was finally included in the analysis giving the very high response rate of 61 per cent of the original distribution list.

From this analysis an identikit was made up of various characteristics exhibited by Britain's farm managers. The basic facts show that nearly all Britain's farm managers are married males aged between 30 and 49 and approximately one-third come from families with a farming background. Public schools accounted for 35 per cent and grammar schools for 45 per cent. Most of the managers had held four or five jobs including their present one, with an average duration of two to four years. If compared with industrial management the figure of 90 per cent of managers holding some kind of formal qualification to carry out their job is pleasantly high. About one-half of the managers were paid on a fixed salary basis but nearly one-third drew bonuses in addition.

The majority of farm managers (60 per cent) were in jobs that required one to three months' notice and just over half enjoyed a basic pension of some kind. Over two-thirds were entitled to two to three weeks' holiday a year but over one-half did not take their full entitlement. Almost 75 per cent of the respondents worked between 50 and 70 hours a week and about one-half claimed that less than 10 per cent of their time was spent on manual work, but approximately 33 per cent estimated that 10 to 50 per cent of their time was spent on manual work.

About one-half of the managers were to be found on farms between 500 and 1500 acres with a trend towards arable systems. Almost two-thirds of the sample worked on farms with a labour force in excess of seven and nearly one-third worked with labour forces of fifteen or more. Although 75 per cent were responsible for such tasks as recruitment and dismissal of staff, buying and selling, very few were responsible for long-term fixed investment decisions. Some 85 per cent had full- or part-time clerical or secretarial assistance.

One surprising fact was that just over one-half (54 per cent) considered themselves to be seriously or slightly underemployed and although for the main part they were well satisfied with the kind of work, personal relationships and freedom, they were a good deal less than satisfied with their general conditions of employment such as salary, security and promotion. It was found that problems involving personnel and personal relationships are the most demanding in managers' opinions and this is supported by the fact that human behaviour is one of the most popular subjects in my experience of Diploma in Management Studies students. Great satisfaction was derived by many farm managers from the notion of 'being one's own boss'. Lack of free time was an often voiced complaint but in spite of the various complaints over 40 per cent of respondents claimed that they were never likely to give up the job of farm manager.

From the point of view of this study the opinion of most of the respondents was that major changes will of necessity be towards more formal management training; it was in fact this recognition which led many of the respondents to join the Farm Managers' Association in the first place.

Giles and Mills followed with Part 2 of their work in February 1971 and this looked at the manager's job in four areas:

1 Training
2 Job description
3 Terms of employment
4 Job satisfaction.

From the sample examined it would appear that the farm manager is basically well qualified, and it would appear that he is certainly better qualified than his industrial counterpart, as 22 per cent held a degree, 66 per cent a diploma, and this percentage was higher still in the group aged under forty. The managers themselves suggested that further qualifications would be required in the future and the report does emphasise the need for post-experience training as well as formal qualifications in management. Again such areas as finance and dealing with 'human problems' were identified as subjects requiring further study.

It was of interest to note that the vast majority of managers felt satisfied with the actual nature of their work, with the personal relationships and with their status as farm managers. For those concerned with management training in agriculture a careful reading of the works cited will be invaluable and close study of the tables will amply repay the time spent.

Work of rural sociologists

Agriculture has far too often in the past been considered as an industry apart and even in academic circles little attention has been paid to work done in the agricultural environment, with the possible exception of economists. However, researchers may well find that work done in such aspects of agriculture as rural sociology may prevent repetition of research work carried out many years previously.

Market researchers could benefit greatly from reading some of the papers published by rural sociologists in the area of innovation and especially in the diffusion of new innovations, and I feel that this chapter would not be complete without reference to some of this work and its value to managers in both industry and agriculture.

An area in which work by rural sociologists has been outstanding is in the work done on the diffusion of innovations, or the study of how innovations spread throughout communities, and these studies deal with the transmission of farm innovations from agricultural scientists to the farmers. Work was being carried out in this tradition as early as the 1920s. A classic work was Ryan and Gross's Hybrid Seed Corn Study, the major findings from which are of value to all concerned with marketing; these are that:

1 The initial use of hybrid seed followed a bell-shaped distribution curve when plotted over time and four adopter categories were classified on the basis of their first use of hybrid seed.

2   Three stages in the adoption process were recognised by the workers:
(a) Awareness or first hearing about the new innovation
(b) Trial, or the first use of the seed corn
(c) Adoption, or 100 per cent use.
3   The period of adoption ranging from awareness to 100 per cent adoption averaged about nine years for all respondents.
4   The average farmer first heard of hybrid seed from a salesman, but his neighbouring farmers were the greatest influence on adoption.

Sociometric methods were used in a later study in an analysis of the adoption of soil conservation methods by Illinois farmers in 1946 in which the influence of the farmers' peers was stressed as an important factor in adoption. Work has been carried out in diffusion studies in the United Kingdom in such areas as bulk milk adoption and these studies are of great value to management in general. Work carried out in all areas of diffusion of innovations has been summarised by Everett M. Rogers and is worthy of further study.

To summarise, agriculture as a major industry is well aware of the need for management training and this is being carried out in colleges and universities, often on a cooperative basis with management centres, to cater for the new entrant to management in agriculture and those wishing to extend their existing knowledge. The Agricultural, Horticultural and Forestry Industries Training Board is very well geared to the short intensive course for the practising farmer and farm manager and those who will require 'topping up' from time to time, and has future development in these areas under active consideration.

Research carried out on how managers spend their time and on the profiles of the farm manager is a very important training aid to enable managers to obtain some comparison with others as to how best to spend the day. In the tradition of research in diffusion of innovation the rural sociologists are giving a useful lead to all interested in marketing, and emphasise the need for multidisciplinary studies.

References

Ansell, D. J. and Giles, A. K., *The Farmer and His Time; An Agricultural Exercise in 'Activity Sampling'*, University of Reading, Department of Agricultural Economics, Miscellaneous Study No. 46, July 1969.

MANAGEMENT DEVELOPMENT IN AGRICULTURE

Giles, A. K. and Mills, F. D., *Farm Managers; Part 1: A summary of data from an enquiry into the profession; a study commissioned by the Farm Management Association*, University of Reading, Department of Agricultural Economics, Miscellaneous Study No. 47, 1970.

Giles, A. K. and Mills, F. D., *More about Farm Managers; Part 2: An enquiry into the profession commissioned by the Farm Management Association*, University of Reading, Department of Agricultural Economics and Management, Miscellaneous Study No. 49, February 1971.

Rogers, Everett M., *Diffusion of Innovations*, The Free Press of Glencoe, 1962.

Ryan, Bryce and Gross, Neal C., 'The Diffusion of Hybrid Seed Corn in Two Iowa Communities', *Rural Sociology*, **8** (1943), 15–24.

Note—Danbury Park Management Centre is now part of the Anglian Regional Management Centre, which has been formed by the North East London Polytechnic in association with the Mid-Essex Technical College and operates as a Faculty of North East London Polytechnic.

20

Management Development in Distribution

K. C. Lawrence, Director of Training, Distributive Industry Training Board

Background of the industry

The basic activities of the distributive industry are buying and selling goods in such a way as to realise a profit. To do this it has to buy what the customer wants, or persuade the customer that he needs what it has bought, at a price and in the quantities which will enable the process to be repeated satisfactorily from both the customers' and the firm's point of view.

Various methods of carrying out these activities effectively have developed and the industry is now one of enormous and increasing diversity. The means of selling vary between wholesaling, retailing by counter service, self-service and mail order. The means of buying vary from direct buying from manufacturers, from agents, from wholesalers, buying through individual buyers to buying by committee. The organisations vary from international organisations with thousands of outlets to the small corner shop—from organisations dealing with one type of goods to those dealing with virtually all types of consumer goods. There are organisations who seek to create particular customer demand, others who react to demands. It could be said of any industry that it is one of change because of new materials, processes, product design and manufacturing techniques but distribution is probably changing more fundamentally and more rapidly than most. If we look around us we can see the external changes. More cars, more parking restrictions, high property values in central sites mean for many retailers fewer customers with more capital tied up in property. The development of shopping precincts, urban development programmes means for many well-established businesses removal from established 'markets' and customer sources.

Problems of rapid change

Social and economic changes have resulted in the customer having different requirements and expectations about the environment, the service and the choice he or she now expects as opposed to those of a very few years ago. At the same time, a very large proportion of the workers in distribution are part-timers, augmenting family income, not particularly interested in long-term career prospects.

The growth of large distributive organisations with enormous buying power has led to a situation where with some merchandise the distributor sets the quality standards for the manufacturer who cannot afford to lose the contract. This, inevitably, has led to such distributors having to employ experts in manufacturing processes, chemists and technologists, who can set and check standards and processing methods.

Thus, management in this industry has to work in an environment of rapid change. This includes changing methods, structures, different forms of competition, changing expectations and attitudes, both of employee and customer.

Imagine going to work one morning to find: a third of the staff are different from those employed last week, the main source of custom about to be removed because of a town redevelopment scheme; because of a revaluation of property, rent on the premises being increased; a change in the weather adversely affecting the sales promotion of a high and expensive item of stock and a competitor down the road undercutting prices on your main lines by a substantial amount.

For those in the distributive industry as proprietors or managers these are some of the problems which may have to be faced as well as the more usual managerial problems of delegation, communication and human relations. For many managers in distribution problems arise from the presence of the vital third party—the customer, a situation rare in most industries.

Organisation structures

The organisation structure behind and around managers and the degree of freedom to operate inevitably vary. In the distributive industry there are branch managers whose main responsibility is to ensure that their store is clean, adequately staffed and meets sales targets set by regional managers, the buying, pricing, product promotion decisions being made centrally on a national front. There are 'buyers' in departmental stores who are responsible for the purchase of particular types of merchandise and for its presentation and sale; the limits on their authority tend to be those of budgets and the company merchandise policy.

There are organisations with central head offices but with the main business being conducted in branches spread across the country. The head office employs experts and specialists covering all aspects of merchandising, buying, financial control, stock control, transportation, etc. For such organisations there are problems of communication, control and training because of the spread of outlets.

There are organisations such as Mail Order houses and departmental stores in which the senior management and specialists are in the same buildings as the majority of the staff. While such organisations do not have the distance difficulties of the multiples they have all the normal managerial problems encountered in any industry.

However, in the final analysis, management, as represented either by a number of people operating in specialist or general areas or by one man, will tend to be related to 'What merchandise to buy and sell?' 'When and from whom it should be bought?' 'At what price?' 'When and at how much should it be sold?' 'How should it be presented?' 'What stocks should be held?' 'How much capital to invest or reinvest in fittings, premises?' The large organisation works in millions of pounds sterling, the small in hundreds. One, possibly, buys from the manufacturer and negotiates quantity, price and brand names—the other from a wholesaler or manufacturers' representative and, more frequently, haggles over the quantity he believes he can sell.

There is, however, a vast difference in the relative effect of the decisions upon those who make them. It is probable that the senior executive of a large organisation has less personally at stake in making his million-pound decision than the owner proprietor in making his hundred-pound decision. In the event of a 'wrong' decision the first might face dismissal with a golden handshake, the latter might face bankruptcy.

The larger organisation will have experts, specialists and facilities to help to provide the information upon which decision are based. It also has the difficulty of ensuring that decisions and information move through the various levels of staff at a speed which will make them effective at the right time. The smaller organisation has to rely much more upon one or two people who need some expertise in all major activities.

Within all this we must recognise the highly competitive nature and environment. Distribution competes to attract the potential customer into contact, through the shop, the catalogue, or the agent or the warehouse. It then has to sell against competition on price, range, service, delivery, etc. By its very nature it is in the hands of the manufacturer or the supplier. Industrial disputes or poor quality manufacture, resulting in short supplies or returned goods, tend to reflect directly on the distributor, rather than the manufacturer. It is more sensitive to economic change than almost any other sector of the economy.

Management development

Against such a background the distributive industry has to develop managers, it has to ensure that by structure, by policy, by selection and by training that management can maintain profitability at a level which will lay the foundations for the future. At the same time, it has to ensure that future generations of managers will be able to deal with an industry which may be operating in fundamentally different ways.

The choice would seem to be to plan to develop through an evolutionary process or change rapidly by a revolution. Clearly, the former is a more realistic and sensible approach. However, it does depend upon defining overall aims and strategies in all activities, having a view of trends and probable developments. Such questions as 'will off centre shopping centres become a normal pattern?'—'is discounting to become a more general practice?' 'Will voluntary groups expand?' 'What effects will such developments have on the business?'—all have to be considered in planning the use and development of all the resources within the company. It could be said of most organisations that the primary emphasis has to be on the development of business in all its facets. There are, however, examples in most industries of organisations whose highly developed management programmes failed to keep them in business because other aspects failed at a point when the development programme was out of step with the operating problems.

Establishing corporate objectives

The first major basic step for any company, but particularly because of the rapidity of change, for distributive organisations, is to determine and constantly update the corporate aims of the firm, both in the long and the short term. It must also ensure that it does not apply outdated solutions to new problems. Management development must be focused on helping people towards the achievement of the organisation's aims and the solution of both corporate and departmental problems. Particularly in companies which believe in training and development, the aim of management training or development is often specifically defined when the total business aim is no more than a vague assumption. There are many examples of succession plans for management without success plans for the business. Management development must be regarded neither as an end in itself nor an optional extra. Just as programmes have to be geared to individual needs so they must be geared to changing organisational objectives and problems.

Thus, it is suggested that the starting point for very many businesses is to establish the 'where are we now' in meaningful, quantitative terms. To do this means posing some of the fairly fundamental questions— 'What business are we in?' 'Who are our customers?' 'How well are we doing—what are the critical and meaningful business ratios?' 'How do we stand?'

More frequently than not, the results of such examinations in distribution indicate the weaknesses which appear in many organisations in most industries. The organisation in terms of the allocation of authority, responsibility for activities, does not match the needs of the company or the measures by which individual performances are judged. The information available to many managers is either inadequate or inappropriate. Their experience or skill is not related to the functions they are supposed to perform and, indeed, those functions are often unclear. In other words, because the objectives have become vague and the organisation inappropriate, managers operate on assumptions, based on previous experience, about both aims and responsibilities and levels of performance.

Having established the starting position, the next series of questions stem from the basic questions 'Where should we be and where do we want to be?' 'What do the general trends indicate?' 'What stops us doing better and what is likely to affect our future performance?' 'When must we be in the new situation?' This leads to an examination of what is effectively preventing the closure of the gap between achievement and hope. The levels at which such questions are posed is vital. They must be asked, originally, at the very top. The levels from which some of the answers should be sought are equally vital; in large companies they have to come from all levels of management and supervision, simply because that is where the real know-how lies. Policy from the top has to be practically applied at all management levels and that demands under-standing and involvement to obtain commitment to the actions which arise.

Indeed, the posing of the questions and the formulation of answers itself constitutes a basic management development programme. In certain cases the first step is, in fact, to persuade senior management that such questions have to be asked and that the answers are not self-evident. This is particularly true in companies enjoying comparative success. To illustrate such an approach, where the need became apparent, let us examine an actual situation in a furniture retailing business.

Case study: furniture retailing

The Managing Director, in examining his accounts, found that while his sales turnover had remained constant, his staff costs had increased and a too high proportion of capital was tied up in stock, consequently, his profits were reduced. A critical tour of the store indicated that the stock range was very wide, sales promotions were uncoordinated in various sections, goods were not grouped conveniently and in some cases did not carry price tags.

The initial reaction to the situation was to put the shop-keeping aspects in order and to let the managers know how little he thought of their performance generally. The steps were fairly clear, to cut down on stocks, to dispose of some at mark-down prices in a sale, to check on displays more frequently and to insist that all goods were price tagged. However, he remembered that he had been through this, or a similar exercise, before; it was, indeed, a recurring cycle of events and while it gave temporary improvement, the overall trend remained the same.

Discussions with individual managers showed that they were very knowledgeable about the merchandise and were very good 'face to face' salesmen. This was to be expected since they were all promoted from the salesfloor and had been with the company some time. The discussions also revealed that they had few statistics available about their department's performance, they had neither budgets nor targets and judged performance on sales turnover, or the absence of customer complaints and by the comments of the Managing Director as he visited departments. As far as they were concerned, business was not too bad but a competitor down the road was having some effect—'because his goods were cheaper'.

It became very clear to the Managing Director that there was no understanding about the firm's market aims, and, therefore, no application of a specific merchandising policy or defined objectives. In general, the general attitude was 'we sell furniture and if we do that successfully we make a profit', and 'our reputation speaks for itself'.

These discussions confirmed his view that some fundamental thinking about and clarification of aims was necessary. He felt he could afford neither the time nor the money to have his managers trained and in any case, realised that such training would serve little purpose unless the company aims were properly defined, and the operating methods refined. On the other hand, he recognised that the company was approaching a crisis point financially and competitively. Rapid change was necessary and would have to be fairly fundamental, both in approach and method, but, at the same time, the business had to be kept running for six days in the week.

His aim was clear, he had to increase profitability and the return on the capital invested. He believed that he could achieve this by:

1   Establishing a specific company image and market aim. History, reputation and competition indicated that the market should be the middle and higher income groups and the image related to the product range and customer service.
2   Limiting the range of stocks and not seeking to compete in particular ranges.
3   Coordinating product and departmental sales promotions.

4   Developing an overall profit-planning system.
5   Establishing departmental performance measures related to profit as well as sales turnover.

He explained the aims and methods to the managers but realised that the situation in which decisions were made at the top had developed men who would not make decisions and who did not contribute ideas other than on 'selling'. This background, together with the vagueness of the current organisation structure, the absence of defined performance criteria or monitoring systems he knew could lead to a reversion to the existing situation once the novelty of change had worn off.

Training or 'individual development' within the existing structure would serve little purpose. To convert sales turnover oriented managers into profit conscious 'resource' managers was itself difficult and would not create change unless the system itself prevented a return to old systems and attitudes. At the same time, no system could work unless those operating it had appropriate knowledge, skill and commitment.

He decided, therefore, that the two processes should go hand in hand, and drew up the following action plan :

1   Discussions between Managing Director and managers about company aims and the role of the Managers in the planned changes
2   Revision of organisation structure. A Merchandising Director appointed to coordinate all merchandising activities
3   Introduction of departmental budgeting system
4   Introduction of unit stock control system based on range analysis
5   Introduction of departmental profit targets
6   Clearance sales to reduce stock holding and limit range
7   Reorganisation of store layout
8   Introduction of system of staff performance appraisal.

Having established the sequence of main operating changes a plan of management involvement, communication and training was instituted. It was decided that no training sessions for managers would be conducted or planned unless the technique and methods were to be put to immediate use by those attending and, conversely, no new methods would be introduced without adequate preparation of those concerned; practice had to rapidly follow theory.

Thus, the Merchandising Director ran in-store sessions on sales analysis and forecasting, the Company Accountant explained budgetary control systems before the introduction of the departmental budgetary system. The Merchandising Director also ran sessions on stock control and range analysis before the unit stock control system was introduced. At each stage, managers were expected to contribute ideas on the application and then put the systems into operation. The definition of departmental targets by the managers followed sessions on target setting, and on the value of particular ratios.

The reorganisation of store layout was conducted by a project team of managers chaired by the Managing Director, the members of the team visited other stores and attended method study courses.

The introduction of performance reviews was preceded by discussions on target setting and augmented by monthly progress meetings in which departmental performances were examined against trading accounts and budgets. The whole programme was planned to be covered in a year but improved business results were apparent within months. Equally apparent was the effect on individual managers. The Managing Director found that he had to force himself not to take over decision-making from some managers, that he had to provide more information 'down the line' than he had previously. Many of the managers who had, initially, resented the changes because of the apparent change from what they regarded as the main function of selling to dealing with 'paper', found that they were deriving greater satisfaction from having a broader view and from making more use of their staff. Whilst retaining a deep interest in merchandise and sales turnover they began to see the overall picture and thought in terms of profitability and cost effectiveness.

In other words, all managers found that by being used themselves and by focusing on business targets they were developing themselves and developing others. Most of them began to determine knowledge and skill needs in themselves and sought ways of satisfying those needs within or outside the company. The qualities to which they looked in their own staff to move into management or supervisory roles ceased to be simply selling expertise or merchandise knowledge. Clearly, a few managers could not cope with the new situation and either resigned or were dismissed.

In this example the situation dictated some of the actions and the time scale over which they had to be conducted. However, the principles which were applied are those which need to be understood and applied in any distributive organisation.

MANAGEMENT DEVELOPMENT IN DISTRIBUTION

Diagnosis of personal development needs

In many cases there is a need for people to move away from merchandise, sales turnover orientation, to being concerned for profitability and business efficiency. This means that there has to be a greater knowledge and awareness of distributive business management and of the means of making the most efficient use of all resources.

Management as a body has the aim of running a successful enterprise and, therefore, individual managers must be aware of what constitutes success for the business. Their measures of performance have to be related to the aim of the company. Aims which are specialist functional aims may not contribute to overall company success—as defined. For example, a sales department's measure of performance may be to achieve high sales turnover and sales per square foot of selling space. To achieve targets in these areas might involve training, development and direction of staff, but high sales turnover does not necessarily mean profitability. Thus, measures to achieve one 'functional' type of success may not contribute significantly to the business's total aim.

The roles of people in the work situation must be determined by the aims and needs of the business and not by the people themselves. People, naturally, will tend to wish to do those things which they do best and in which they have the greatest self-confidence. Thus, one finds sales managers who sell but do not manage, who concentrate on sales turnover and not profit; on doing not delegating or developing others.

The actions which one takes to train and develop people must be linked to early application of methods and techniques. Frequently one finds managers, or trainee managers, being given training in certain techniques which they cannot put into practice. The result is either frustration in the job or rejection of the theories or techniques in a practical application.

The structure in terms of communication lines, responsibilities and authority must be designed and operated in such a way that managers are not frustrated in their endeavours to achieve realistic levels of performance. There is little point in showing branch managers how to improve stock turn or improve the return on capital in the premises yet, at the same time, so limiting their authority to make decisions that they can only criticise the decisions made centrally without, themselves, being able to affect the results at their own branch.

The application of ready-made prescriptions under the heading of 'management development' such as appraisal, succession planning, job rotation or courses, if applied without proper diagnosis may do no more than treat the symptoms and obscure the disease.

Management development must be total management development from top to bottom. If managers are to develop individually at the lower and middle levels, top management itself has to develop, and to accept that limiting freedom of action or access to information, to certain levels or individuals, will stunt development—a plant cannot grow beyond the confines of the box—unless it destroys the box. If management is concerned with the efficient utilisation of all resources, managers have to be developed who are able, and given the freedom to influence the deployment and development of those resources. This means that they have to be aware of and competent with the most effective techniques and encouraged to adopt them.

Overall, the distributive industry has to cope with changes, it is affected by and effects changes in society and in the economy. However, in the final analysis management development is not the concern of an industry, it is the concern of individual companies who, in the short term, wish to survive and lay the foundations for improving their prosperity in the longer term. Equally, it is the concern of individual managers, whose performance and future job prospects depend upon their ability to be successful on a managerial front. In the distributive industry shorter and longer terms may be different from manufacturing industry. It can take years to take a project like 'Concorde' from original idea to production, during which time new managerial methods and approaches can be developed along with the main line project. In distribution the need to change from counter service to self service, from local buying to central buying may be a matter of weeks or months and management has to change and develop at that pace. While the manufacturer and the customer are major influences, distributive management has to be aware of the fact that it has to change at a speed dictated from elsewhere as well as being able to bring about changes in its own way at a pace which is established by its own ability to change. Thus, in distribution, successful management has to be pragmatic and practical. It has to face and answer problems which almost inevitably appear more immediate than in manufacturing industries. Yet it has to avoid the solution to the immediate problem becoming the cause of a longer term crisis. Management development has to be designed to produce flexibility in outlook and approach; the ability to plan for and operate within changing situations. Distributive managers have to be flexible but not aimless.

It is generally suggested that the ability of British industry to produce well-designed, well-made goods has been often dissipated by an apparent inability to market them. This may stem from a belief that quality will, in the end, speak for itself, and that sales and profit will follow. Distribution may have a similar problem in believing that good merchandise, good service and acceptable prices will attract custom. Such a view may obscure the fact that profitability stems from the effective use of all resources, and may require some basic theories of customer service to be abandoned in the interests of business success. Business success, in terms of profit or return on capital, requires structures, methods and measures of performance to be designed in those terms. It requires management to be developed towards that aim and not with the aim of their being able to use fashionable management or distributive techniques, however viable they might appear to be in theory. The industry has also to avoid the rejection of new theories or techniques simply because 'distribution is different'.

There are organisations in the distributive industry of whom it could be said that their way of conducting business, their approach to management, their selection, development and use of talent is unequalled by any industry. These are the companies that have led the way in change and who in practice synthesise the views expressed in this chapter. Their business results are good, their financial position secure, their long-term competitive position secure, their standing in the stock market strong, all of which is reflected in the customer/staff and staff/manager relationship.

It may be felt that there would be value in citing the systems and philosophies of such companies as examples of and to the distributive industry. This, in my view, would be similar to providing a route map from London to Manchester and then suggesting that it is a pattern for any journey of similar distance.

The history, environment and current structures and situations will vary from company to company. Experience, background, knowledge and ability will vary from individual to individual. Management Development is concerned with the development of the body of management and with the development of individuals in, or to move into, management in a particular company. It must be planned to satisfy specific needs and to achieve specific aims and therefore there can be no general solution.

In general this chapter has concentrated upon 'business' problems and change. It may be felt that it has ignored the problems and possible methods of approaching the development of individual managers. To ignore this would be like considering road safety without considering people. However, the people in distribution are no different from people in any other industry, either individually or as a body. The large majority of managers will have achieved their present position as a result of experience and success in jobs below the one they have at present. Their job skill and knowledge will be more based on experience than on theory. Some, but probably not the required proportion, will be people who were recruited or joined the industry as management trainees. Each type poses problems. The older more experienced manager is, naturally, more resistant to change, particularly when it appears to nullify the value of his previous experience.

The buyer who becomes a shop manager and then finds that 'buying' is to be controlled centrally, using quantitative techniques based on computer models may resent the system and feel frustrated. The younger entrants, completely *au fait* with the latest techniques and principles, may become frustrated because they cannot apply them. This is not peculiar to distribution. Indeed, this industry possibly has fewer resisters to change than most, simply because of its nature.

Very frequently the problem in distribution is not a lack of belief or a failure to see a need to develop people but lack of facilities or an apparent lack of opportunity. In some cases this is more apparent than real because the jargon, the examples and the approach to management development tends to be that of the manufacturing or processing industry. Overall the industry averages between five and ten people in an establishment and that fact, together with the differences in the situations described earlier, would appear to support the view that 'distribution is different'.

The purpose of this chapter has been to show that in distribution the emphasis has to be on monitoring the existing situation, constantly defining and redefining aims and objectives in the 'full business sense', and in involving management by a proper planned balance of theory and practice. It also seeks to emphasise that in distribution situations can change and develop managers, just as managers can change and develop situations. It is vital for the prosperity of a company and the satisfaction of the people concerned, that the right balance is achieved. This requires the recognition that the development of people is an integral part of distributive corporate planning and action, whether the company is large or small.

21

Management Development in Education

Samuel Hughes, Headmaster, Burnage High School, Manchester

In a letter dated 1839 Arnold of Rugby wrote : 'as to what regards the position of a schoolmaster in society you are well aware that it has not yet obtained that respect in England as to be able to stand by itself in public opinion as a liberal profession; it owes the rank which it holds to its connexion with the profession of a clergyman, for *that* is acknowledged universally in England to be the profession of a gentleman'. Arnold was himself in holy orders and, had he not died relatively young, would probably have ended up a bishop. He liked his staff to be ordained but forbade them curacies lest they be distracted from their main occupation of teaching. The equation of the schoolmaster and the clergyman has worn thin over the years but the basic similarity in pastoral function has never completely disappeared. For anyone to suggest that Arnold could best be updated by substituting 'manager' for 'clergyman' would still be regarded in many quarters as both inappropriate and undesirable. Less than a dozen years ago a headmaster who had the temerity to suggest at a conference that managerial training would be a most suitable preparation for his and similar posts was told by the speaker following him to take his nonsensical rubbish to the factory floor where it rightly belonged and where it should properly remain.

Attitudes, however, have altered, largely because conditions have changed. In the field of secondary education, with which this chapter is concerned, change has been rapid and widespread. In the 1950s a secondary school of over 1000 pupils was a rarity; now such a number is considered quite usual. As recently as 1965 a conference on the organisation of 'large schools' was open to heads of schools with 800 or more on roll. In 1970 the head of a school whose size had doubled in four years unwittingly remarked 'When my school was a relatively small one of 800 . . .'. Secondary reorganisation, by creating comprehensive schools, has tended to establish fewer schools and larger schools. When Manchester went comprehensive overnight in 1967, 59 schools were reduced to 24. All schools, because of the trend among schoolchildren to stay on longer, have tended to become larger. Many schools have become very large indeed, are still growing and will most certainly continue to grow even more after the school-leaving age has been raised to 16 in 1972.

When large schools emerge it is rarely because of simple growth along existing lines. A comprehensive school is not just a grammar school multiplied by two or three. More often than not it represents a grammar school combined with one or two secondary modern schools with perhaps a technical high school thrown in for good measure. Nor can a comprehensive school be regarded simply as the sum of its component parts. It is usually a highly complex organisation with different abilities and aptitudes among its pupils. Expectations of both pupils and parents will vary enormously, achievements cover a wide range and attitudes reflect these differences. A grammar school head used to a staff of 30 or 40, mainly graduates, all of whom were part of a system with widely accepted norms of performance and behaviour, might find himself presiding over a staff of 80 or 90 men and women with a wide range of qualifications and experience and called upon to fashion with them a curriculum embracing the whole spectrum of ability from Oxbridge entrant to near-illiterate and to create the machinery of a social organisation taking in both the most receptive conformist and the most antagonistic rebel. Someone has described the new comprehensive schools as 'plural societies with collective schizophrenia'; the problems of size, great in themselves, are accentuated by those of complexity.

Comparing headmastering today with the smaller and less complicated process of the 1940s, it is not difficult to identify other pressures which have mounted. One is much more conscious of financial considerations : the increasing share of the gross national product devoted to education, the largest single slice of which goes to secondary education, the costing exercises which need to be made to assess claim and counter-claim on resources in a school, the struggle against inflation. After years of relative legislative calm in the post-1944 period the 1960s have brought sharp reminders that education is an important operation of the body politic, that schools and the structure in which they function are subject to political dictation. Nowhere has this been more keenly felt than in secondary schools and if another kind of political activism has more strikingly affected higher education in the form of student unrest, there are few schools where the traditional bases of authority have not been questioned by both staff and pupils. Schools are not merely moulds, they are also very much the mirrors of a society in which turbulence and change figure prominently. Nor is educational change just structural. A tremendous reappraisal of the content and method of curricula and examinations is going on at the same time. The pedagogic explosion in content is almost as violent as the revolution in form—and all are happening not just simultaneously but also at a bewildering pace.

In such a situation it is small wonder that heads of schools are inclined to see their positions as being vastly different from what they were a few years ago. It is not possible to meet the problems of the heterogeneous, multiple, changing societies which make up our schools simply by resolving like Boxer in *Animal Farm* to work harder. One has to learn to work no less hard but differently, to turn to advantage the experience of others similarly placed in other occupations and enterprises. The parallel with the manager in industry and public administration has become obvious. Accordingly there has been a willingness to reach out for help from the principles and practices of management science, to give support to courses of in-service training aimed at discovering what can apply to education. It is not an easy search. Even after the initial reluctance and suspicion have been overcome heads of schools have found that management science is not precise like a physical science with concepts and laws readily applicable because of their universal acceptance. They have found it to be derivative, debatable and frequently couched in unfamiliar language. Often they have been puzzled and apt, in consequence, to seize upon the simplified, perhaps oversimplified, statement as being the whole truth. When—for instance—it has been suggested that the manager had a function to plan, to coordinate and to assess then the headmaster could recognise that this was what he had been doing in his school, in greater or lesser degree. Like Molière's M. Jourdain he had been speaking a kind of managerial prose, unwittingly, for a long time. As with many managers outside education heads have frequently been practising ahead of precept and then intensifying their practice once it was confirmed by precept.

Planning and identification of objectives

The planning role has always been implicitly accepted. Even in the small single-purpose school heads accepted that they needed to draw up arrangements for forthcoming events and developments. But the demands on them were often diminished by the organisation taking care of itself as it were. Fundamental appraisal was rarely needed. A grammar school was a grammar school and if a headmaster were to query the purpose and method of the school over which he had been appointed to preside then he was either incompetent or a busybody. He simply had to see that it ran efficiently, got on well with staff, parents, governors and pupils, pursue academic excellence, show willing by teaching himself, secure good examination results and keep a high standard of uniform. For the headmasters of modern schools it was different, for the idea of the secondary modern school was new and its purposes needed to be considered from fundamentals. After the war it was not enough merely to produce an up-dated elementary school. Heads had to adjust to the longer school life created by the raising of the leaving age to 15 in 1947 and to decide on objectives when the pressure for external examinations began to mount in the 1950s. Under the tripartite system the range of ability was undoubtedly greater in the modern school than in any other kind and the purposes of the school open to wider interpretation, the influence of local conditions unquestionably stronger and the pursuit for 'parity of esteem' more pressing. The technical schools, where they existed, had even more question marks hanging over them. Were they to aim to be as good as but different from the grammar schools, or quality modern schools, or trade-schools with a strong vocational bias, or new versions of the intermediate or central schools from which many of them sprang? Even in such schools fundamental purpose was often neglected, or grew up almost by accident.

The head of a large comprehensive school today has as starting point for all his planning, to think out his overall philosophy as a conscious, deliberate act. The ethos which he seeks to establish for his school has to be clear in his mind. It need not be a process of logical, creative thinking carried out in splendid isolation and then beautifully codified and handed down like the tablets. It will probably bear the influence of other minds and experiences, be the product of discussion and debate with senior colleagues, be enjoined by the conditions and limitations of catchment, locality, intake, staff recruitment, physical resources and so on. It is hardly likely to be original and will probably have parts plagiarised from other similar schools. It may (though it rarely is) be written out at length and in detail, but, whether spelled out or not, the head needs to have a clear idea of his overall objectives and to make them known as necessary reference points or guidelines for his staff at all times. Without such action the school may wander on, impelled by the daily motion of attendance, teaching and learning, but lacking a sense of purpose. Without known attitudes, too, conflicting postures may be taken on many issues, baffling to pupils and staff alike because of their inconsistency. Worse still a collection of accepted attitudes replacing a conscious code may spring up as a result of decisions taken on the spur of the moment, on the corridor, off the cuff. In the setting of the comprehensive school with so many different elements and so many disparate and conflicting objectives possible the head as overall planner has to decide his goals and determine his priorities. Let one, though an important, example suffice to illustrate this: should the school pursue academic excellence, individual advancement, the development of talent, or should it stress communal values, the importance of service, the development of social consciousness? And if the head thinks that both sets of values should be sought after simultaneously with what proportion of urgency and with what priority?

The working out of overall philosophy is only a starting point for the very practical problems of planning which the head has to face. A major one flows from it: what is to be the academic—the teaching/learning—pattern of the school? In theory the British headmaster enjoys considerable freedom in this part of his planning. He is not subject to outside dictation as are his counterparts in some countries where curricula, even timetables, are laid down by national or local bodies. But in practice he is subject to various constraints which he ignores at his peril: physical limitations such as staffing, buildings and finance, national needs, parental expectation, examination content and fashion, higher educational demands. This results in a national pattern which is broadly similar when compared with foreign patterns but inside which it would be difficult to find two schools with identical curricula.

The vast majority of heads opt for a common general course for the first few years of the secondary course in which the ingredients are fairly predictable—English, mathematics, science, history, geography, art, craft, foreign language, physical education, together with the one compulsory subject, religious instruction. Several decisions, however, have to be made even at this stage : whether there shall be any choice at all to pupils (usually there is none at this point), whether there shall be any attempt to 'stream' by ability, what shall be the relative weightings given to the various subjects, whether 'subjects' shall be retained at all or give way to 'integrated' or 'interdisciplinary' studies.

The question of streaming is obviously connected with the need for overall philosophy, especially at present when the argument for non-streaming in the secondary school gathers weight and support and can no longer be dismissed as the idiosyncracy of the freakish few. Whether lower forms are streamed or not, by the time they reach middle school they pose further problems of decision-making. How many and which foreign languages? Separate or combined sciences? What is the place of craft/aesthetic subjects? Should all pupils take all subjects? Few schools follow a compulsory pattern and increasingly heads resort to offering a choice of courses on a *table-d'hôte* principle or a series of choices *à la carte*. Examples of the former are academic, general, commercial, engineering, catering, building courses in which the subjects are grouped and the pupil opts for the total course. In the latter case the school insists on a mandatory element covering English and mathematics and the pupil adds four or five other subjects drawn from overlapping or complementary pools of subjects. Decisions of many kinds now have to be made—the arrangement of the pools, the limit of choice, the viability of small subject groups—and whether he realises it or not the head's decisions will be coloured by his underlying attitudes.

At present, two separate public examination systems, the General Certificate of Education at ordinary level and the new Certificate of Secondary Education exist side by side to be taken by pupils who are 16 years old. Courses and examinations for the two systems are quite different in the majority of subjects and decisions about who does what have to be made two years before the examination in several cases. There is even the decision whether the pupils shall take any examination at all—whether it be a form of by-passing because the pupil is very good or of rejection because the pupil is not considered good enough. In either case the establishment of criteria is a duty which the head cannot evade.

The responsibility of devising the academic framework is far from over by the 16-plus stage. The sixth form of today has changed, perhaps imperceptibly to the outsider during the past decade. Generally it is larger in number, for many pupils stay on today if only for no better reason than that the entry qualification in many professions and occupations has been raised from the ordinary to the advanced level of GCE. Aspirations for higher education has intensified and opportunities for it have increased. The sixth form no longer consists of a small band of potential undergraduates who have surmounted a fairly high academic hurdle to gain admittance to it; in fact, overall, the future university entrant is in a minority. Academic planning therefore has to take into account the new category of sixth-former, at the same time addressing itself to the continuing yet changing needs of the old—particularly the demand for new subjects and new treatment of old ones and the growing recognition that the total academic development of the sixth-former needs a measure of general education be it general studies or optional extras, or 'minority' non-examinable extras. The 'majority' need persists and the head has to address himself yearly to the way in which he arranges his pools of options of advanced-level subjects so that they make sense, offer opportunity and also have relevance to the middle-school system of options through which the pupils have earlier passed.

Management of resources

A year or two ago at one of the in-service courses for headteachers a speaker from industry stated that the good manager had 'to obtain the best out of the resources available—money, materials, time and people'. The good headmaster would accept a similar obligation but would want to change the order of the resources. The head in the independent school, be it boarding or not, has a financial balancing act to perform—the services provided and the salaries paid must correspond with the fees raised, or vice versa. The head in the local authority school is freed from this responsibility. But like the administrator in any service or non-profit making organisation he must accept a large measure of financial dependence. There are few local authorities that hand over a global sum to their headmasters from which they supply all the needs of the school. Generally the head is granted an allowance based on the number and age of his pupils—his capitation allowance—for the purchase of text-books, exercise books and teaching materials. There are frequently additions for special purposes such as field-work and study courses or to meet special needs such as an immigrant influx. Examination fees are usually not charged to the school and items of capital expenditure and furniture, repairs and renovation are borne by the authority. The capitation allowance—always insufficient—is chicken feed by industrial standards and the head even of a school of over 1000 pupils is probably dispensing finances only of the order of £5000 per year. The subdivision of this sum is a matter of considerable comparative importance to the various parts of the school, and it needs to be carefully and fairly made. But the total is low, the operation of very limited duration, variability with other resources or factors non-existent and there is no possibility of transferring items from one account to another. So financial control can be ruled out. Despite that, however, finances do loom large in the life of the school especially because all the many extracurricular activities which are undertaken—the running of a magazine, the staging of a play, the travel of teams, to mention but a few—need money, the raising and disbursing of which can become a major preoccupation. Obviously the head will need to be much involved, though if he is wise he will seek ways of involving other members of staff in the non-capitation finances, possibly by the creation of a finance committee.

Materials, like finance, are likely to be a small part of the whole, externally supplied and financed and subject to little variability. They are insignificant compared with the stock-in-trade of a wholesale firm or the raw materials or finished goods of a factory. However, the other two resources mentioned—time and people—are of paramount importance in a school. Time there seems to be in abundance—whole years of pupils' lives, whole working days of teachers' labour—yet it is priceless beyond measure. It needs consideration in many different ways. There is for instance the need for the head to have his sequence of time right and his assessment of the time needed for various task performances more or less correct. All planning is 'forward' planning and the head needs always to be a jump ahead of those around him : 'I shall be up before you are awake, afield before you are up and breakfasted before you are afield' says Bathsheba in *Far from the Madding Crowd* to her astonished farm labourers. In a school the head has frequently to be 'living ahead' of the moment, making projections of class sizes and course needs, translating the implications of present actions into future models. This is especially the case in the summer term when the head is concerned with the pattern of the new school year ahead and, in his mind, has already lifted the school a whole year. His model is one in which 2 alpha is already 3 alpha—and it is not uncommon in his consultations with staff to run into misunderstanding because he and they are on a different time-band.

Another entirely different dimension of time is the use the head makes of his own time. It is still considered slightly indecent or unprofessional for the head to give up time, or rather create time by giving up other things, so that he can address himself to the problems of managing his school. Heads still tend to fill up their days with the trivial round and common task and then sacrifice their nights to the formulation of policy.

The greatest obligation, however, must be the ordering aright of pupils' and teachers' time. All theory on curriculum has to be translated into the reality of pupils and staff being at set places at set times, spending daily and weekly allocations of time on set pursuits. The instrument for this important operation, the timetable, becomes the strongest single weapon in the hands of the head. Through it he shapes his grand design for his school. Itself it demands time for the various processes which are necessary for its final completion. It is a demanding operation in terms of size alone : a school of 60 teaching groups each following a seven-period day five days of the week would need a 2100-piece timetable even if there were no subdivisions for options and specialisms. In effect such an organisation would probably end up with 2300 'pieces' or more—a jigsaw without a known solution beforehand and one in which an error might mean two teachers to one form or, worse still, a form without a teacher.

It is common nowadays in the large schools to find the initial timetable planning beginning in the Easter term for a timetable to operate from the following September. The starting point has to be the timetable in current use, a consideration of its effectiveness, deficiencies, any known changes likely to be caused by numbers at various levels, subject changes and other relevant factors. This information must be consolidated by the head and passed on by him with a preliminary or tentative distribution sheet covering the whole school to the heads of the various subject departments.

Then follows a period of discussion, at first unilaterally between the head and the departmental heads for their reaction and then a plenary meeting with all heads to gain universal acceptance of the distribution. It is far better to iron out differences at this stage than to wait for individual disagreement later, especially as concessions at various points are needed.

The next stage is to ascertain the likely figures for option groups where they operate to find the consequent staffing requirements for the various groups and sets. Staff allocation has then to be made with the head of school looking at preliminary proposals from departmental heads and considering the load of the individual teachers especially those who may 'belong' to several departments. This has to be pushed to a fine point of detail, the head determining who is going to teach what, and the final distribution of time balanced. Once this is known the head will have to consider whether he needs to advertise for new staff in the light of the revealed needs, known resignations and retirements, though some of this has been proceeding at the same time as earlier steps.

Now the starting point of the construction of the timetable is almost reached, but not before a list of requirements and desiderata has been drawn up covering such considerations as the availability of specialist rooms, the times when part-time members of staff may be used, the needs of those staff who commute between buildings if the school is on more than one site, the requests for television or radio periods—and many more. This is virtually a briefing or programming operation. The head may be doing this for himself but most likely he is preparing it for the benefit of the timetable constructors who can relieve him at this point. These, frequently volunteers at senior staff level, may need two or three weeks or more depending on the size of the school, its complexity and the degree of sophistication which it is felt it can tolerate in this most difficult operation. The head can never totally opt out: there will be snags not foreseen and clashes which can be resolved only at the highest level. Whatever method is used for the construction, peg boards, pasteboards or paper, pencil and rubber, once it is done the work is not yet completed, for the whole has to be meticulously checked, copied, broken down for distribution. It is hardly surprising that in recent years much research has gone into the mechanics of timetabling. A calculus to help with early and middle stages is evolving and before long the first computer-compiled timetables will be in operation.

The timetable is a means of designating people—staff and pupils—to their allotted tasks throughout the teaching day. But the relationship between head and both categories of this particular kind of 'resource' is not confined solely to lesson time. The school is a community in which the classroom process of learning and teaching is a part but only a part. With pupils the head can no longer expect to have the same degree of intimate personal knowledge which he could possess in the smaller establishment. He will know a large number of pupils—for the best, for the worst and for a variety of other, often fortuitous, reasons. He will frequently be unable to put a name to a face on encounter, or a face to a name on reference but he has no excuse for not knowing all about the vast generality of his pupils and for not knowing in considerable detail about a large number of representative individuals. He will have little opportunity for an extensive teaching programme himself. Indeed it could well be argued that his main function is to ensure that others have the best possible situations for teaching even though by talent, training and experience he could teach his pupils better than many of the staff he employs. His job is not to teach pupils but to see that his staff do, and when his staff becomes so large that the bulk of his time is devoted to managing them then he has moved in effect into the position of a manager of a group of professional practitioners.

Organisation structure

In a school, this kind of personnel management has to embrace two quite different functions. One is that which covers the various areas of learning/teaching, the academic organisation of the school. The existence of various subjects or disciplines inside schools can be traced as far back as the Greeks; the recognition of separate 'departments' in secondary schools belongs to the day before yesterday. Yet, though less than two decades old the practice is universal. The head has to determine what shall be the nature, size and areas of the various departments in his school, appoint or assist in the appointing of his heads of department and allocate staff to them. Until a few years ago the departmental divisions were simply the subject divisions writ large and this still remains the usual practice. Obviously some departments, like English or mathematics, are bound to be comparatively large and likely to continue separate from the rest. But increasingly subjects are being grouped so that separate subject departments like chemistry or physics are giving way to larger amalgamations of departments of science. New and sometimes mystifying groupings like those of 'humanities', 'technical subjects', 'communications' and 'creative activities' are appearing and only the individual school will know its particular ingredients. The development is an interesting one. In one sense it may reflect a growing realisation that the subject divisions are arbitrary and inhibiting and is therefore academic in origin. In another it may unconsciously be recognising the managerial precept that there is a limit to the number of subordinates with whom the manager can deal. However convenient the development is not without danger in the setting of the school. The effect of concentrating departments is to produce a comparatively narrow, vertical structure in which the newcomers at the bottom of such an arrangement are made conscious of their inferior position and the long way they may have to go before becoming a head of department themselves. It is a bleak prospect if you happen to be 14th in a science department! It is, too, in contrast with the accepted norm of professional behaviour and attitude. The teacher is autonomous in his classroom and although team-teaching is spreading it is still very much a minority practice. The teacher does not sell his services independently like a solicitor or a dentist but he does like to feel that he has a right to professional dignity. There is as well a suspicion that many of the departmental concentrations are artificial with administrative rather than educational considerations uppermost. For both reasons a more shallow arrangement of departments may be organisationally less commendable but educationally and personally more desirable.

The second structure which the head has to devise is that which covers the non-teaching organisation of the school. This embraces the administrative and pastoral functions, the volume of activity which the school as a vast aggregate of individuals generates. The English system of education has produced two distinct patterns, that of the boarding school with its houses as the bases for living and general supervision, and that of the day school mainly based on the form. The modern comprehensive school has to try to ensure that the individual pupil is not submerged by the sheer weight and size of the organisation. Many heads, to inculcate a sense of belonging, have consciously copied some of the elements of the house system; in some areas purpose-built schools have been designed to give architectural substance to the idea. In other schools the absence of physical amenities has denied any choice to the head, or he may have inherited a form of organisation which hardly excites him but which he feels he cannot alter. Whatever the system—'houses' with group tutors, or 'years' with form teachers, or a mixture of the two—the head needs to be clear what is expected at every level. Many of the traditional supervisory duties attaching to the office of the head will be passed down to a growing middle level of school administrator—the house master or the year master. And many problems stop there.

Once a conscious attempt to create machinery of school government is made the inevitable development is the need to define the powers, expectations and relationships between the various members of it. Since so much in this field was based on customary usage there is still some reluctance to embark upon attempts at role definitions. Where a school staff enters willingly upon the exercise, however, it can be most useful in both the doing and in the final product. Nor is it as formidable as it might first appear. In one school the staff produced a ten-point definition of the functions of an academic head of department which is duplicated and known to them all. It reads :

Duties of head of department.

1   He will work closely with all members of his department to ensure the effective teaching of his subject.
2   To this end he will hold regular full meetings of his department, together with informal meetings and sub-meetings as occasion demands.
3   He will be responsible for the preparation and periodic revision of all schemes of work applicable to his subject, the choice of papers and syllabuses of internal examinations and the preparation of working syllabuses to that end.
4   He will determine the teaching methods and techniques which are to be used in the teaching of his subject.
5   He will supervise all internal examination papers and mark schemes and present skeletal samples of worked scripts as required by the headmaster.
6   He will supervise the activities of all student teachers teaching or observing his subject and prepare a report on their work at the end of their practice.
7   He will assess the financial needs of his department, present his case at the beginning of each financial year to the headmaster and make known any current adjustment of need.
8   He will prepare requisitions within the terms of his allowance, check the arrival and inventory of new books and materials, keep the

necessary stock books and perform the annual stock-taking and checking.

9 He will liaise with other heads of department to secure integrated courses wherever possible. He will make recommendations to the librarians for the inclusion of books applicable to his subject in library ordering.

10 He will have an eye to the changing nature of his subject, try to keep abreast of specialist content and method, be mindful of curriculum development and in-service training and generally advise the headmaster on matters relating to his subject and its place in the curriculum.

In the same school an advertisement for the vacant position as Head of Upper School carried additional notes which set out the duties which had been similarly drawn up:

1 He will act as the head's representative as and when requested to do so.

2 He will participate in the process of overall planning and decision-making and help as required in the determination and construction of timetables.

3 He will be responsible for the establishment and coordination of the work in the Upper School in consultation with the various heads of department.

4 He will supervise the teaching and pastoral duties of the teachers in Upper School and encourage extracurricular enterprise.

5 He will supervise the non-teaching staff of the Upper School, help in their recruitment and appointment and report on their efficiency.

6 He will be responsible for the fabric and furniture of Upper School.

7 He will be answerable to the headmaster for the discipline, welfare and progress of the boys in Upper School and cooperate with outside agencies on their behalf, either directly or through his year masters.

8 He will acquaint himself in whatever way he can with the work and activities of Lower School.

It is impossible, however, to indicate the informal pattern which has grown up and which will probably change with the newcomer.

Several points are worth making at this stage. An important one is that the two patterns of organisation, academic and pastoral, produce hierarchies which, when set out in tabular form, appear quite separate. In school the staff must appear in both hierarchies for every teacher has both a pastoral and an academic role. So a master may be fourth in a modern languages department in the academic hierarchy but a second-year master; another can be head of the technical department and fifth-form master 'working' under the fifth-year master. This interlocking or overlapping duality is accepted without question. Another point is that although the definitions of function may be suspect as setting limits to performance or expectation, in practice they rarely operate in that way. They are not becoming some new type of rule book. The definition of the Head of Upper School is helpful here; it specifically refers to the 'informal' pattern, and schools like other organisations are apt to grow outside the defined shapes set out for them.

A much more important matter is the principle of delegation which underlies the practice. The head is quite deliberately shedding much of his power and several of his functions. Already the attributes of good delegation are beginning to take shape and be recognised. The detailed 'job description' above is but one. Another is that once delegation has been made it needs to be as extensive as possible and vested at every point with the measure of power which is needed to give decision-makers at lower levels the authority to carry out their decisions. One difficulty is to gain widespread acceptance of it. It may come relatively quickly inside the school—pupils and staff soon come to know whom to see—but the process of acceptance by parents and outside agencies is slow to develop. The head himself needs to train himself to be tolerant to his delegates, to intervene as little as possible, not to have his hand perpetually on the overrider switch. Above all, the designing of delegation should be as forward-looking as possible for the large schools of today have to be rather special training grounds for their future leaders who cannot, like the present generation of older heads, hope to serve an apprenticeship in smaller schools, for these are fast disappearing.

The senior levels of administration in large schools are passing through a fascinating stage of development. In a purely technical sense a new kind of administrator is emerging to supervise the growth of 'office-business' which has proliferated in recent years. The head's secretary of yesteryear who probably coped with everything single-handed is now transformed into a registrar or administrative officer presiding over a busy staff of six or seven. The increase in the volume of the typewritten word is staggering not least as an ancillary to the work of the classroom. The duplicators are rarely still and the telephone, as in all organisations, perpetually ringing. How far this growth is the product of extended activities, size and concentration and how far self-generated is anyone's guess.

In the wider context of the school, the roles of senior members of staff have been subject to just as much change. The official recognition of the post of deputy headmaster is as recent as 1956, though before that date the grammar schools had their 'senior masters' and the secondary modern schools their 'first assistants'. The office was never clearly defined and the practice differed widely. Generally, however, it included all or a major portion of three widely accepted roles—that of 'stand-in' when the head was absent, that of performer of certain prescribed tasks such as the disciplining of defaulters, duty rosters, help with timetable and some teaching and that of 'piggy-in-the-middle'. The last of the three, which made the deputy the greatest of the intermediaries, was perhaps his most important function, to be the guide, comforter and friend of both staff and pupils, the approachable figure, the leader of the common-room and at the same time the touchstone for the head, the antidote to high-magisterial loneliness. The deputy in the new setting can no longer perform all these roles and as the head himself delegates more of his power downwards the danger is that the deputy may be the most over-worked member of the staff. This is being mitigated in several ways: the growth of the idea of a 'top-management' group in which the executive role of the deputy is recognised, the growing importance in the level of operation below that of deputy—that of senior master or senior mistress—and, most timely and essentially, the recognition in the Burnham Award of 1971 that large schools may qualify for two deputies and that a new formula for arriving at their salaries shall be mandatory. The next step may very well be the abandonment of the name of deputy and its replacement by some more realistic title such as associate or assistant headmaster.

For this will only be the recognition that the head does not 'go it alone'. His system of delegation is a guarantee that he does not work himself into the ground. He will further buttress himself by involving staff in consultation at every level and, if he is wise, embrace the new philosophy of participation by staff according to which assistants claim a much greater share in arriving at decisions affecting their activities, their standing and their relationships. Sometimes the principle of delegation which implies the overall prerogative of the head is in conflict with that of participation which implies some diminution in it. There is a further complication nowadays in that the senior pupils of schools do not so readily accept their inferior, submissive position without question. The existence of school councils and working parties is still a responsible and fairly innocuous development, but there are dangerous and disruptive influences standing on the touchlines which need careful attention.

Communications

The need for the head to be attentive extends, of course, to the running of his organisation at all points. It could very well be said that having broken the large mass down into smaller manageable units he then has the problem of ensuring that the bits function. This is a continuing problem of coordination and supervision, again for which he can no longer be wholly and personally responsible himself. But he can devise means for this. One area which calls for special attention is that of communication with all the members of his school. With his pupils his communication may be universal through assemblies, though if he is sensible he will recognise that what he says is often not listened to, and if heard not heeded; or it may be trivial because that is all that is left after his various intermediaries have dealt with it, or cataclysmic because that is what they have been unable or chosen not to cope with. In the new position in which he is placed the head will probably best act indirectly through the leaders of the smaller unit rather than directly himself. With his staff he cannot, even if he wished, talk all the day and every day. Nor is there need to. The actual day-by-day contact formally through information meetings of short duration or informally at breaks is still of infinite value, especially for the informal and personal exchange. But increasingly the written word has to be used—the daily or weekly bulletin, the occasional set of arrangements or orders, the extremely valuable discussion papers in which the head or someone deputed by him sets out the facts and the arguments prior to a meeting. The style has tended to become more simple and direct, more like the tabloids than *The Times*, but undoubtedly more effective none the less. Even with meetings and papers, however, there are bound to be misunderstandings. The growth of a new kind of guard against these—the staff coordinating committee or some such body—is evidence of a new need and the response to it.

Evaluation

No matter how attentive to the workings of his organisation a head is, he would, if pressed, find it extremely hard to claim that he knew just how effective it was. For institutions which claim to assess the performance of their pupils so exactly and are regarded by the outside world as institutions of perpetual testing and quantitative measurement, schools are singularly ill-equipped at this stage to evaluate their own overall performance. The earlier educational devices which operated to assess the working of individual teachers, the mainly physical controls of daily visitation, inspection of exercises, presentation of record-books have largely disappeared. The periodic inspection by Her Majesty's Inspectors or LEA Inspectors is falling into disuse or being modified into an advisory process. Yet the need for assessment remains: schools cannot proceed without indicators of individual progress and the refinement of new examination techniques and continuous assessment are welcome. But no one yet has devised any instrument for measuring the overall productivity of a school and its examination results tell only part of the story. The creation of the means to evaluate the performance of staff is widely recognised as one of the great needs of our time. Until that is done the head may develop extensively as both planner and coordinator, but as an assessor he will still be acting on impression or on incomplete and inadequate information. In this sense he is probably less well equipped than his counterparts in industry. But not everything can come at once. The new-model headmaster is as recent as the new-model school over which he is called to preside. The response to the new conditions has already been considerable, thoughtful and, if at times hesitant, at any rate serious and sincere. The new habit of looking critically at performance is a lesson which heads themselves are learning from management theory and practice and some are proving quite good pupils.

Index